The Forgotten Japanese

Miyamoto Tsuneichi.
Kagoshima Prefecture. 1962.
Photograph by Haga Hideo.

The Forgotten Japanese

Encounters with Rural Life and Folklore

Miyamoto Tsuneichi

Translated by Jeffrey S. Irish

Stone Bridge Press • Berkeley, California

Published by
Stone Bridge Press
P.O. Box 8208
Berkeley, CA 94707
TEL 510-524-8732 • sbp@stonebridge.com • www.stonebridge.com

Originally published as *Wasurerareta Nihonjin* in 1960 in Japan by Miraisha Publishers.

All photographs by the author unless otherwise noted.

Translation ©2010 Jeffrey S. Irish, based on the April 1971 edition with additional chapters.

Japanese names appear in customary order, family name first.

Jacket design by Linda Ronan with photographs by Haga Hideo (*top*) and Miyamoto Tsuneichi (*below*).

Printed in the United States of America.

2014 2013 2012 2011 2010   10 9 8 7 6 5 4 3 2 1

LIBRARY OF CONGRESS CATALOGING-IN-PUBLICATION DATA
Miyamoto, Tsuneichi, 1907–1981.
  [Wasurerareta Nihonjin. English.]
  The forgotten Japanese: encounters with rural life and folklore / Miyamoto Tsuneichi, translated by Jeffrey S. Irish.
    p. cm.
  Includes bibliographical references and index.
  ISBN 978-1-933330-80-8 (alk. paper)
    1. Japan—Social life and customs. 2. Japan—Description and travel. I. Irish, Jeffrey. II. Title.
  DS821.M615 2009
  952.03'3—dc22
                    2009024242

Table of Contents

Part Two | Village Stories

Translator's Introduction

Miyamoto Tsuneichi (1907–81) is one of Japan's greatest ethnologists and one of her best kept secrets. Over a period of thirty years, Miyamoto walked some one hundred thousand miles in search of the meaning of life in rural Japan. He found it in the songs and stories, in the living and working habits of its fishermen, farmers, and mountain men and women. Born into a farming family on an island in Japan's Inland Sea, Miyamoto was first a folklorist, an observer, and recorder who wrote more than eighty books and took ninety-five thousand photographs. But he did not stop there. He took what he had learned on the road and became a key government advisor, an advocate for the social and economic invigoration of rural communities weakened by outmigration and encumbered with an aging population.

Miyamoto's parents were unable to pay for his education beyond junior high school, so after a year farming at home he set out to look for work in Osaka. Miyamoto was sixteen when his father sent him off with advice that would greatly influence his approach to life and to his work as an ethnographer:

1. When you take a train, look out the window at the condition of the fields and crops, the size of the homes, the

kind of roofs they have. When you arrive at a station, watch carefully to see who is getting on or off. Observe their clothing and luggage. From this you will know if the place is wealthy or poor, whether it is a place where people work hard or not.

2. When you visit a city or town for the first time, always climb up someplace high to see where you are. Look for temples and for the forests that grow on shrine grounds. Look too at the nature of the homes and fields, and the surrounding mountains. If something at the top of a mountain catches your eye, go to it. If you take a good look from above, you will almost never lose your way.

3. If you have any money, try the local food and you will know the nature of life there.

4. If you have time, walk as much as you can. You will learn many things.

5. It's not difficult to make money, but it's hard to spend it wisely. Don't forget that.

6. I'm unable to provide for your education, so I ask nothing of you. Do as you like, but take care of yourself. Think of yourself as disowned until you reach thirty, but thereafter, remember your parents.

7. If you become sick or have troubles you cannot resolve alone, then come back home. We will always be waiting for you.

8. This is no longer an age in which children care for their parents. It's an age when parents care for their children. Otherwise the world will not improve.

9. Whatever you think is good, give it a try. We will not criticize your failures.

10. Look at what others have missed. There's always something important to be found. There's no need to rush. Whatever road you choose in life, walk it with purpose.

In Osaka, after working for the post office for several years and putting himself through teacher's college, Miyamoto took a job as an elementary school teacher. When time permitted, he explored the countryside outside Osaka and began asking people about their lives. At twenty-two, Miyamoto came down with tuberculosis and returned home to Ōshima Island to convalesce, but two years later he was back in Osaka, teaching elementary school and researching rural life.

In 1935, when Miyamoto was twenty-eight, he met Shibusawa Keizō, grandson of Shibusawa Eiichi, one of Japan's most successful entrepreneurs. Ten years Miyamoto's senior, Shibusawa was a banker and an avid ethnologist devoted to the study of the common people and their contributions to Japanese culture. He established the "Attic Museum" in a building on his own private property in Tokyo, which became a gathering place for Japanese tools and folk crafts, and for the young ethnologists whom Shibusawa engaged—and generously sponsored—in a wide variety of research efforts.

In 1939, at age thirty-two, Miyamoto resigned his job as an elementary school teacher and began walking and researching full time. With Shibusawa's untiring encouragement and financial support, and often on government or academic assignment, Miyamoto would walk, look, and listen for much of the remainder of his life. In 1941 he went to Shikoku, the smallest of Japan's four main islands, and heard stories that would become the basis for "Tosa Genji" and "Tosa Terakawa Night Tale" herein. Physically unfit to fight in the war, Miyamoto performed research for the government with regard to farm productivity and land reform. The war intensified around him and when Osaka was bombed in July, 1945, Miyamoto lost all of his research notes.

Having studied the resettlement of communities that had been devastated by landslides and flooding late in the nineteenth century—described in "Totsukawa Landslide" and "New Totsukawa"—Miyamoto helped communities that had been destroyed in the war resettle to Hokkaido. As an agricultural advisor to the Japanese government and later as a member of various interdisciplinary research teams, Miyamoto continued to explore and study villages that fished, farmed, and lumbered for their livelihood. In the early 1950s he began his first serious study of Japan's islands, work that would contribute to the establishment of the Remote Island Development Act and to his becoming the first director of the Remote Island Development Council in 1953. His related travels to the island of Tsushima in 1950 and repeatedly thereafter would inform his writings in the first three chapters of this book.

Despite the return of tuberculosis in 1953, Miyamoto turned his incomparable energy to the study of forestry, visiting more than two hundred mountain communities in the mid- to late 1950s. The more he traveled, the more Miyamoto learned about fishing, farming, hunting, and logging, and about the ways in which individuals and communities fail, survive, and sometimes thrive.

Miyamoto encouraged rural communities to develop and sell products that were uniquely their own as a means of financial survival. On the island of Sado, for example, he advised farmers to grow a variety of persimmon that was unique to the area, and persimmons remain an important cash crop to this day. A persimmon farmer on Sado Island was known to have said, "Miyamoto gave us this factory, this port, and more importantly, he gave us pride in our lives." Such examples can be found throughout Japan, in the thousands of villages Miyamoto visited as he walked the country. To this day there are monkey grinders, *taiko* drummers, countless museums of local culture, and local products that were spurred along and inspired by this man of rare energy and practical insight. And to this day, Sano Shinichi, Miyamoto's primary biographer, continues to give talks about him; Miyamoto Tsuneichi reading groups read his books; and Sakamoto Nagatoshi tours with his monologue reenactment of "Tosa Genji."

The Forgotten Japanese was first published in 1960. It is a collection of life stories and vignettes as told by men and women in their seventies, eighties, and nineties, people Miyamoto met during his research and travels. It is an eye-opener even for the Japanese; a look at life in rural Japan between 1850 and 1960 that introduces us to farmers, carpenters, and fortune-tellers who are adventurous, curious, mischievous, and resourceful. Through their lives we witness Japan's modernization, and we are offered glimpses of important moments in her history as well. These are the stories of common people; this is history and culture from the ground level. A carpenter is drafted to fight against the shogun's army in a war that signals the end of the Tokugawa period. An old man describes the shogun's final flight from Osaka, requisitioning a small boat to take him to safety. But the storyteller is as interested in the fate of the common boatman as in that of his famous passenger. We learn of families that are too poor to care for their own children and others who take them in, of outlandish priests, and of long and grueling hours of farm work. A woman tells of her travels to see the world. A woodsman talks of wolves, goblins, and fox spirits. A grandfather sings ballads to his grandson. When a boy is lost, the villagers go searching, knowing him well enough to suspect where he might have gone. We encounter a woman with leprosy on a narrow mountain path, and attend a village meeting that lasts through the night. We are introduced to fishermen, hunters, wood carvers, mountain ascetics; to people from every imaginable trade and livelihood. We witness men pulling carts, then horses pulling carts, and finally the arrival of paved roads and cars.

Vestiges of what Miyamoto found on his travels are still to be found in rural Japan to this day. While the bullet train has extended its reach into much of rural Japan and thatched roofs have been replaced by ceramic tiles, many rural Japanese continue to heat their baths with firewood, and individual communities hold meetings much like those Miyamoto experienced. The way of life that appeared to be nearing its end in Miyamoto's time is still nearing its end today. It may finally disappear as the last of those born in the Meiji period pass away, their values and memories lost with them.

With the exception of the photographs in which Miyamoto appears, a photograph of Sakon Kumata in chapter 9 and a photograph of Tanaka Umeji in chapter 10, all photographs were taken by the author. Those that did not appear in the original Japanese version of *The Forgotten Japanese* were selected from among the ninety-five thousand photographs taken by Miyamoto with, for the most part, his Olympus Pen camera. The maps have been redrawn and expanded upon here to provide greater clarity and context. In an effort to make this compelling description of life in rural Japan all the more accessible, the chapter order has been changed slightly and the chapters have been arranged in two parts. In the first, we join Miyamoto on the road where we are introduced to his research methods and then offered accounts of individual lives, each a unique window on life in rural Japan. In the second, we step back to look at whole communities as they respond to a variety of crises and hardships. Only when the original text was redundant or where elaborate geographical details interrupted the flow of the writing have omissions been made. A glossary provides information regarding people, places, events, and concepts that may not be familiar to the reader.

In Japan, a younger person will often address someone older as "Grandpa," "Grandma," "Uncle," or "Aunt," though they are not related in any way. In the text that follows, Miyamoto often does this as well, out of affection and respect, and toward the establishment of a rapport that then led to the many frank and open conversations we find herein.

The Forgotten Japanese (original Japanese title: *Wasurerareta Nihonjin*) is now in its fifty-seventh printing in Japan. It has never been translated into English. This translation is based on a longer version of *The Forgotten Japanese*, prepared by the author as the tenth volume in a collection of his published works.

ACKNOWLEDGMENTS

I would like to thank Miyamoto Tsuneichi's eldest son, Chiharu, for his kind permission to translate his father's work. I am also grateful to Messrs. Okamoto, Takasaki, and Takagi of the Suō Ōshima Cultural Exchange Center—where Miyamoto's writings, photographs, and a vast collection of fishing, farming, and other tools are kept—for their assistance in the selection of photographs and in the checking of innumerable facts. Stewart Wachs, Jerry Irish, and Anne Connolly read, edited, and offered valuable advice with regard to the manuscript. Inagaki Naotomo, one of Miyamoto's students, talked with me at length about his teacher while Sano Shinichi's biography of and lectures regarding Miyamoto provided me with a new perspective on his life. Tsuda Yōjirō of Iwanami Shoten generously shared important photographic data while Iwao Sudo and Haga Hideo allowed me to make use of their photographs of Miyamoto. Kikuno Kenichirō drew the maps and Kodama Tatsurō performed the map graphics. Nakamura Kōji introduced me to the wonderful world of Miyamoto Tsuneichi, and Ken, John, and Stewart at the *Kyoto Journal* encouraged me to pursue this translation. The elderly members of my village served as a sounding board regarding life before the war, and Sayaka kept me going for the years that I disappeared into the vast world of this book and this man. Finally, I thank Peter Goodman of Stone Bridge Press who took on, and stuck with, this important story, helping it to find its way into the English language some fifty years after its Japanese debut.

Jeffrey S. Irish
Kagoshima Prefecture
Japan

Author's Preface

[Originally an Afterword to the 1971 edition]

I set out to write these accounts with an interest in depicting old people as transmitters of knowledge. Then, part way through, I started to think about how I might depict the environment in which the elderly lived when they were young, and how it was that they had lived their lives. I was not interested in mere reminiscences but in considering how these people were linked to the present and thinking about the role that they had played. Because my interests changed along the way and new aims were added, this collection lacks unity. What is more, the only elderly person from eastern Japan included here is Grandpa Takagi Seiichi; no one else is touched upon. Therefore, these are the lives of elderly people living against the backdrop of society in central and western Japan.

With Japan's capital in Tokyo and many scholars gathered there as well, the tendency in current Japanese scholarship is to view matters with Tokyo at the center. And when one thinks of the countryside, the portion of Japan that lies east of the center has become the standard. For example, in the postwar period a lot of attention has been paid to the abuse of daughters by their mothers-in-law. Certainly this is a problem that must be considered, and it occurs in places where fathers are particularly dominant [especially in eastern Japan]. On the other hand, it would appear that there is even more tormenting of mothers-in-law by their daughters, but this matter is given little attention, probably because mothers-in-law lack the means or the power to appeal to the media. With regard to marriage as well, before the middle of the Meiji period [the 1890s], how would the number of daughters who married according to their parents' wishes and those who married on the strength of their own will have compared? It would appear that in western Japan, there were more examples of the latter than of the former.

Even within a single era, various regional differences can be found, but we must not simply divide them into the advanced and the backward. We tend to view people of previous generations and those living in the lower strata of society in a trifling manner. And though we may have a propensity to feel a sort of pathos, I think it is necessary for us to put ourselves in the position of others and to think like they do.

I would like to say something about my intentions and methods in listening to and writing down the words of the old people I have gathered here. First, wanting to see all of Japan, I set out in 1939 and walked the country, going where impulse led me. I traveled in this way until the end of the war, and it was on those travels that I met the elderly men Tosa Genji, Tanaka Umeji, and Takagi Seiichi.

After the war, I returned home and became a farmer, remaining home most of the time until 1952. Prior to that I had returned to help plant and harvest rice and to harvest tangerines. Through such experiences I had developed a deep interest in agricultural methods, and as a farmer I think I am in the possession of above-average skills. So, after the war, at the times of year when there was little farm work to do, I returned to the places I had traveled before the war, visited people I had become close to, and spread information about agricultural methods. I also researched farming communities on the side. Fortunately, wherever I went, I was able at a glance to generally estimate the level of that area's agricultural methods, the nature of their farm management, the degree to which forestry had evolved, and the like. Thanks to this, I was able to enter a village and talk immediately and intimately with the old and young and to the women there, forgoing uninteresting concerns and anxieties.

Thereafter, I looked as closely and thoroughly as I could at a specific area. For example, I went to all of the villages on the island that is my home. I talked with the people I met along the way and tried to answer whatever questions confronted me. Also, from the mid-1920s until about 1945, I walked most of the villages in the Sennan District of Osaka and in the Ikoma District of Nara Prefecture. In this way, I came to understand how each individual community had come into existence and how the people there had lived over time. In a similar fashion, I walked the islands of the Inland Sea. I also made an effort to return repeatedly to the same areas and to participate in research for academic associations.

I continued in this way until 1952, but fell ill and had to stop traveling for a time. Since 1955, I have put my energy into the study of mountain villages. I have written reports on research for academic associations and, with the help of funding from the Forestry Agency and the Central Depository for Agriculture and Forestry, studied some areas continuously for six years, together with a group of colleagues who formed a research group. We are now writing a report with regard to our study of seventy villages.

My method is to go to the village in question and walk around once to see what kind of village it is. Next, I go to the local government office and look in their storage for documents from the Meiji period and after. Then, making use of these documents, I confirm matters I have questions about with the local officials. Similarly, I visit the Forest Owners Association and the Agricultural Association. If, during the course of this work, I learn of the existence of particularly old documents, I visit the homes of the older families and hand copy whatever is necessary. I also select several farming households and research each of them individually, taking about half a day per household. If I am able to complete three homes—one in the morning, one in the afternoon, and another at night—that is ideal. When I ask my fellow researchers to do this work, they are even more efficient.

With the questions raised by the old family documents and with the local government documents in mind, I then meet with the village elderly and begin by asking these questions. Thereafter I encourage the people to speak as freely as possible. In this way I come to have a good understanding of their concerns. And in the meantime I am taught a wide variety of things. "Nagura Talk" is the record of just such an occasion.

During this time I also create opportunities to meet with housewives and young people in small discussion groups. I listen to what they have to say and I talk as well. On these occasions I am able to deduce a number of problems. But what I most want to know is what in their human relations—what in this environment—gave the producers of this local culture their energy.

A countless number of local people have participated in our studies and cooperated with us. I have almost never been obstructed, objected to, or turned away. Of course, there are times when I have imposed myself on people who were reluctant, but it is rare that nothing can be done and I have been forced to give up. I think this may come from my being a person of the past, of old customs. I am ever grateful that others do not try to accommodate me, but talk in a way that is true to who they are. And I think that one of my tasks is to convey their words to others, doing my best not to alter them. I am pleased that a paper monument is being made to these essentially anonymous people.

When it was decided that *The Forgotten Japanese* would be included in a collection of my writings, I added "The Story of Kawame," "The Totsukawa Landslide," "Birth of the New Totsukawa Village," and "Wanderers." Though these are somewhat different in their content from the life histories, I have added them so it will be known that history is not only made by special, famous people, but by a large number of common people, often from worlds that themselves have been forgotten.

While writing these old people's stories, I too have somehow become old. There were many things I wanted to write down, but my notetaking was inadequate or the materials were lost. My memory has grown faint, and in many cases I have forgotten altogether; and so the history of the people lies in that which is thus buried.

Miyamoto Tsuneichi
February 14, 1971

Part One

Life Stories

Chronology

Edo period   1603–1868
Meiji period   1868–1912
Taishō period   1912–26
Shōwa period   1926–89

*An elderly woman in Aomori
Prefecture, one among thousands
who shared their life stories with
Miyamoto. August 1966.*

Chapter 1

Meetings

[Tsushima Island, Nagasaki Prefecture, July–August 1950]

The village of Ina lies on the west coast of Tsushima, near its northern end, and long ago whale was hunted there. I was in the village for three days, and early on the second I woke to the sound of a conch shell being blown. I was told that a village meeting would be held. When I went out in the morning and passed near the shrine, a large number of people were gathered in the forest there. I called on one of the village's old families and asked them about various things. After noon, when I passed the shrine again, I saw that people were still there, talking. I wondered if they had talked on without a break for lunch and was curious to know just what they might be deliberating. Without asking, I returned to my lodging and visited the home of the village headman in the afternoon. The headman, who was still young, was away at the meeting, but an old man, his father, was at home.

In this village only the heads of rural samurai households took on the headman's role, a position the old man had also held when he was young. The farmers had a representative as well, and together they made various decisions regarding the village.

In the course of asking the headman's father all sorts of things, I learned that there was a register box containing the village's records that had been passed down for many generations. When

I inquired whether I might be able to see these documents, he told me they were not at his discretion to show. The box had a key that was in the possession of the headman and could only be opened in the presence of the farmers' representative. I asked if I might be shown the contents in the presence of these two men, and the old man sent someone to the meeting to bring them back. When I explained the situation, they were happy to open the box and show me, and they did just that. I spent the entire night transcribing the main parts but, being dreadfully tired from my travels, my work was inefficient.

When morning came I went to the house of the old man and asked, "Might I borrow these old documents for a time?" The old man said we would have to ask his son. Apparently the village meeting continued on this day as well, and his son had gone off to attend. So once again the old man sent someone to bring him back. The son said that matters of this sort must be brought before the meeting and everyone's opinion heard, so he took the parts of the old documents I wanted to borrow and, saying that he would ask everyone's opinion, he departed. Noon came, but he had not returned. It turned three, and still he had not come back. When I asked the old man, "What on earth could they be discussing?" he said, "There are many matters to be decided . . ."

As I had thought to go to Sago, more than seven miles to the north, that same day, I became increasingly anxious and decided that I would try going to the meeting. The old man agreed to come along with me. More than twenty people sat on the wood floor inside the meeting hall while others crouched under the trees outside, talking in small groups. They appeared to be talking idly, but this was not the case. When I asked what was going on, I was told that when something is decided in the village, they will sometimes talk for days until everyone is satisfied. After gathering and hearing an explanation from the headman, the villagers talk things over in their respective community groups and take their conclusions to the headman. If an agreement is not reached, they return to their groups and discuss the matter further. Sometimes a person with other business to attend to will go home. But the headman and the representative, in their capacity as listeners, mediators, and unifiers, must remain.

Deliberations had continued in this manner for two days without concern for whether it was day or night. The previous night their talk had apparently lasted nearly until dawn. When a person became sleepy or had nothing more to say, they went home. It seems that the matter of my wanting to borrow old documents had been brought up in the morning, but when I arrived at the meeting a conclusion had yet to be reached. They had not been discussing the old documents from the morning until three in the afternoon. Other matters were being discussed but, in time, several people had brought up the matter of the documents.

I was not there at the time, but I was given a summary afterwards. The headman had introduced the matter, explaining that "a professor doing research on Tsushima for the Federation of Nine Academic Societies has come to investigate matters regarding Ina. He says that old official documents are necessary for him to learn about Ina's past, and he has asked if we might loan them to him." He then added, "We've never loaned them out before. Because this is the village's important documentary evidence, we should all discuss it thoroughly." The topic of discussion then shifted to another matter.

In time, an old man who was quite familiar with the old days told a story. "Long ago, the master of the house in the oldest and highest-ranked rural samurai family died, and his child, who was still quite young, took over. At this time an old man who was a relative of the family came along. After asking to be shown documents that authenticated the status of the family that had been passed down by the household, he took them. No matter how they pleaded with the old man to return the documents, he refused, and made as if his house was the oldest in the village." Once a discussion of this and related matters had passed through the entire group, the subject was changed.

After some time had passed the matter of the old documents was brought up once again, when someone said, "We've all heard

*Village meeting hall in rural
Okayama Prefecture.
January–February 1953.*

that old documents were in the village's register box, but this is the first time we've seen its contents. I haven't heard tell of any good coming of having these papers, so if our showing them to a stranger might be of some help, why don't we?" Then, for a time, there was talk of things that had been tucked away in people's homes until someone had come along with an eye for their value, and the good things that had come of showing them. After a variety of other small talk, the conversation once again shifted to other matters.

It was upon such a scene that I arrived. The headman summed up what had transpired, and I thought that at this rate a conclusion would probably not be reached easily. After everyone had spoken their mind, an old man called out in quite a loud voice, "From the looks of him he doesn't appear to be a bad person, so how about we make a decision?" Those who had been in discussion outside came to the window, and they all looked at me. I explained what was written in the old documents. In the old days, when a whale was caught, young women would put on beautiful kimonos and makeup and go to see it. Because it was wrong to do such a thing, a document had been drafted to stop such behavior. I told them of this and other documents. Then everyone talked for a while about the whale-hunting days. The talk seemed ever so leisurely and yet it evolved bit by bit. When they had talked for more than an hour, the old man who had brought me there asked the entire group, "What do you say? Since he's gone to this trouble, how about we loan them to him?" Someone responded, "If you say so, I don't think anyone will object." At this the headman offered, "In that case, I will take responsibility." Then and there I wrote up an IOU, and the headman read it aloud, asking, "Is this OK?" Voices came from the group saying "Yes, that will be fine." The headman then took the documents that had been placed on the wood floor in front of him that morning and handed them to me. I thanked him and went outside, but the old man who had brought me there remained behind. I wonder how long the discussion continued after that.

An image of that village meeting is deeply engrained in my memory. This system of holding meetings is not something that began recently. In Ina the records of village agreements dated back nearly two hundred years. Those are the records that remain, but I expect there were village meetings even before that. An old man over seventy told me that when he was a child things were done much as they are now. The only difference was that long ago, if a person was hungry, they didn't leave to eat. Rather, someone brought a box lunch from home, which was eaten while the conversation continued. If night came before the discussion had ended, some slept right there. Others talked until morning, and this carried on until a conclusion was reached. I was told that for the most part even the more difficult matters could be resolved in three days. This required patience but, at any rate, they didn't push themselves. They discussed matters until everyone was satisfied. So when a conclusion was reached, it had to be strictly abided by. These were not discussions of theory. In considering something, people shared every relevant precedent they could think of.

Such deliberation was not unique to the village of Ina. In

Chiromo, a village on the east coast of Tsushima that I visited some ten days later, when I asked if they could show me their old documents, representatives of the four villages along Chiromo Bay gathered and taught me deeply just how important meetings are. I learned that meetings of the representatives of these four villages have continued for more than four hundred years, ever since they began hunting dolphin together in the bay. When I said that I wanted to see their communally owned documents, the representative of Chiromo said, "Let's send a messenger to the other representatives," and I, thinking nothing of it, made do with a simple "Thank you." As it would happen, the messenger had to go by rowboat to a representative's house that was at the back end of the bay. It was two and a half miles one way. More than three hours passed from the time of my request until the messenger returned to tell us that he had contacted the representatives of the other three villages. When I spread out a map, I realized what trouble I had caused them.

Another hour passed, and the three representatives arrived by boat. Finely dressed in traditional *haori* [half-coats], they all carried fans. It being summer, they must have been hot, but it seemed that meetings of the representatives were stern affairs. They told me that they wanted to discuss things for a time, so I went to another house to make inquiries. At about nine at night I was called back to the representative's house where the meeting was being held. I arrived to find the four representatives gathered in the front room. They had deliberated without eating dinner. The representative of Chiromo said, "We have decided that you cannot take the documents with you, but you can look at them for one full day." The reason: the quantity of fish that had been caught in the communal nets was inscribed in the account books, and they couldn't allow such information to leak out. This being quite reasonable I said, "That would be fine." The representative of Chiromo cut the seal on the register box and opened the lid. Confirming the number of books inside, he handed them to me. Then dinner was brought out on small wooden tables, and as I had not eaten yet, I partook as well. These aging lacquered tables had small compartments that contained rice, boiled taro stems, and pickled eggplant. I was told that since long ago this had been the protocol at gatherings of this sort. While we ate, the four men told stories of catching dolphin in the old days, and most likely such talk had continued throughout their deliberations from five until nine o'clock. If I had been there, I would like to have written down every single one of their stories.

I was up all night that night too, transcribing the account books. Feeling somewhat melancholy, I stepped out into the moonlit night. In front of the house was a bay and across it the distinct line of low, dark mountains. A wind blew across the ocean, and the moonlight was finely chopped by the waves. There, by the shore, an old woman from my lodging was spinning thread all through the night, "Because the moon is beautiful . . ." Working, she enjoyed the moonlight and the cool night breeze.

I pressed on with my transcription work during the day too, and in the evening, when I had finally finished, I went to the home of the representative to return the account books. That night while I went to one of the old families in the village and made inquiries there, again the three representatives gathered in the home of the Chiromo representative, placed the account books back in the register box, sealed it, and at around midnight, returned to their respective villages. I had finished my inquiries and was on my way back to my lodgings when I heard voices from the shore and saw the light of a pine torch. I arrived at the shore just as the representatives were getting into a boat to return home. Feeling truly bad for having put these men to such trouble for the past two days, I attempted to hand them money I had wrapped in paper, saying it was to pay for the *sake* consumed at the meal we had shared. But they refused to take it, explaining, "It was our duty." When the boat departed I thanked them, calling out, "I'm sorry to have troubled you and thank you very much." To this, one of the representatives responded, "Now I have performed my duties," and saying this he rowed off across the sea in the moonlight.

I have written these stories in great detail because I want it to be known in concrete terms how the villages of old appeared, when and under what circumstances a handing down of traditions was necessary, and what it meant for villagers to discuss old conventions. I am not saying that all villages in Japan were this way. But at least in the villages to the west of Kyoto and Osaka, village meetings of this sort have taken place since long ago. At these assemblies it would appear that no distinction was made between rural samurai and farmers. In the order of succession from feudal lords and their retainers down to farmers, the status of farmers was low, but when it came to being a member of a village community, their ideas seem to have been treated equally.

When I was looking at the old documents of a place nearby, also near the north end of Tsushima, I found a passage that was almost three hundred years old. It was a criticism of a rural samurai family in the village that was directly descended from the Sō clan [who had once controlled Tsushima] saying that it was inexcusable that they sent only their manservant to meetings. This would suggest that the rural samurai himself normally attended such meetings—showing his face and speaking his mind like all others—and that he would have had to listen to what the other villagers had to say as well. When the rural samurai interacted with their retainers and landless younger brothers who had formed branch families, they probably put on airs with them. But when it came to interactions with common villagers, and there was no lord–vassal relationship, it was only natural for villagers to file a grievance when the rural samurai skipped meetings.

Just the same, numerous distinctions remained. Rural samurai and farmers could not intermarry; only the rural samurai could perform a scene from Kabuki on the occasion of the *Bon* festival [Festival of the Dead]; and so on. When one looks only at such distinctions, the class system appears to have been strong, but when one looks at life in the villages, there were many instances of a rural samurai working a farmer's land. And this situation was by no means limited to Tsushima.

In this we can see that villages had their own distinct life. I imagine that at village meetings there were many instances where matters were not settled using today's logic. Rather, people would have told parables and no doubt likened the matter at hand to their own lives and experience in a way that was easy to convey and easy for others to understand. In the middle of the discussion, time was set aside to cool down. If there were objections, fine, and for a time things would be left like that. When, in time, a voice came out in favor, that opinion would be left to stand and everyone would think together about it. In the end the person in charge would make a decision. In this way there were likely few unpleasant feelings, even in a small village where people came face to face with one another every day. At the same time, it is clear that these village meetings held authority.

There was a register box in every village on Tsushima, and these held records of agreements that had been reached. It was in this way that, supported by the passing down of institutions, customs, and beliefs, self-government was effected. And while the opportunity for everyone to speak of their own experiences and observations certainly did serve to strengthen their unity and bring order to village life, it also impeded the village's forward progress.

Chapter 2

Folksongs

[Tsushima Island, Nagasaki Prefecture, July 1950 and July 1951]

As I had been delayed in the village of Ina, it was after five o'clock when I departed. Even though it was summer when the days are long, the sun was already on its way down. From Ina to the back end of Sago is a little over seven miles. Although I couldn't be sure, if I hurried I might just be able to arrive with a little daylight left. At any rate, I departed with the thought of hurrying, and then someone from the place where I'd been staying came chasing after me. "Some people came to Ina from Sago to buy wood, and since they'll be heading back now it would be good to join them."

When I reached the edge of the village, three men stood there talking, their horses tied to a tree. Seeing me, they said, "So you're the one that's going to Sago. If that's so, how about making the trip on the back of a horse? Today we came here thinking to buy some lumber, but since it hasn't been cut yet we're going back light in the rear." I was grateful, but being poor, after calculating the cost of riding, I declined. "Then we'll tie your shoulder bag on one of our horses," they offered, so I had them strap my rucksack on. "You walk on ahead," one told me. "We have to buy some gasoline to take back, and we'll catch up with you directly."

I set off hurriedly, relieved of my burden. After Ina, the village of Shitaru appeared and the evening sun on the ocean inlet there was beautiful. While I was walking on the road along the shore, the three men on horseback came up from behind and passed me, looking gallant. It was just like in the drawing of farmers off to get fish, running their horses, in the legend of Ishiyama Temple. They were dressed in light, short-sleeved kimonos, drawers down to their knees, and straw sandals.

It was all fine and good to look admiringly at their retreating figures, but in almost no time they'd disappeared from view. Relying on my map, I passed through Shitaru and started along a road through the mountains, but the men on horseback were nowhere to be seen. Completely at a loss, I asked someone working in a field if anyone had passed on horseback. "They were going at quite a pace," he replied.

I had thirty-three pounds of rice in my knapsack, along with a change of clothes. Much like in medieval times, one had to carry rice to travel in Tsushima in 1950. Without this rice, more often than not, I'd have been imposing on the farmers I stayed with, for in Tsushima rice was scarce. That aside, I'd not asked the three men their names, or where in Sago they lived. The valley in Sago runs about two and a half miles north to south, and there are six tiny villages in that stretch. I thought things looked bad, but anyway I'd try walking as far as I could. If I took a wrong turn I could always sleep out in the mountains.

In May of that year, when Izumi Sei-ichi (a professor at the University of Tokyo) had come here to do preliminary research, he'd gotten lost on the road from Sago to Ina. He'd set off from Sago past noon, thinking he'd easily come out in Ina by evening, but he had become utterly lost, and didn't arrive in Ina until ten that night. Izumi-san had warned me, "In many places in the north of Tsushima, the narrow road is the main one, so you have to be careful." I could see that it was just as he'd said. When I came to places where the valley narrowed and, moreover, where the road divided into two, I was suddenly at a loss. There were no signposts or anything. So I tried walking both roads and looked for the presence or absence of a horse's hoof. Then I took the road with the hoofprints.

Walking along in this way, it occurred to me that this was probably what the roads had been like in medieval times and before. In addition to being narrow, the road was overgrown with trees, and without the slightest chance of a view there wasn't even a way to confirm where I was. I can well imagine taking the same road many times and still getting lost. Until you've walked a road like this, it's hard to understand those stories about people being led astray by foxes and raccoon dogs [an animal related to dogs and wolves but more closely resembling the raccoon in appearance and temperament]. And at night these roads are absolutely unwalkable. The sun was probably still shining on the upper slopes of the mountains around me, but this narrow valley road was already as dark as night.

Walking along, I could hear voices somewhere. It sounded like they were calling out. For all I knew they were calling me, so I tried calling too, in a loud voice. And while doing this, I walked in the direction from which the voices had come. I climbed up the valley and came to a pass. But even up there, as the forest was dense, there was no view at all.

At the top of the pass, the three men were waiting, their horses tied to a tree. I paused to catch my breath, and when I said rather emotionally that it was no easy task to walk the roads in these mountains with absolutely no visibility, an old man of nearly seventy said, "There's a good solution for that. Speak out, so others will know you're walking here now." When I asked him in what manner I should speak out, he answered, "Sing. If you're singing and someone else is on the same mountain, they'll hear your voice. If they're from the same village, they'll know who it is, and they'll sing too. If the person is near enough that you can make out the words, then you call out to them. By simply doing that, each knows at least the direction the other is heading, and what they will be doing there. So if you get lost, as long as someone has heard you singing, they can imagine what happened and where." I found that to be rather convincing and realized that a knowledge of folksongs is necessary when walking a mountain road such as this one. When I asked the old man if he would sing, he replied, "Let's wait until we've started walking again," and mounted his horse. The road descended through uneven rocks. Astride his horse, the old man held the reins with one hand and the saddle with the other to keep his body from sliding forward and falling, for although there was a saddle it had no stirrups. He explained that the reason for the absence of stirrups was to reduce the chance of an injury; in mountains such as these, one can get thrown from a horse if one gets caught up in the drooping branches. Walking together like this, I came to feel that the folksongs these people sang and every detail of the way they rode their horses were accumulations of a deep wisdom about life itself.

Then, sitting on that unstable saddle, the old man began to sing. And from the moment he began I was struck with admiration. This was definitely a packhorse driver's song. It was not rhythmical and refined like the songs of the Matsumae and Esashi packhorse drivers, which have become parlor songs. It had the simple artlessness of a horseman's song, and although the old man was approaching seventy, his voice truly carried well. Atop his horse, he seemed to be lost within his own song. I followed him, running along behind.

When the road became a little better and the valley more open, we came upon a village called Nakayama. The houses, about ten in all, were scattered here and there among the fields. Though the sun had already gone down, none of the houses had lit their lamps yet. At every house the people could be seen out front, putting things in order or talking. The red fire burning for a bath at one house made an impression on me. A young man stood in front of that home, removing dirt from a hoe.

When the man on the horse asked the young man if he wanted to come over, he responded, "At *Bon*." This being *Bon* on

the old calendar, the festival would be some ten days later. "You
haven't come much this year." "Yeah, the last time was in May."
The young man stretched his back and looked at us. He was a
bright, round-faced, and sturdily built youth. While it was nearly
five miles from Nakayama to Sago Valley, these were neighboring communities. Yet he was saying that since New Year's, he'd
only been to Sago the one time in May. There's no radio or newspaper, no Saturday or Sunday. Life here is still without plays or
movies. When I asked, "Do you spend all your time working?"
The old man answered, "No, we make a picnic lunch and go over
to Chūzan (a village on the coast) for shellfish in among the
rocks, and to fish. We have fun." Another of the men on horseback said, "This old man has a good voice, so he's had quite a lot
of good fun." I thought this was because he was enraptured with
his own singing and that this had brightened his life, but there
was another meaning to what the man had said.

We continued on from Nakayama along a valley road, and at the
upper reaches of the Sago River the road descended alongside the
stream. Sometimes on the right bank, sometimes on the left, the
road passed on whichever side offered even a bit of flat ground.
In many places I had to traverse the river from right to left or
from left to right, and each time I would pull off my shoes and
socks, roll up my pants, and make the crossing barefoot while the
men on horseback splashed their way across. When I reached the
other bank, I would hurriedly wipe my feet, put on my socks and
shoes, and run after them, for they'd have already gone far ahead.
Soon I was exhausted, completely out of breath.

I'd not eaten lunch. Even here on Tsushima if I stayed at an
inn I'd be given breakfast, lunch, and dinner. But when I asked
farmers to put me up, while they'd eat breakfast and dinner, many
ate no lunch to speak of. It was rare to have any meal that was
worthy of being served on a tray. When the farmers were hungry, they'd eat whatever was on hand. Most of them didn't have

watches. Even if for argument's sake they did, they didn't have radios or the like, so there was no fixed time. Families with children in elementary school would have some notion of time, but the average farmer wasn't bound by what we call time. When I broke my watch during my travels, I came to know what the world was like without one.

Because I was traveling to study Tsushima for the Federation of Nine Academic Societies, when I had left Izuhara, the island's main town, I'd been provisioned with a little more than thirty-three pounds of rice, the amount necessary for the completion of my research. But actually a fair amount had been taken out. The archaeology team had to employ laborers, and they had to be given food. Since allotments hadn't been made for them by the food supply office, deductions were made from those of us who were on the island for long-term research. I had received a per-day ration of one pound of rice, so as a rule I had to skip lunch.

When I walked the island, I did my best to stay with farmers, and for lunch some of them made do with sweet potato powder, others with nothing at all. In one house where I was asking questions of an old man, he didn't eat lunch, even when midday had come. When I suggested that he eat and that we could talk afterward, he answered, "I'm not working today," and made no move to eat. The idea of "no work, no meal" seemed to be alive and well in this area. So when I was able to buy sweets, I'd make do with them for lunch, but in Ina I'd skipped lunch altogether. On this trip, however, getting up at six every morning, listening and taking notes until midnight or one, and copying old documents, no matter how excited I may have been, the fatigue was merciless. And what is more, since the top of the pass I'd been at a constant run for more than two and a half miles. If I hadn't run, I could not have kept up.

At last I'd become desperate, and while crossing the river I put my face in the water and drank with abandon. I took off the wing-collared shirt I'd been wearing and my pants and wore only my undershirt and trunks. Dressed like this a little sweat wouldn't hurt. I balled up my shirt and pants, tied them with my belt, and slung them over my shoulder. Wearing my heavy work shoes and looking rather heroic, I ran on once again. Because I'd fallen a little behind, I heard one of the men call out to me. When I caught up they asked, "Are you tired?" "What? No!" I dissembled, though I was having a bit of a rough time of it.

What appeared to be a five- or six-day moon was now in the sky. It was approaching half full, and the night road was bright.

The old man had sung the horseman's song for the better part of an hour atop his horse. Tripping along after him, I ventured to ask, "Are there also *Bon* dance songs?"

"No, *Bon* dancing has already faded away."

"But the songs are still around, aren't they?"

"It's not that they're not, but . . ."

"Then, one of those."

"Well, then one epic ballad . . ." agreed the old man, and he then began a *Bon* epic, the Ōeyama Epic. It was a truly quiet song and seemed to contain an old Buddhist tale.

According to my grandfather Ichigorō, the Hyōgo Epic was the oldest. And I'd heard that his own song pulled water, so to speak, from the stream of the Hyōgo Epic, but I'd never dreamed that I would hear, from an old man in the valley of Sago, in the north of Tsushima, a song almost no different in cadence from my grandfather's. The Ōeyama Epic tells of when Yorimitsu slays the young man Ōeyama, who takes the guise of a demon and steals from others, and it's thought that the lyrics of this song are relatively old.

The old man also sang the Otsuya Seishin and Shiraito epics, among others. And finally we came to where we could see the light of fires in the homes in the valley of Sago. Every time we passed in front of a house, the horses whinnied. The ones the three men rode were all males. And at every home, a mare was tied. With each house we passed, the stallions were drawn to the mares and tried to head in their direction. There is a line in a *haiku* about "a horse neighing when a horse passes," and it was just so. There's a knack to pulling in the reins when passing in front of a home, and it was no time for a song. Anyway,

I'd arrived in Eko, in Sago Valley, having run more than seven miles. The man who'd helped me with my load said, "Tonight come to my house and spend the night," so I parted with the other two and settled in at a farmhouse in the middle of rice paddies. And that night I listened to stories about the valley of Sago until after midnight.

The next day, I visited Old Man Suzuki who, already four years over eighty, was said to be the best singer in the valley. He was behind his house in the shade, making grass sandals. "Grandpa, I heard you're the best singer in Sago, so I've come hoping you'd give me a chance to listen."

"Where are you from? You say you're from Tokyo? That's where the emperor lives. These days the emperor has come on hard times." After that we talked of various things and gradually, in time, he appeared to be in good spirits. Saying, "Maybe I'll sing one song," he started the Ōeyama Epic. He was old and got out of breath, but definitely sang better than the old man of the night before. He had a practiced voice and could truly turn a verse. In places he even resembled one of those ballad singers accompanied by a *samisen*. I sat cross-legged on the ground, listening with my eyes closed. When he'd sung to the end, he simply said, "I'm out of breath, it's no good," and didn't make a move to sing any more thereafter.

On the island of Tsushima there are six miracle-working goddesses of mercy. Traveling to worship these six Kannon first became popular around the end of medieval times. Men and women would form groups and go on a pilgrimage. In Sago there was also a hall for the Goddess of Mercy, and these flocks of pilgrims would come along and stay in the people's homes. When this happened the young people in the village would go and sing, in turns, with the pilgrims. They competed based on the quality of a verse or a phrase, and in the end they would bet all sorts of things. The men would even make the women wager their own bodies. Apparently it was rare for a woman to ask a man to bet his own body, but at any rate, they would go that far. Old Man Suzuki had never lost in such a sing-off with the women. And, it was said, he had slept with nearly all of the beautiful women who had come along on pilgrimages. That was what had been meant the night before about the old man having enjoyed himself because he sang well. Anyway, in the north end of Tsushima, young men and women sang and danced together until around the end of the Meiji period. A fire was lit in the yard in front of the house where the pilgrims were staying, and the pilgrims and village youth would have sing-offs and even dance-offs, forgetting the passing of the night. At such times no distinction was made between married and unmarried women.

Songs were not just sung. They were accompanied by movement and sung back and forth. No doubt Old Man Suzuki was not only in the possession of a good voice but was also the most skilled in these parts at all the rest as well.

In the following year, 1951, I returned to Tsushima for research. I heard the most folksongs in Sasuna, near Sago. One evening I arrived in Sasuna, together with Shibusawa-sensei, chief of this research, and the women of the village performed a Kabuki dance for us. They sang each passage of the story of *Chūshingura*, and the dance with which they accompanied it was truly refined. I became friendly with the old woman who sang. Remarking that I thought this area should have a lot of songs, I asked if she might sing for me. She consented with pleasure, and told me to come over that night.

After finishing dinner at the place I was staying, I waited. When it had grown late, she came to get me. I went along carrying a bottle of *sake*. Four grandmothers, all over sixty, had gathered, and there were young people there as well. One of the older women said, "First *you've* got to start things off by singing," so I sang a verse from the *Bon* festival dance from my hometown.

The women who sang for Miyamoto, seeing him off at the local pier. July 1951.

They said that it was much like their own, and the grandmothers happily began to sing. To moisten their throats I poured them *sake*, and they drank freely. That was when the singing really started. Their voices were pretty. Thinking that if I took out my notebook I'd ruin the mood, I decided only to listen. When one woman had sung and grown short of breath, the next would begin. Many of the songs were from the Kabuki stage, and there was always dancing with the hands. Moving their hips, standing on their knees, although they danced only with their upper bodies, they radiated beauty from deep within. I was unable to see them simply as old farming women.

The young, seated men were attacked and disparaged by the older women, who called them artless monkeys. I learned that *Bon* festival dancing had thrived in Tsushima and that there was *Bon* dancing in nearly every inlet, up every creek. During this *Bon* dancing, they also had a scene from Kabuki, and it had become an important occasion for the learning of folksongs as well. But in Sasuna, for some reason, *Bon* dancing had fallen out of practice. This, it would seem, had reduced the number of opportunities for the elderly to pass on their knowledge to the young.

When the old women had sung, they demanded a song of me as well. I don't know all that many songs, but for every three times they asked, I'd sing once. This, I thought, is how singing competitions came to pass. As the singing became more excited, more and more of the lyrics had to do with sex. The young people shrieked with elation, but the old women remained relatively composed. It had grown late, and the singing voices were loud, so people in the neighborhood gathered in front of the house. The singing continued in this way until about three. Of course, during that time there was also animated conversation. And so it was that I first came to have a notion, though faint, of what sing-offs in these parts had been like.

Chapter 3

Grandpa Kajita Tomigorō

[Tsushima Island, Nagasaki Prefecture, July 1950]

I called on Grandpa Kajita Tomigorō on a clear, bright morning late in July 1950, in the Azamo section of Tsutsu Village, on the island of Tsushima. Earlier at the post office, in the course of a conversation with the postmaster about various aspects of this village, I had learned that only one person from among the village's first settlers was still alive. That was Grandpa Kajita. "Try visiting him," the postmaster encouraged me. "He's over eighty, but in good health, and he's quite capable of conversation."

Here was a person who had watched a village grow from its very beginnings. This was really something. I took my leave of the postmaster and went to visit the home of Grandpa Kajita nearby. He had retired from his position as head of the household and was living with his elderly wife. His son lived in the house just below theirs, where he also ran a confectionery store. I found Grandpa sitting and making fishing tackle on the wooden floor of a house that was blackened inside by the soot from wood fires.

I greeted him, saying, "Grandpa, I hear you were born in Kuka, in Yamaguchi Prefecture. I'm from Nishigata, to the east of Kuka. So I feel nostalgic, coming to visit you . . ."

"Really, you're from Nishigata? You've come a long way,"

he mused. "It's been ages since I've been to Kuka. I imagine it's changed a lot."

The old man spoke entirely in the language of my home, so right from the start he didn't feel like a stranger. And when I said, "I was thinking maybe you could tell me about things from the distant past . . ." he started to speak without hesitation.

It was long ago that I first came here. I was seven at the time, and I didn't know east from west. I'd had bad luck with my parents. My father had died on me when I was just three and my mother around that same time. My brothers all died young as well, so, as for relations, I had just one grandmother and she took me in. Then, as it happened, there was a man named Masamura Jisaburō who didn't have any children; he said he'd try raising me, so I went to live with him and stayed until I was seven. I don't recall much from my childhood. My grandmother's family, they were confectioners. Sometimes I'd go there and be given a toffee to lick, and I looked forward to that.

You ask how it is that I came here to Azamo? Well, they had what were called *meshi morai* [literally, "food receivers"] on Kuka's large fishing boats. It was custom to put five- or six-year-old orphans on these boats, and I was placed on one too. As fishing boats go these were large, with five or six people on a vessel. But they didn't fish off the coast of Kuka. Instead, they all went far away. Since way back, Kuka's fishermen had been going to Tsuno Island in Nagato to fish for sea bream, half a dozen boats to a group. The oldest among these fishermen would become the "big captain" and when they went over to Tsuno he did all the bargaining with the people there, and decided both where they'd fish and where they'd lodge at night. After that everyone worked as they pleased. Then, when it came time to return, all of the crews and the locals would gather together to talk and the big captain would address the people of Tsuno Island, saying, "There were no troubles, so all went well." And the fishermen would all return to Kuka. On the way, their boats traveled in pairs and helped one another out when there was an accident.

They didn't just go to Tsuno Island. Some fishing crews went to Karatsu, too, on the west side of Kyushu. And in time they were even able to go to Tsushima. The Kuka fishermen were the first to make the journey. I've heard that, long before I was born, a feudal lord from Hiroshima married off his daughter to Lord Sō Sukekuni in Tsushima. After that, people started to go back and forth between Hiroshima and Tsushima, fishermen included. Crews from Hiroshima would come and fish off the coast of Kuka and probably the guys from Kuka heard their big stories right there because the Kuka fishermen came back with some tall tales. The visitors claimed there were fish in Tsushima that were fabulously large, and that the sea was filled with fish. Well, if there were that many fish, the Kuka fishermen wanted to go too, and so they followed the crews from Mukainada, in Hiroshima, and crossed over to Tsushima. That was all more than thirty years before I was born.

As it happened, the boat I was put on was going to Tsushima. I'll never forget. It was in 1876. We left Kuka and it took any number of days before we arrived here. On windy days, we'd attach a tiny sail to the bow of the boat. When there was no wind, we'd put the oars in. When we got as far as Hakata, we took on *miso*, soy sauce, salt, and rice. Then we waited for good weather on Genkai Island, at the mouth of Hakata's harbor, and when we thought the weather would hold for a few days, we departed. My young mind couldn't believe that the first boat I'd ever been on was suddenly going to Tsushima. The little town of Kuka had been my playground, and now wherever I looked there were only waves. The boat wouldn't stay still. We were rocked up and down and it was more than I could bear, so I held on to the side and just watched the big waves. The adults were something else, rowing along on the tops of those big

Boy sleeping on fishing nets.
Yamaguchi Prefecture.
August 1962.

waves. They rowed even at night, and I was relieved when we arrived at Iki Island. Climbing up on the hill at Katsumoto, on Iki, we could see mountains far to the north. When I was told that this was probably Tsushima, I was discouraged to think we still had that far to go.

As an orphaned child taken aboard, I didn't have any work to do. I was supposed to just play quietly on the boat. It was so small, though, and there was really no way to amuse myself so it did get boring, but the fishermen all doted on me and I somehow made it through. On the boat, when night fell, I'd take a cloth patchwork kimono from the stern and, covering myself with that, would burrow down under the rush mats. On rainy days, I'd make a roof of these rush mats and do nothing but sleep all day.

We were in Katsumoto for a number of days waiting for fair weather again, and then after a full day at sea we arrived in the castle town of Izuhara [on Tsushima]. I was amazed to find a town like this on an island at the other end of the sea. In those days some of the homes in Izuhara had tiled roofs but many still had rocks on their roofs. The feudal lord made his rounds of the island on horseback. He wore a hat and an open-backed half-coat and was a truly splendid sight.

It must have been around the time of the fall festival that we arrived in Tsushima. We'd left Kuka after *Bon*, but the weather was bad and it had taken the better part of a month.

We contracted with a seafood wholesaler in Izuhara, and because he was going to build a storage shed in Azamo that year, the boat I was on came here. Nowadays, Azamo is a fine, civilized town, but when I first came here, this bay was all dark and grown up with trees. See that grove of chinquapin trees across the bay, those big trees growing packed close together? In these parts, trees like that were growing all over. And there were big rocks in the bay, so it wasn't the kind of place you'd moor a boat. What's more, there were no people. The trees grew right down to water's edge, so close that their branches touched the sea. There was just one shed atop the promontory at the border of Azamo and Little Azamo, and it looked like it might blow over. Someone from Hirado had put in a net for yellowtail just below, and the shed was for the net's caretaker.

Properly speaking, Azamo was in a forest dedicated to Priest Tendō, so people were not supposed to live here. Around here, such places were called *shige*, and the people really feared them. They'd say, "That's Tendō's *shige* so you shouldn't live there, you mustn't do anything that will defile it." The beach in the back of the bay was called "No Admission Beach" and no one was permitted to go there.

You ask why it was that people from Kuka came to live in such a place? There were a lot of samurai in Tsushima, and traditions were strictly observed in all the villages. We fishermen didn't have etiquette or manners, so we weren't able to associate with others there. It didn't matter to us if we suffered divine punishment, and figuring it would be best to just live amongst ourselves, with people who got along well, we decided to build a shed in Azamo and live here.

So you want me to talk a bit more about what happened before that? Well, anything earlier was from stories I heard from the grown-ups so I don't know much. Tsushima is near Korea, and I heard that the Japanese often went to Korea secretly [because Japan was still closed at the time], to buy ginseng. I often heard about ginseng. It was really costly, and what you could hold in the palm of your hand was worth many gold pieces. It just wouldn't grow in Japan, so people went secretly to buy it.

The moneychanger Gohei was the boss. People would refer to "the moneychanger of Kaga," or to "Kaga where the moneychanger is." Gohei was a shipping agent and the wealthiest man in Kaga. When he came to Tsushima, he wore a Japanese kimono and raised a Japanese flag, but when he'd passed Tsushima he raised a Korean flag, wore Korean clothing, and, having become a Korean, made the crossing. Aside from the moneychangers, there were more Gohei imitations than could be counted. Eluding government officials located in Tsushima, they went to Korea as well. And there were far more of them than the government could handle.

The government placed a lookout on Teppō [Gun] Point, west of Azamo, on the southwest end of Tsushima. When they sighted a fishing boat that had set out rowing west from the Kō Peninsula, which juts far out into the ocean east of Azamo, they'd fire a warning gunshot into the air. If the boat didn't start back east, they'd come rowing out of the Tsutsu Bay in a longboat. These boats were narrow and long. They had eighteen oars and were so fast it seemed they were flying. They'd even beaten steamships in a race.

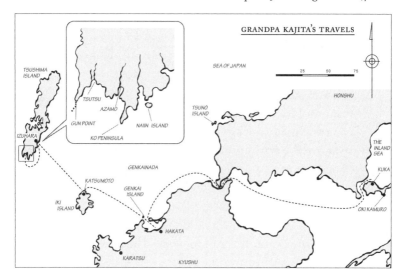

With all those oars, they were also called "centipedes" and everyone feared them.

When the gun was fired from Teppō Point, the rowers in Tsutsu Bay would ready themselves. When a second shot was fired, they'd come out rowing. Nearly all the fishing boats were caught. And when they were caught, they were taken to Izuhara and subjected to water torture. They'd force the fishermen's mouths open and pour water in and they'd choke. It was more painful than a person could bear. Fearing that, the fishermen did their best not to go west of Kō Peninsula.

As it happens, nearly three miles out from Kō Peninsula there was a place called Ōse, the number-one fishing spot for sea bream in Tsushima. There were big fish there. At times they caught sea bream there that were three feet from eye to tail, bigger than any you might see these days. It was that kind of fishing spot, so everyone went. And before they knew it, the wind and tides would take the fishermen out to the west. A gun would go off, the longboat would come along, and they'd run for it, scattering like baby spiders. Those who fell behind were caught, and though they'd committed no crime, they too were subjected to water torture. It was like dancing on the edge of the boiling pot of hell.

When night fell, the fishermen would anchor and spend the night east of there, off the coast from Naiin, in the shadow of Naiin Island. They called that place "Sails Down," and it was the best-hidden anchorage.

Then, after the Meiji Restoration [1868], fishing boats were allowed west of the Kō Peninsula. The Kuka fishermen jumped for joy. The sea bream there were coming from the west so, without a doubt, there were even more sea bream off the coast from Tsutsu, and that's where all the fishermen rushed to be. Sure enough, the fish were there for the catching. The ocean was full of them. The people of Tsutsu allowed fishing offshore, but didn't permit people to moor their boats there, so when night fell these fishermen would go back to Naiin Island.

Well, one day something terrible happened. It was December 15, 1872. The sun had sparkled a bit in the morning, and when it sparkles, a wind will come up. Not thinking much of it, though, the Kuka fishermen headed out, offshore from Tsutsu. Past noon, a terrific northerly began to blow. They say the air grew damp and salty, and Tsutsu, right there in front of their eyes, grew dim and hard to see. They rowed for Tsutsu with all their might, but nearly everyone was swept out to sea and died. Altogether forty-four people went missing, and the great Katsuemon was among them. The man was thought to be a fishing god. Katsuemon could look at the weather, the tide, at fish . . . he was never off the mark about anything having to do with fishing. But even Katsuemon died, and to this day that storm is referred to as the Katsuemon Storm.

Most everyone living along the sea between Kuka and Tsushima knew Katsuemon. If someone mentioned "Katsuemon from Kuka" others would think, "Oh, the fishing god." If someone asked Katsuemon, "What'll the weather be tomorrow?" ten times out of ten it would be as Katsuemon had said. But even Katsuemon was capable of an oversight. Apparently he'd said, "What an unpleasant day!" on his way out, and he never came back.

The people of Tsutsu were hard on outsiders, but they were all good people and they held a memorial service at the Eisen Temple for the forty-four who had died. And to this day, the souls of the dead are enshrined there. Sometimes, on the night of December 15, the people of Tsutsu see the spirits of the forty-four fishermen walking in from the sea, towards the Eisen Temple.

But even after such a large accident, the people of Kuka didn't stop coming to Tsushima. It's said that on that day, one of the boats had capsized and drifted away with a father and son clinging to it. They were exceptionally lucky, for they drifted and drifted, to the ocean off Hirado, and were saved by the people there. This father and son returned to Kuka and told others, "Our boat capsized because waves came in over the bow and stern. Mount wide boards in your bow and stern, and your boats will be stronger in the waves." After hearing this, fishermen started doing just that. And when waves rose up they spilled back to the sea and didn't swamp the boat. In any case, after that, there was never an occasion when as many as forty or fifty people died.

There's an explanation for why we came to live in Azamo. The year before I came to Tsushima, in December of 1875, an eight-oared longboat from Tsutsu went to Izuhara to make a payment to the authorities there. When they were on their way back, a terrible westerly blew, and they were beaten by waves and overturned off the Kō Peninsula. They were found by a large fishing boat from Kuka which, after uprighting the longboat, rowed back to Naiin, nursed the crew, and brought them back to Tsutsu. The people of Tsutsu were overjoyed and they said, "We're truly in your debt. As a token of our thanks, we'll do whatever you ask of us." So the people from Kuka said, "In that case, can you allow us to live along the Azamo Bay?"

"We can do almost anything you ask for," they replied, "but that place is *shige* and you'd be cursed."

To which the Kukans said, "It doesn't matter if there's a curse. Besides, now we're living in an age where a living god, the emperor, rules Japan, so Priest Tendō won't do us any harm." So, with permission to build a shed in Azamo, they returned to Kuka.

The following year, the year they built a shed here, that was when I first came. When I say we built a shed, that was not something we fishermen could do. First, a merchant from Izuhara named Kameya Hisabei came, felled trees, cleared the land, and built a shed. The roof was made of cedar that had been cut down and split into boards. Bamboo was then placed over these cedar planks, with rocks on top of that to hold it all in place. The shed's posts were made with logs that were sunk right into the ground, and its walls were lined with straw mats. There wasn't a floor— just straw mats placed on the ground—but just the same, the place made me feel like a lord. Until then, every day I'd only been living on waves. I'd wake to the sound of them striking the side of the boat. It's nothing when you get used to it, but as a child of seven I wanted to try sleeping in a house on land.

I've been calling it a shed, but it was really more like a storehouse. A clerk and apprentice came from Kameya's store in Izuhara, and they'd buy the fish we caught, gut them, salt them, and take them back there. Most every day a boat would come from Izuhara, and when they did, they'd bring the kind of things fishermen want: rice, *miso*, tobacco, and the like. We'd come back from sea, enter the shed, and buy the various things we needed. After that, everyone would sit indoors by a fire that burned quietly in the sunken hearth and talk late into the night.

All the talk was frightful for a child, for fishermen's stories are all about encounters with rough seas. And in the old days, for some reason, there were lots of monsters. Off the coast of Kuka, on a drizzly night, like clockwork, a voice would come up from deep down in the ocean, saying, "Give me a ladle, give me a barrel." That was the cry of a sea monster, and if you gave him a ladle, he'd use it to fill the boat with water and sink it. And Genkainada [a stretch of ocean between Tsushima and the Kyushu mainland] was a place where sea spirits often appeared. Everyone delighted in the telling of such stories, but we small children were seized with fear.

I wasn't the only orphan who had been brought along. Every boat had a *meshi morai*, so there were probably seven or eight of us. I'd go into the shed and there'd be others, so I had someone to play with and wasn't bored.

The thing that caused the most trouble for the fishermen was the harbor. Countless big rocks along the shore left no place to moor a boat. The inlet at Old Azamo was large and could have made for a good harbor, but there were only a few of us, and it was just too hard for us to clear, so we decided to use Little Azamo, and set to clearing a harbor there.

Clearing a harbor meant removing the rocks that were lying around in it. People are resourceful, and after some thought the fishermen came up with a way to clear out the big rocks: When the tide was out and the sea was shallow, they'd put a boat on either side of a rock. Then they'd lay down a log across the two boats, and the strong fellows among them would dive into the water with a large rope made of wisteria vines and wrap it around the rock. And last, they'd tie the other end of the rope to the log which they'd slung between the boats. When the tide came in, the boats would rise and the rock too would float free, suspended in the ocean. Then they'd row their boats out and drop the rock in a deep spot. Using two boats and one turn of the tide, they could only move one rock. But working patiently, they managed to make a place where the boats could moor. All of us celebrated when the work was done but then a big storm came, bringing the rocks up with it again and making a mess of the harbor.

The fishermen had dumped the rocks in a bad place and it was decided they had to take them much farther out. And so they did. That was no ordinary effort. As a child, all I could do was watch, but in my own childish way I was impressed by how hard they worked. And you know, they did all of that between fishing runs.

In that way, the New Year passed and about the time the trees were coming into leaf we returned to Kuka. Back there, I was once again in Masamura's keep and, as before, I helped out with the making of confections at my grandmother's house. Then, when fall came, I came to Tsushima as a *meshi morai*. I repeated this until I turned ten, and since somehow or other I'd learned how to prepare meals, after that I went along as the cook. This work was for children who had yet to come of age, or for men who were over sixty. You'd eat what you were given and the pay was scanty, but poor families would send their children from early on to be cooks on fishing boats so that they'd have fewer mouths to feed.

By that time, I'd come to understand most of what was going on around me. It would have been fine to be a confectioner in Kuka, but since I had very few kin and could do whatever I wanted, wherever I wanted, I decided on the life of a fisherman and set out in earnest to learn how to fish.

After that, Azamo became more and more civilized. Everyone had a saw and hoe and they cut down trees and turned the soil. They cleared small plots and took to growing vegetables, and somehow made this place livable.

In only five or six years, between 1876 and 1882, Azamo changed beyond recognition. And while I'd thought of it as a very distant place, around that time boats were made stronger and their sails bigger, so they could go from Kuka to Tsushima in five or six days. Azamo became a place you could go to easily, in no time at all, as if you were going next door. And that happened with only a few small changes in the way boats were made. On top of that, in Azamo, though they were only sheds, we had homes. The more crude among them had knotty log posts and walls made from the branches of chinquapin trees, but when we came in from the sea at night, we had a place to sleep.

We weren't educated. We didn't know how to read or write and could hardly count money. We knew nothing of how they were keeping the accounts at the Kameya storehouse, and we asked Master Kameya to make Masamura Kunihira of Kuka the clerk there. Do you know of Kunihira? He was a great man. In Kuka, he could have lived with his hands in his pockets. After all, he was a gentleman. But he came to this remote place and became the storehouse clerk. The storehouse may have been Master Kameya's, but being a man of understanding, he employed Kunihira. And we worked and left everything up to Kunihira.

Kunihira told us, "This storehouse should be owned by someone from Kuka. Things aren't going well these days because Kameya doesn't know how to do business. Living in Tsushima, he doesn't understand the outside world, so he's losing out all the time. It's not like in the days of the feudal lords. People these days are shrewd, and nothing will come of this business if it's handled in Kameya's large-hearted manner. We must bring someone competent from Kuka to handle the business here. I can look after things, but I have work to do in Kuka, so I can't devote all my energies to this place." It was agreed that what Kunihira had said was quite reasonable and so Goshima Shinsuke was brought here to replace him. This guy came along and gave a kind of structure to Azamo. He was a deep thinker too and he said, "No doubt, in the future, things will open up as far as Korea. When that happens, Azamo will be right in the middle between Korea and Japan. All the fishing boats going to Korea will pass through here. To prepare for that time, we must all settle here. Nothing will come of going back to Kuka whenever winter comes. Those who can bring their parents and siblings should do so." And saying this, he built himself a house with dirt walls.

Eventually everyone built houses. I was still young, so I was going back and forth between Kuka and Azamo, and in those days it was popular to leave Kuka for Hawaii. While a day of work in Kuka only paid thirteen *sen* [100 *sen* = 1 yen], in Hawaii you'd get fifty. Saying they wanted better earnings, people left, one after the other. But I was now a fisherman and had decided to spend my life catching fish, so I didn't change my mind. And besides, I was catching a lot of fish. Try catching 150–250 pounds of sea bream in a day. Your fingers and arms start to hurt. They're all big fish. You feel one on your line and try pulling, but it doesn't come up. Just when you think you've snagged a rock, the fish starts jerking on the line. It's no easy task to handle and humor it, and pull it up to the side of the boat. It's like persuading a woman who hates you. You try this trick and that, letting the line out and pulling it in, and if you're not careful, the line will be cut. On the other hand, there's no greater happiness than when you bring one up. Try catching ten such sea bream in a single day. You'll generally feel pretty good, and at night you'll want to have a drink. At times like that, you don't think about things like making money. I just felt that fishing was fascinating. It was a mystery to me why everyone in the world wouldn't want to become a fisherman.

You know, it's not like catching little sea bream off the coast of Kuka. Before long we weren't just fishing at Ōse. Twelve to fifteen miles farther out was another shoal, and we discovered lots of sea bream there too. I couldn't believe my eyes. And it wasn't just sea bream. We found an incredible number of swordfish—lots of big ones swimming with their fins up out of the water. But we didn't know how to catch them, and we talked it over, saying "If we caught these, who knows how much money we'd make."

There were lots of yellowtail, too. But Kuka fishermen

specialized in sea bream, so we didn't know how to catch yellowtail. If only someone could come and catch them. The whole situation was really frustrating.

Then, when I was coming back from Kuka, I met some fishermen from Okikamuro (in the Tōwa Township, Ōshima District, Yamaguchi Prefecture) in Hakata. I asked them, "Do you want to try going to Tsushima? There are fabulously large fish. You catch them, and you catch them, but there are more than you can catch."

"Are there yellowtail?" they asked.

"You want yellowtail? I said. "If you went to Tsushima you'd be amazed. When the yellowtail come, there are so many that the water level rises."

"Is that true?"

"Would I lie?"

So it came to be that fishermen from Okikamuro came to Tsushima. That was 1887, and I'd become a competent young man. Those guys from Okikamuro knew how to fish yellowtail, and they came here and caught an appalling amount. They needed a storehouse, so they got Kuranari of Izuhara to be their wholesaler. He was a good man and treated them well. The yellowtail fishing spot was off Teppō Point, but they worked out of Azamo and developed Naka Azamo.

Just as it had been in Little Azamo, it was hard work clearing rocks out of the inlet, but by that time people knew how to get dynamite and break up the rocks with it. More fishing boats were also coming to these parts, and they made sure that each boat that came into the harbor slung a rock onboard and took it offshore, so clearing the harbor was easier than it had been in Little Azamo. Once the rocks had been cleared away, the harbor in Naka Azamo was larger and deeper, a good port.

You can't build a harbor all at once, and though I said it was easier, it probably took about thirty years for it to get like it is now. A harbor that only held four or five boats

Azamo, Tsushima,
Nagasaki Prefecture.
July 1950.

when the fishermen from Okikamuro first came sheltered more
than five hundred by the middle
of the 1920s, and larger boats
were able to come in too. You know, the energy and drive
that fishermen have shouldn't be taken lightly.

Up until late in the 1890s most of the homes in Azamo
were sheds. They were truly crude. Then, in the same year
that there was a war, in 1894 or 1895 [the years of the Sino-
Japanese war], a big wind blew. I'd never seen a wind like
that. Little Azamo is in a hollow so it wasn't hit so bad, but
in Naka Azamo the wind was channeled right in, and a lot
of houses were blown over. I heard tell of a family who was
sitting by their hearth when a huge gust suddenly came,
picked their house up, and carried it eight to ten yards. The
house was flattened. It's said that the family suddenly realized they were sitting outdoors. That's just how bad the
typhoon was.

Well, things couldn't go on like that. Typhoons would
come again in the future, and stronger homes had to be
built. There's a place called Sare, near Okikamuro, and we

brought a tile maker from there and had him make roof tiles. While there were stone roofs in other parts of Tsushima, this was the only place with tile roofs from early on. Tsushima was known for its hawks, crows, and stone roofs, but only here in Azamo we had tile roofs and plaster walls and rows of nice homes. People came from Tsutsu to have a look.

People really started to settle here late in the 1880s. In those days one could often see fox fire burning over on the other side of the inlet. It was rather unsettling. And on a really quiet night, there was sometimes a sound like the world being torn apart. People said this was probably Priest Tendō taking flight. By the late 1890s, the number of houses had grown to a hundred, and about seventy boats came from the Kii Domain to fish yellowtail every year. The harbor became lively, and we stopped seeing the fox fire or hearing the sound of Priest Tendō in flight. It seems that in this world we live in, people are at the top.

Around that time I got married and decided to live out my life here, and because we couldn't get by on fishing alone, I taught my wife what I'd learned as a boy about how to make sweets. I'd go out to sea while my wife made sweets at home and sold them. In that way, we made a humble living.

There was a lot that was interesting and much that was sad. But as a person with no talents, fishing was about all that interested me. As for what was sad, the time when my wife suffered a loss was about all. Fifty years living with her, that was the happiest thing of all.

I've been talking for quite a while. Shall we take a break?

Chapter 4

Nagura Talk

[Aichi Prefecture, October 1956 and May 1957]

Here I'd like to try conveying the nature of village life through stories told by elderly people from Nagura Village in Aichi Prefecture [located on Honshu, Japan's main island].

Nagura is in the mountains of Mikawa, near the border of Shinanō. To reach Nagura, one takes a train through the mountains and along the contours of valleys to a stop called Taguchi, and from there a bus that first climbs to the actual town of Taguchi, set upon a plateau. Taguchi developed as a stopover on the Ina Road that connects Toyohashi and Iida of Shinanō. Continuing from here, one drops down into a valley, only to climb again on a winding road up a steep slope to a high pass. This is Nobezaka, or what the villagers call *Banzai Pass*. Look north from the top of Banzai Pass and you'll see a plateau with gently undulating hills. This is Nagura, and its homes are scattered here and there at an elevation of 2,000 to 2,500 feet. After climbing such a steep mountain road, encountering this scenery is unexpected. On the plateau, winter is cold and spring comes late.

Life was hard here at first. The records tell of a time when more than half of the population deserted one of the Nagura communities. However, the people who live here are truly hard-working, and they have managed to build a village that is very nearly the ideal for a rural village in Japan today.

When the Human Relations Integrated Research Group, led by Professor Muramatsu of the Psychiatry Department at Nagoya University, decided to study this village, I was given the opportunity to participate. I visited Nagura in the fall of 1956. Thereafter, I went twice more, and was able to get a close look at the state of the village.

There are two types of villages in Japan: those where large landholders own most of the land, which is worked by many tenant farmers, and those in which land ownership is relatively balanced. In the latter case, even if it comes to pass that someone becomes a large landowner, often they will not thrive for long. Many researchers are interested in villages where landowners and tenants are distinct, but few take a second look at villages of the more balanced type. Accordingly, I'm making an effort to closely study such villages, and, based on their number, I've come to think there may be even more villages of this type than of the other. Nagura is a typical example: while there were large landholders in the beginning, they did not continue for long.

Although the villagers are living in the mountains, in a village of this sort one can observe a certain modernity in their character. In Nagura, there lives a farmer by the name of Sawada Hisao who is quite knowledgeable of local history. Respected by his fellow villagers, he was a great help to me at the time of my research. I was studying Ōkubo, Inosawa, and Yashirowaki [individual communities located within Nagura Village], and when I told Sawada-san that I wanted to hold a roundtable talk with old folks, he called together four people. So it was that Kaneda Shigesaburō of Inosawa, Gotō Hideyoshi of Ōkubo, and Kaneda Kanehira and [Ms.] Ogasawara Shiu of Yashirowaki—all of whom were older than seventy—gathered in a temple in Ōkubo. Moderating, Sawada-san kept their conversation lively.

At that time I heard and was most impressed by the story of Kanehira-san working in his rice paddies until late, and

Nagura,
Aichi Prefecture.
May 1957.

particularly in the paddy in front of Shigekazu-san's house, where he worked until eight or nine at night. Kanehira-san said that he was able to work particularly late in front of Shigekazu-san's house "by the light of a fire that was always lit until late in the front room." At this, Ogasawara Shiu-san explained that such a fire was not lit every night, but on the days Kanehira-san was working, assuming that he would once again be working late.

In fact, until this was discussed at the roundtable, one party had not told the other of their good will, and the latter had been under the impression that these were just people who stayed up late. I suspect that in village communities there are unseen instances, like this one, of people helping one another. Of course, to the contrary, there are unseen instances of people dragging one another down as well.

ROUNDTABLE DISCUSSION

Kaneda Kanehira: Well, it was probably when the road was built that this village really began to change. I was eight at the time, so that must have been 1892. I was born in January of 1885.

Kaneda Shigesaburō: Yes, things changed after the road

was built. Being four years older than you, I remember a
lot from those days. That was when Harada Jinpachirō was
mayor. As a child, Mayor Harada had been adopted by a
liquor-store owner who was the village head in Shimizu.
Though he'd been adopted, he was a great man. He was
related by blood to Furuhashi Genrokurō of Inabu, the fin-
est character in these parts. Harada fraternized both with
him and with Kanehira Akiyoshi of Enshū. Furuhashi was
a member of the prefectural assembly, and he broke his back
trying to get a prefectural highway from Taguchi to Inabu.
Then around 1891 a guy named Gotō became prefectural assemblyman, and he was the one that turned the Ina Road,
which passed from Taguchi through to Tsugu, into a prefectural highway.

Gotō: Yes, that was the way it was. I have a clear memory
of that as well. Over in Ōdaira, near Sachisa's place, a shack
was built for cooking, and a lot of laborers were brought in
to do the construction work. That was probably the most
outsiders we ever had descend upon this village.

Kaneda Kanehira: That contractor was a good and reliable
man. What was his name? It was so long ago . . .

Kaneda Shigesaburō: I think he was called Itako Yoshi,
though I can't recall how he wrote his name. That man stole
another man's wife. Her name was Okoma-san, and she was
a good woman who many men fell for. When the work was
done and it was time to leave, Okoma-san disappeared as
well. All told, it was good to have a road that could accommodate cars. Before that, there was just a narrow path that
climbed up the valley to the top of Nobezaka. Shortly after
the road was completed, the Sino-Japanese war began . . .

Gotō: Yes, that became Banzai Pass.

Kaneda Shigesaburō: When the people of the village
sent off soldiers, they'd go to the top of the pass and yell

"*banzai!*" But that lacked warmth because when the soldier said his goodbyes and headed down from the pass he would disappear from view at once. So we began making our sendoffs seven or eight hundred yards this side of the pass, at the north end of Ichibaguchi. That was where we'd yell "*banzai!*" The person departing would then wave while walking. And we'd stand there and wave back. It took a little while before the road would bend and they were no longer in sight. We were loath to part. At the time of the Russo-Japanese war, of the Japanese-German war [World War I] and of the recent war, when soldiers were enlisted, we sent them all off there. So there was something about leaving the village that was emotionally weighted.

Gotō: That's the way it was. When I'd go away somewhere and come back to Banzai Pass, it felt good when our village came into sight. In those days there were still a lot of forest fires. They were usually caused by someone smoking in the mountains, and their discarded cigarette butt would start a fire. So, along the new road they've built these rest areas here and there, pits dug in the dirt with signs that say SMOKING AREA. The old road didn't have things like that.

Kaneda Shigesaburō: The police had those rest stops made. They did a lot to make people guard against fires. Until that road was complete, all the cargo was carried by horses, and once the horses got used to the work, a single person could pull about five packhorses at once. A bell would be attached to the bridle, and those made by Ōsone in Nagoya were said to have a fine sound.

Ogasawara: Those bells went "*sharanko, sharanko.*" That was truly a fine sound. You could listen to the sound of the bell and know where the packhorse was from. And the packhorse drivers sang. A man in this village by the name of Koma-san was a skilled singer. He stuttered, was short-tempered, and beat his wife all the time because, he said, she wouldn't listen to him. But when he arrived at the top of the pass, he'd start singing in a voice that really carried. Though far off, he could be heard clearly from his own house. And when his wife heard him singing, she would light the fire for his bath. That song was his signal for her to prepare his bath.

Kaneda Kanehira: Yes, that was Kaneda Komakichi. He had nothing to recommend him, but he sang so well that everyone was enraptured by his voice . . .

Ogasawara: There were those who actually fell in love with that voice. His wife, for one.

Kaneda Kanehira: Any person, unless they're an idiot, has something they can do better than anyone else.

Ogasawara: A woman shouldn't spend her whole life with a man who has no merits to speak of. The wife is attracted to *something* in her old man, and the husband is drawn to something in his wife as well. Even if she's a fool, if a woman is attractive down there, her man won't leave her. But just the same, we women were at a disadvantage. Because we have the monthly hindrance. . . . Women suffered a lot because of that. There were so many superstitious people in these parts, and they made a real fuss about that time of the month, so in the past every house had a *himaya*, a separate shed. When menstruation began we'd stay there, and we even had a separate stove to cook with. It was said that if we ate with the family, the family fire would be defiled. But when I was about fifteen that custom became much less common. That change too may have been because of the road built for cars. In Ure, on the other side of this mountain, they had *himaya* until just recently. Around here, although the sheds disappeared early, when a woman has her period she's still not to offer tea at the family's Buddhist altar. And for twelve days she's not to enter the areas dedicated to the local deities.

Kaneda Shigesaburō: To Harada Jinpachirō's house, which was also the liquor store in Shimizu, they attached an awning and made that the *himaya*. It was about four square yards in size.

Ogasawara: When a woman had her period she wasn't supposed to wear a man's *geta* [wooden clogs] either. And even now, old people like me don't hang our undergarments in the direct sunlight or spread them out to dry. My young daughter-in-law doesn't have these rules, but I hang mine in the shade, because it wouldn't feel right.

Kaneda Shigesaburō: Women were at a disadvantage with regard to everything. Even though the world changed rapidly for men when the road was completed. . . . As for what changed, the first thing was that the packhorses were replaced by carts and horse-drawn wagons. In this village, a guy by the name of Goichi was the first to have a horse-drawn wagon. After that, those who could manage a horse had a wagon. At one time there were sixteen horse-drawn wagons in this village. Anyway, for the thirty years after the wagons came, this village was full of life. There was so much work.

Gotō: The number of carts grew, too. In Nagura alone there were fifty cart-pullers. Young men who'd been hired on or adopted by farming families often became cartmen when they set up independent branch families. After the fall harvest was in, they'd go to work as cart-pullers.

Kaneda Shigesaburō: There were cart-pullers in every community but Inosawa. And that community had no horse-drawn wagons either. The horse-drawn wagons had four wheels and the carts had two. Using these, freight was carried between here and Taguchi. People in Taguchi then carried this cargo on to Ebi. From Ebi it would get carried to Shinshiro, and in that way the goods went all the way to Toyohashi. And where the freight was transferred, those places grew rapidly. In Taguchi, for example, there were less than ten houses up until the end of the Meiji period [1912]. It had long been a luggage transfer point on the Ina Road, and there were stores there, but it was a lonely place. Yet when freight was brought in on carts and transferred there, the number of houses suddenly grew.

Gotō: Until around the end of Meiji, Inabashi (on the Iida Road) had more houses than Taguchi. The liquor store in Inabashi made *miso*. You'd pay ten *sen* for that miso and they'd put it in a wrapper of woven barley straw. In the days before carts, we'd carry that on our backs in *shoiko* [wood-framed backpacks] and we'd get one *sen* of compensation. When carts came along, we were able to carry a lot more cargo. And not just *miso* and soy sauce. However, if one is to speak of the cargo that came from Inabashi, it was really only *miso* and soy sauce. When the number of carts grew, we did even less traffic with Inabashi while our comings and goings with Taguchi grew. We could take rice to Taguchi, buy *miso* there, and bring it back. Or we'd take wood boards. Originally we'd pulled a horse as far as Ebi to buy things like salt, straw mats, and bamboo hats. That was the cheapest place, but when the carts started coming through, the oil shop in Taguchi began to sell salt, and in time you could find everything you were looking for right there in Taguchi. And you could get twenty to thirty *sen* in one day taking boards there. Before that, such work hadn't existed.

Kaneda Shigesaburō: Until around the beginning of Meiji [1868], all the food and clothing in this village was plain. And if you grew rice, in the old days the yield was poor. In Ōkubo and Inosawa, lots of the paddies brought in even less than five bushels of rice. That's less than one third of what you can get now.

In those days more *hie* [millet] was grown here than anything else. It was grown in the barley fields. Around the time the barley came into ears we sowed millet between the rows. By the time the barley matured and was harvested, the millet was a vivid green. Once the millet had ripened and been cut, it was tied into bundles and propped up here and there in the field. When it had dried well, we'd cut the ears with a razor or knife. The ears were then spread out on straw mats to dry and pounded with a mallet to separate out the seeds, which were next put through a sieve to take out the chaff and then pounded on a mortar. People ate millet and it was also used as fodder for their horses. A half-gallon of millet and a pint of beans were cooked, mixed together, and fed to the horse once a day. The horses were better fed than us humans.

People mostly ate *hezurimeshi* [a mixture of rice, greens, and grains]. We'd boil dried greens, give the water we'd boiled them in to the horse, finely chop the greens and mix them with millet and rice before cooking it. Long ago the mixture was about half rice and half millet, but in the 1890s less millet was grown, and the proportion of millet used was one-third as much as rice. We'd add a little bit of salt, too. It was customary for the boys to be well cared for, so when *hezurimeshi* was cooked, the rice was kept separate for them to eat, and the rest of the ingredients were mixed together. There was scarcely any rice in what the adults ate. Barley was also added in place of millet. *Miso* soup was generally the side dish. But on the first, fifteenth, and twenty-eighth of each month, we had rice boiled with *adzuki* beans, and that was really tasty.

Millet did pretty well even in years when other crops fared poorly. Bugs didn't infest it, and, no matter how many years you kept it, the taste didn't change. For this reason we all stored millet in the community storehouse. It was probably around 1885 when Furuhashi-san, working for an association to help the poor, had everyone put aside millet for famine relief. We'd had a community storehouse since way back, but we'd stopped using it in the beginning of Meiji. But he brought that practice back. In the beginning, we put the millet in straw bags, but later we switched to bamboo baskets.

In those days, most farming families kept a stock of two years' worth of food. Rice was stored unhusked, and when a new crop was harvested you'd start eating last year's rice. Until then you were eating rice from two years before. On the rare occasion that you'd eat new rice, it was so tasty you'd smack your lips. A good farmer was someone who ate his way from one old stock of grains to the next. That being the case, you'd go nearly your whole life without eating tasty rice! If you didn't put up with that, you wouldn't get through the famine years. And you'd take good measure of a family in the village that was following this practice. If you had a daughter, you'd marry her into that family because it's the hardest thing having your own daughter right there in front of you with nothing to eat.

Gotō: Even now there aren't many families that eat just rice. People say you get *beriberi* [a condition resulting from a vitamin B1 deficiency] from eating only rice, so most people mix in some barley.

Ogasawara: I think it was in the late 1890s that we pretty much stopped eating rice mixed with greens. My family had been especially poor, so we had a hard time coming up with something to eat. When I was six, I went to work as a nursemaid, taking care of another family's children, and I did that until I was nine. A six-year-old these days is childish, but in my day we were treated as grown-ups. When I turned ten I was sent out to cut grass for the livestock. And at sixteen I was married. These days sixteen-year-olds are junior high school students. At the time my husband Keitarō was twenty-three. Because I'd worked, I hadn't been to a single day of elementary school. My husband was from near Okazaki and was adopted into the Matsuzawa family. His mother was widowed early and, having a lot of children, she found it was hard to raise them all, so she came to this village and asked the Matsuzawas to adopt him. He grew up as their child. A house was built for him on the Matsuzawa's property, and he set up a branch family and took me as his wife. He had the house and grounds, but no money at all. Since there was no mother-in-law and no sisters, my parents and others told me the situation would probably be easy, and I had a mind to marry. We were together for sixty years. A quiet man, he'd go through a day hardly saying a word. But he did twice as much work as the next man. That was his good point . . .

Kaneda Kanehira: He sure was a hard worker. I could keep up with most anyone, but your old man was something else. For a small man, he sure could work.

Ogasawara: We were poor, but since we took that for granted we had no complaints. When I think of it now, we really put up with a lot. Those days, for a girl to go to school, she'd have to be from an awfully fine home. When I was little, the only girls who went to school were Sawada-san's mother and the daughter from the liquor store. When the liquor store's daughter quit going, Sawada-san's mother quit too. In those days the boys really teased the girls.

Kaneda Kanehira: Not many boys went to school either. If eight boys graduated from the advanced course in one year, that was a lot.

Ogasawara: We poor families went to great pains to scratch our way through. More than anything, we had to be frugal with food. In my house, we mainly ate *daikon* radish mixed with rice. We grew a lot of *daikon*, cut it into strips, and dried it. We'd freeze it over the winter. We also hung it out to dry, whole, and pickled it. *Daikon* was in our rice *and* it was the side dish. Just the same, when we boiled strips of the radish slowly with seaweed and bamboo shoots and ate it in the mountains, it was delicious. Before noon, I'd put the rice bucket in a sack and the cooked vegetables in a wood bucket and take these to our field on the mountain. But when millet-rice was replaced by barley-rice, we pretty much stopped eating the vegetables. You could say our lives had gotten that much better. At first, I'd cook the barley at night and put it aside, and then the next day I'd mix it with rice and cook it again, but later we started eating ground barley.

Kaneda Shigesaburō: We drank a lot of tea. We grew tea from the beginning. In May we'd all pick the new leaves and rub them together between our hands. Every house had a tea bucket. We'd put the tea leaves in it, sprinkle in a little salt, pour the hot water, and mix it with a tea whisk. It was good when there were a lot of bubbles, so we'd dip out the bubbly parts into tea cups with a tea dipper and drink it. *Sanka* [mountain gypsies] would come along and sell us tea whisks. They were big, about eight to ten inches long. It was said that if you gave a person young tea in the morning before they headed out, they were protected from injury.

As for the tea bucket, it didn't have handles. It was big, and probably held a gallon or more. I still have one. I use it to wash rice. We didn't have one-handled tea buckets either. The one-handled buckets were for salt water. In the old days, every house had a salt-water bucket. In the mornings we'd fill the bucket with water, drop a little salt in, and purify the house inside and out. When we no longer purified our houses, we started making the one-handled buckets larger and using them to wash rice.

Kaneda Kanehira: Speaking of change, lighting changed a lot too. When we were little, oil lamps were still being used. Before that there were portable candlesticks. They'd place an iron dish with legs on top of a stand made from a round slice of wood, fill the dish with oil and light it on fire. In the case of the oil lamps, there was a box under the legs, and that was where you put a variety of pine wood that had a lot of resin. With an adze or an axe, we'd finely chop pine roots and knots. The better-off families had paper-enclosed oil lights. In this village, when we first started raising silkworms, we still had oil lamps. Then, early in the 1890s, they were replaced by metal box lanterns with narrow wicks. Oil lamps were somehow not suited for the raising of silkworms. Lamps came into use late in the 1890s, shortly after the arrival of metal box lanterns. Around that time indoor fire pits suddenly disappeared as well. Until then, every home had a fire pit cut into the floor of the kitchen, and a large pothook hanging from the ceiling. In no time at all, they were replaced by *kotatsu* [foot-warming braziers].

Ogasawara: Well, in the old days, we ate things that didn't even taste good, and we worked hard. My husband didn't take off his straw sandals from the time he got up in the morning until he went to bed at night. He even wore them when he took a nap. We lived together for sixty years, but I never saw him really laugh. Kanehira-san, you sure worked hard too.

Kaneda Kanehira: I didn't like to be outdone. Of all the farm work, tilling the paddies was the hardest. I'd till a quarter of an acre in a day. We'd wear bamboo shin guards while we turned the soil to avoid hitting our legs with our pronged hoes.

Gotō: We did the paddy tilling as a community because the work was just too hard to do alone. The healthy among us would get in a line and hoe. Usually about eight people lined up. Being a hard worker, Kanehira-san would hoe six rows at a time. We'd be hoeing four and could hardly keep up. So sometimes we'd take shortcuts. After a whole day turning the soil, I'd have twenty-five blisters on my hands. And they would become calluses.

Kaneda Kanehira: I sure worked. Pronged hoes in the old days were large. They weighed six-and-a-half pounds and had prongs that were fourteen inches long. With the handle, they weighed more than eight pounds. You'd swing that from morning to night. With only a hoe, I tilled three and a half acres. And I grew as much rice as the next guy. In 1906, I brought in five tons of rice. There was also rice I didn't bag, so I probably had eighteen bushels for every quarter acre. When you're working that much land alone, you can't go home as long as the sun is up. I worked until midnight to pay for rice seedlings, and there were times when I returned home to find that my children had put out their own bedding and were hidden deep under the covers, asleep.

Ogasawara: You really were the hardest worker in this village. When you were working in your family's paddy below Shigekazu's house, his father would say, "Tonight we must not close the storm doors because Kanehira-san is still working." And saying that, they'd keep things so that the front light could be seen.

Kaneda Kanehira: Oh, so that's how it was. I'd always been grateful because that family kept their front light burning late, and since I could see the end of my hoe, I was able to work into the night. Meanwhile, I sure ate! Can't say whether it was tasty or not, but I ate five times a day. I'd wake up at three in the morning and eat *ochanoko* [a light meal], and then go to the mountain to gather firewood. I'd come back and eat breakfast around nine. That was always one bowl of rice. Lunch was sometime between noon and two o'clock, and I'd usually eat that in some field in the mountains or at the paddy. At five, I'd eat what was called *yoija* [another meal] and then dinner was at nine. When we all worked together turning soil in the paddies, someone would call us to a meal by pounding on a wooden board. Then we'd all come in from the paddies and eat *yoija*. When we were working, we'd be waiting for the sound of the board being struck. After that, we'd work till dark, until we couldn't see our hands.

Gotō: It's not as if everyone worked like Kanehira-san.
There were lazy folks among us, guys like Priest Yosō. He
took care of the temple. For generations this place had been
looked after by a head priest, but the temple records are
blank from 1878 to 1889. That was when Priest Yosō was in
charge. In the old days, the temple had a paddy and field
that the priest farmed. So Priest Yosō farmed as well, and
when there was a funeral or memorial service, he'd put on
his robes and go. His wife's name was Omitsu, and they
had two children, Yoshio and Hiroshi. The priest and his
wife fought constantly. Since the village was quiet and the
temple was up high, we could all hear them fighting. "I'm
going to kill you!" "Drop dead!" They'd go at it from early in
the morning, in voices that carried throughout the village.
And since the priest was always taking exception to something, we took to calling him Priest Protest. Just the same,
we needed him to take care of funerals, so we said nothing.
But finally, when he'd gone so far as to pawn the temple's
death register to borrow money and then also pickled vegetables in the temple bell, there was really nothing we could
do but kick him out. He worked as a packhorse driver for a
while, but that didn't continue for long either, and he went
to Toyohashi. I don't know what he did next. As for the
temple, after that Sekishū Oshō came here from the Fuku-
da Temple in Taguchi to fill in part-time.

Sawada: The fall of Priest Yosō was probably also related
to the rise in Shinto funerals. Just at the time of the Meiji
Restoration and the anti-Buddhist movement, Satō Kiyo-
nori and Furuhashi Genrokurō of Inabashi reached an
agreement to promote the Shinto religion, and fifty people
in Nagura became followers of Shinto. As a result, the
power of the Buddhist temple fell off markedly. Priest Yosō
was here right about that time, and before him there had
been a priest by the name of Chitetsu. Looking at the writings he left behind, he wrote well and in a fine hand and I

think was quite a scholar, but without permission he had cut down and sold the temple's trees and had to pay a fine for getting on the wrong side of the law. And he too may have lost his job as a priest.

Kaneda Shigesaburō: When I think about it, it doesn't seem like things have changed, but really before you know it they change a lot. In the old days the whole village had thatched roofs. The Haradas' house was about the only place with shingles, and it's still as it was back then, though the eaves used to be a bit longer, and they used to have a big *sake* storehouse in the back. All the other homes were thatched, so we needed a large supply of reeds. But now the shingles have been replaced with tiles, and there are only two or three houses with thatch.

Gotō: Things have really changed. These days I don't hear talk of young men visiting girls at night either. When we were young, we'd go to the ends of the earth if we heard about a beautiful girl. I went on foot all the way to Ena District in Mino. That's probably eight to ten miles. After finishing dinner, I'd cross over the mountains. It was hard work. There's a song that goes:

> *When we were young*
> *we'd frequent Ena*
> *and dawn would come*
> *to the riverbed there.*

That's the way it was. You'd sneak into a girl's house, and while you were fooling around, the sun would come up. Sawada-san, you ask if there was a girl I liked? If I didn't, I wouldn't have made the trip. And it was boring just playing with the girls in the neighborhood. I wanted to do something reckless.

Kaneda Shigesaburō: It would have been pretty dull in the old days too without what people now call a "thrill." It was nothing to get close to a girl. If she happened by, you'd call out to her. Tell two or three jokes, and if she responded, that was proof of her interest. Then, when night came, you'd call on her. She wouldn't refuse you. If her parents were strict, it was best to enter the house quietly. The parents usually slept in the storage room, and the children slept in the kitchen or near the dirt floor. This was easy work. Pee on the runners, and the door slid open without a sound. That kept it from squeaking. Then I'd roll up my *obi* [a sash worn around the waist] and, pressing down on one end, I'd unroll it, watching it unfurl all the way across the room. If I walked softly on the *obi*, the floorboards made almost no noise. It was easy to tell the difference between a girl and a boy in the dark—the boys had shaved heads, and the girls' hair was all done up and scented. You could tell a girl right away by smelling. And when you got under the futon, unlike these days, the girls weren't wearing panties. That's how we all played, because there were no other pleasures to speak of. At times tragedies did occur, but that's no different from nowadays.

Ogasawara: You ask about the bullying of wives by their mothers-in-law? They say there was a lot of that in the old days, but now that you mention it, I don't recall any in this village.

Gotō: There was in Kawaguchi.

Ogasawara: Well, that mother-in-law was not normal. She was half crazy.

Kaneda Shigesaburō: Well, yes. In this village, over a period of seventy years, that was the only obvious instance of a mother-in-law and daughter-in-law not getting along and causing family troubles. We heard rumors about certain families, but those were not normal families. Each was different in some way. People often talk of mothers-in-law bullying their daughters-in-law, but when it comes time to

*Participants in the roundtable.
Nagura, Aichi Prefecture.
January 1961.*

look for such a case, surprisingly there aren't any. There may be more cases of wives bullying their mothers-in-law!

Ogasawara: There *is* that in every house, in large or small amounts. Women's lives have become easier, and with that change, they've become that much less scrupulous.

Kaneda Kanehira [speaking to Ogasawara-san]: Grandma, you're a perfectionist, so as for things being rough on daughters-in-law . . .

Ogasawara: That's not true. She's who she is, and I'm who I am. I don't push for things my daughter-in-law doesn't like. I hang my underwear in the shade because it's been that way since I was little. I feel bad showing something dirty to the sun. But I don't tell my daughter-in-law not to. Why would I want to do something that's not to her liking since, whether I like it or not, I'll need her to take care of me when I die? You're the same, aren't you?

Kaneda Kanehira: That's true. I retired from being head of

the family because I didn't want to always be scolding my children. And on my own, I can work without worrying about anyone else.

Ogasawara: Yes, those of us who've worked hard all our lives don't feel right unless we're working, even now that we're old. That's our nature, and it can't be helped. No matter what anyone says, we have to be allowed to work.

Kaneda Kanehira: Yes, and I certainly didn't retire with the idea of taking it easy.

Ogasawara: The young people these days don't work.

Gotō: But your son has a reputation as a hard worker.

Ogasawara: What are you saying? He doesn't work half as hard as his father did. Compared to his father, he's a playboy. But even so, he's able to eat. It's easier to get by than it was in the old days, so I don't complain. When we were young, we could work twice as hard as they do now and still not get by.

Gotō: Yes, and after all, young people today are superior to us.

Ogasawara: That's the way it is. In all his life, my husband was never the head of the village. He wasn't the kind of man who could do that. And here's my son, the village head. I worried he might not be up to it, but he's doing the job without troubling anyone. So it seems everyone's moved up in the world.

Kaneda Shigesaburō: Yes, they've moved up. In the old days we'd never have even thought of planting rice in May. Now they drive power tillers and can plow a paddy while smoking a cigarette. And they bring in twice as much rice. This would be a great world if only we didn't have wars.

As for the talk earlier about how the houses have changed, it's just as you said. A carpenter came along from Hida and introduced shingle roofs. Then, when sericulture became popular, people added a second floor to raise silk-worms. Silkworms deepened everyone's pockets.

Before we came to raise silkworms, about all there was around here that made money were *ai* [indigo], tea, tobacco, and horses. We had a lot of horses. They were called "Nagura horses," and every house had two or three. There were houses with as many as ten. A lot of packhorses plied the Ina Road, from Taguchi, through Tsugu and on to Shinshū, and also the Iida Road, from Inabu, through Neba and on to Shinshū. Those horses came from Nagura. And because horses were kept in the homes, the houses have been large since way back.

We made good indigo, and we put it in straw bags and took it to Ebi. And there were those who came here to purchase it. Tanigorō, a dyer from Taguchi, came to buy indigo. There was a dyer in Inabashi who came as well. The dyer in Taguchi only dyed thread, but the dyer from Inabashi brought a skilled artisan up from the city and dyed not only thread but designs and patterns on fabric.

We also made good tobacco. Tobacco grown in the mountains was popular because it had little resin, and folks even came from Toyohashi to buy it.

When we sold goods, it was always at the price the merchant proposed. It's not like we could say, "The price you are offering is cheap so make it higher." They bought on their own terms. So no matter how much time passed, we farmers couldn't raise our heads.

Selling was hard, but buying was hard, too. If you wanted to prepare a wedding trousseau, you had to go west to Asuke or south as far as Shinshiro. When the road was completed, the Manrin Store from Asuke began to pull a wagon up here to sell their goods, and everyone was quite pleased. That was when the silkworm arrived.

Sawada: Prior to this, we had actually raised some silk-worms, but they were all raised naturally. Then Kaneda

Tomisaburō of Yokote went to Tomioka, in Gunma Prefecture, to study sericulture. Back then it was rare for someone to go that far away, but the village wanted to develop relations with Gunma Prefecture to establish sericulture. An instructor in silkworm culture came from the Kyōshin Company which was in Gunma, and we built rooms to raise silkworms. The silkworm rooms in Katō-san's house in Inosawa and in Kaneda Kunio's house were completed in 1905 and, starting around that time, an increasing number of silkworm rooms were built. In the beginning, we carried the cocoons to Akechi in Gifu Prefecture.

Kaneda Shigesaburō: In 1874 a silk mill was built in these parts. Imaizumi Hanshichi built it on the grounds of the Imperial residence in Inabu. At the time, we fed the silkworms leaves from wild mulberry trees. To help them spin their cocoons we'd go to the mountain to cut hemlock branches, and spread them out on our straw mats. The silkworms would spin their cocoons there, or in wrappers we made out of straw. Then we'd use small, wooden box cocoon-holders, or "centipede" cocoon-holders. Those were replaced with "reformed" cocoon-holders in the Taishō period [1912–26] and by "collapsible" cocoon-holders in the Shōwa period [1926–89].

Not wanting to be entirely at the mercy of the merchants, and feeling the need to have some say in the matter, at the end of the Taishō period we began selling the cocoons as a cooperative. But before that, we set up a cooperative association for raising the silkworms. In 1916 the people of Terawaki set up the East Nagura Sericulture Association. We gathered in Honda-san's house. Honda-san was a reliable man, and there was this guy Sakae-san who was a devoted follower and took care of things. So we brought the cocoons all to one place to sell them. The merchants would then come along and say what they were willing to pay, and we'd sell to the one who offered the highest price. This was a good system, and silk producers from Manba, Ichinose, and Yashirowaki joined the association. And buyers, pleased that they could buy in bulk, started coming from Shinshiro, Inabu, and Yabushita. But as the number of members of the sericulture association grew, there wasn't a building spacious enough for all the cocoons to be gathered, so in each community a place was built for the handing over of cocoons. The association split apart, and those who led the breakaway formed the Sericulture Implementation Association.

When this cooperative sale of cocoons began, life rapidly improved.

Gotō: And when the buses and trucks started coming in the late 1920s, things changed again. Carts and horse-drawn wagons abruptly fell into ruin. Gotō Waki and Tsukada Kinsaku held out to the end with their horse-drawn wagon, but finally, around 1955, they replaced it with a truck.

Now, with the bus coming through here, one can easily go out to Taguchi and board a train from there. And for shopping one can go beyond Shinshiro, to Toyohashi. Without even noticing, we've stopped sending people off at Banzai Pass.

NAGURA REVISITED (MAY 1957)

When I returned to Nagura in May, 1957 and told Matsuzawa Kiichi, an old man living in Yashirowaki, about the roundtable discussion held at the temple, he explained, "I wanted to go too, but I was in poor health at the time...." Then, sitting on the edge of his verandah, gazing out on neighbors working in the paddies and at the houses in Tochida and Ōhira beyond, Matsuzawa-san spoke from morning to night. Here is the first part of what he said.

* * * * *

Ogasawara Shiu's husband, Keitarō, was adopted into our family as a child. I don't think I was born yet, but in those days Keitarō's birthplace, Nishi Mikawa, must have been a place where life was especially hard. A lot of people from over there brought their extra children in this direction. Like many families, Keitarō's was poor, and his mother brought him around our village, stopping everywhere, and finally leaving him in my house before going home. She'd go to someone's house and say, "Please put us up for one night." No one would decline such a request. They'd invite her to sit beside their fire pit in the kitchen, and put out the evening meal. They'd talk together for a time before everyone went off to sleep. Keitarō and his mother would curl up beside the fire pit. Well, the boy's mother found this so utterly sad. For all she knew, if she were to leave her boy in that house, he'd be made to sleep there all alone. Imagining this, she was unable to ask them to take him in, and when the following morning came she'd leave, saying, "Thank you for everything," and be sent off with, "It was nothing."

In this way, a mother could go from house to house, and if she was not taken with the prospective parents, there was no need to leave the child in their care. Keitarō's mother likewise walked all over, but it seems no family was to her liking. Then she came to my house and Moto, my grandmother, was here. After dinner they talked for a time and everyone went to their rooms, but Grandmother Moto said, "What a cute boy. I'll sleep with him and hold him," and the boy went to sleep at once in her arms. Witnessing this, his mother cried and was happy, knowing she could leave her child in this house. Apparently saying, "I ask this of you," she left. Thereafter, Keitarō grew up sleeping in Grandmother Moto's arms. When he was grown, he returned to his parents' home to see them, but he was unable to live there, so this became his home. I called him Brother

Keita, and he helped me in all manner of things. He built
a house on these grounds and set up a branch family. Shiu-
san, his wife, is the daughter of Katō, who lives up the hill,
and the both of them being of strong character, they worked
together and built a large house here.

In this village a number of homes have children who
were taken in and later started their own branch families,
and most of them came from the direction of Nishi Mikawa. These children were neither thought of as domestic
servants nor treated harshly, but it was uncommon for the
family's fortune to be shared with them. Rather, it was
handed down to those who were adopted as successors.

Mine is one of the older families in this village. We
continued for hundreds of years as one household without ever having a branch family. However, my grandfather
Tomisaku didn't father any children, so he adopted a boy by
the name of Kuniyoshi from Kamitsugu to succeed him. It
turned out that Kuniyoshi was scarcely able to read or write.
My grandfather, figuring that if he was going to adopt one,
he might as well adopt another, then took in Komesaku
from Taguchi as a son. Komesaku was quite a fine person,
and my grandfather came to depend on him. This second
boy was my father. But because Grandfather Tomisaku
had also adopted Kuniyoshi to succeed him, it wasn't as if
he could not share his property. Dividing things 60/40, he
also built a house for Komesaku. And though they were not
blood relations, my father's generation treated one another
as kinfolk. Mind you, relatives were given an important role
at celebrations and funerals, and they helped one another
when there was work to be done.

* * * * *

Since way back, every once in a while someone would come
along on their travels to a place like this one, deep in the
mountains, and settle down. One who came to our house

was a man by the name of Furukawa Yahei. In our old family register you can see that he was from Miyata Village in
the Shimagami District of Osaka, that he came and settled
here in 1878, and that his name was added to the Matsuzawa Komesaku register. Dressed as a pilgrim and skilled
at telling people's fortunes, he was apparently already quite
advanced in years when he settled here. He set down his
belongings at my house, and for some reason or other he
stayed. Since he was old, we built him a small house in
front of my own and had him live there. It's not as if he
asked us to take him in or that we asked him to stay. Back
then there was a lot of that sort of thing. He knew how to
read and write, so perhaps it was thought that he would be
of some use. In those days most farmers didn't know how
to write, so it was common to turn to a scribe. But it was
already the Meiji period. There was a village government
by then, and, with a man like Harada Jinpachirō as village
head, there was probably no real need for a scribe. Below
the village there's a temple called Entsū, and it was under
the pretext of being the temple's caretaker that Furukawa
Yahei stayed on.

Furukawa traveled with his wife and they were quite
an intimate pair. She was an extraordinary woman. I hear
tell that she once left her bamboo hat behind while traveling. She would not listen to Yahei when he said, "We've
already come five miles, let's let it be and buy a new one
somewhere." It's said they walked back the five miles and
brought the hat back with them. When Yahei asked, "Why
are you so attached to that hat?" she undid the seam and
took out a ten-yen note. Showing it to him, she said, "Because this money will be of use to us in an emergency."
She was prudent in that way. They were a close couple, but
didn't have any children. They both died here on this land
and we held their funerals at my house. When they passed
away, there was no one in Osaka to tell, so it ended there.
There were people like that in the old days who had a past

they didn't want to talk about. And the people in our village didn't ask.

After Furukawa Yahei became caretaker of Entsū Temple, people took to calling him "Mr. Priest." Several people became his pupils, among them Tsuchiya Yoshimutsu's father. One man whose stories you heard at the roundtable, Kaneda Shigesaburō, was also one of the priest's students. The priest had the power to see into people's hearts. Shigesaburō was in training to be a carpenter specializing in the building of shrines, and when he was twelve years old he came to this house to work. Observing him, the priest said, "You have the power to become a fortune-teller." Shigesaburō thought nothing of it, but later he did become a diviner, and in these parts he's well known for it. He's traveled as far as Nagoya to the west and beyond Hamamatsu to the east, offering prayers and telling fortunes. And they often prove to be on the mark. Four or five times he took me to Ondake [a holy mountain in Nagano Prefecture].

* * * * *

My parents often told me that in a community everyone must make an effort to get along well, and if everybody just works hard, in no time they'll all get along. In the old days it seems the people of Yashirowaki were terribly poor, and more than half of the land in this community belonged to Sawada-san of Ōhira. It probably came to be that way when, in a famine year, people borrowed rice from the Sawadas and lost their land. Then, when the Sawadas were half in ruin themselves, the land all reverted to the original owners.

In Ōkubo there was also a family called Hyakkoku Gohei. They were large-scale farmers with a fief that yielded more than five hundred bushels of rice. But without doing anything wrong and without being lazy either, in the natural course of things they lost everything and the land reverted to the common farmers.

That kind of thing happens these days too. See that
house over there, the farmhouse above the paddies? That's
Suzuki Kazu's house. It looks quite dapper now, but before,
it was about to collapse. Kazu-san's father Ishisaburō was
quite a drinker. Ultimately he mortgaged his paddies and
fields to Tōgendō, a doctor in Yuya, for 360 yen. Then he
drank that money away. Ishisaburō's mortgage was lost and
with it, his property. Until then, the Suzukis had been one
of the better-off families in these parts. They even had three
branch families.

But Ishisaburō drank himself to death, and his son was
taken by the army. The mother, now alone, worked and took
care of the house. But she was still young, and the people
of the village gossiped about this and that. Whether or not
something was going on, a woman couldn't live alone. It's
only natural to depend on someone who is nice to you, but
I hoped her son would return quickly from the war. Every
day I watched the smoke that came from the roof of that
house. After the war had ended, there were days without
smoke, probably days when the mother was not at home.
If only, I thought, the son could return home before the
house fell into ruin! Well, he did come back, fortunately,
and in place of sputtery smoke, a purple smoke rose up. I
was relieved, seeing that they finally had something proper
to burn.

The son had returned, however, to find himself a tenant farmer and, not being able to survive on farming alone,
I heard that he was dealing on the black market. I figured
that whatever he did, as long as he was able to eat, in time
he'd settle down. And then one morning I woke up and
casually looked out and would you know, that house was
in a halo of light. I was taken aback, although it was actually nothing to speak of. My house faces west and with the
mountain east of here, the sun is late to strike. Kazu-san's
house faces east and the sun hits there early. When the sun
has yet to reach my house, it's already on Kazu-san's. There's

a wide paddy between our homes, and when the light of the morning sun strikes the water in the paddy and is reflected up onto Kazu-san's house, it is lit from two angles. The house appears to glow, and the windows on the second floor shine as bright as gold. I don't know how to explain it, but in the old days it didn't glitter like that. So, anyway, I was surprised. I thought that surely good things would come to that house.

And then one day, when I was walking on the road over there, I ran into Kazu-san, so I told him, "Your house has a halo over it. Surely good will come, so work hard." He was pleased and said, "Grandpa, I'll visit early in the morning if you'll show me just once the view of my house from yours." Thinking that was the least I could do I waited for him. He came early in the morning, and the two of us waited for the sun to rise.

The sky was a deep transparent blue, and suddenly the sun struck the western mountains, then gradually moved lower. It hit Kazu-san's house, then the paddy in front, and the dew on the grass around Kazu-san's house. When I said, "Isn't it wonderful?," Kazu-san answered, "Truly. Is that my house?" and for a time was speechless. And then he said, "I've never looked at my house like this before. It sure is nice. Thanks to you, I feel cheered up." Very pleased, he went home.

Shortly after that there was the liberation of farmland [land reforms shortly after World War II that sought to reduce tenant farming and absentee landlords]. Kazu's family had sold their land to Tōgendō, but they'd continued to grow rice on it and pay rent. Then it came to pass that the land was returned to them. So, when all was said and done, Kazu's father had profited to the extent that he'd been able to drink to his heart's desire. There are those who say, with some envy, "things worked out well for Kazu-san." And as he's a serious and dutiful son, they say, "It's thanks to Kazu-san's virtue," rather than speak ill of him. Since then, one good thing after another has befallen that family. He married well, and there's no longer anyone who is critical of the mother. And it hasn't only been Kazu-san's family that has prospered. Of the homes I can see from here, there isn't a one that you could say is in a bad way now. There was one in the shadow of this mountain that was in a pitiful state, but there too the son finally started pulling his weight, and they seem to be fine now. This place is heaven on earth.

The other day Kazu-san came by and asked, "Grandpa, did you notice that I built new racks for drying rice at my place?"

"I know, I know," I told him. "With those racks, in your lifetime, you can hang as much rice as you want."

"I'm grateful to you, Grandpa. Thinking you were probably watching, I went out and bought first-rate chestnut wood and built it with that. It's eight inches in diameter so I think it'll be good for many generations to come." He seemed so pleased. They say that a family that builds a strong rice rack will amass a fortune.

Watching from here like this, without even exchanging a word, I can tell just how each family's doing, as if they were right there in front of me. And when they're all doing well, I breathe a sigh of relief. When all's said and done, there's nothing better than when the community prospers.

* * * * *

Though the people in Yashirowaki get along well, there are quarrels and times when folks talk ill of one another. But feuding among poor people won't make them rich. What they really need is resourcefulness. It's one thing to work and work, but nothing will come of just working like a cow or a horse. We all worked well together in this community, but in the beginning that's all that we did. I don't know why, but in Yashirowaki only two or three families other than my own had *oiko* [wooden backpack frames]. It's strange to think of farming without one, but farmers didn't have carpentry tools. As for metalware, about all they had were pots and kettles, knives, hoes, and scythes. No one had a saw, a plane, or a chisel. And without a carpenter living nearby, you couldn't have a wooden frame made for you. So people borrowed frames from the families that had them. My own family had nearly twenty *oiko*. But people would break them and return them that way, which was more than my father could bear. When he complained, saying, "I've had enough! Make your own *oiko*. You can figure out how to make one without asking a carpenter," then everyone in the community just found a way to make them. That's all there was to it. And when they all had wooden backpack frames, everyone got a lot more work done. People simply became more resourceful. So these days, there are few who depend on others.

There really aren't many quarrels, probably thanks to this community having been so poor since way back. No one was out-and-out rich. And the job of community head is rotated through the families one at a time. Even tenant farmers have been community heads, and that practice of taking turns continues now, and not just here; all the communities in the area are that way.

This being the case, when taking a wife, no one was particular about the social standing of a family. If there was a girl of age among your kin, you'd marry her in order to incur as little expense as possible. Aside from that, many couples became friendly on their own, and usually their parents gave their consent later. And it goes without saying that visiting young women under the cover of night was popular. If you were interested in a girl, you'd seek her out and visit frequently. But not everyone did that. Each person has their own nature, and while there were fellows with a lot of energy, there were also those without it. There were also some guys with such a strong drive that they couldn't make do with one girl. They'd visit the girl over there and then see the girl over here. Because the girls married at sixteen or seventeen, it's not as if they had known a lot of boys. Probably half were married without having experienced a night visit. Actually, the young men most often frequented the homes of girls that had missed the chance to marry, or who had divorced and come back home. And so, when the pairs that played in this way got married, in many cases the woman was older. Those couples got along well.

Even when a boy would pay such secret visits, the girl's parents would feign ignorance. If young people went too far, one of the parents might clear their throat. But most boys didn't do anything too rash, since they had to maintain relationships with the girls' parents during the daytime.

Were there cases, seventy years ago, of parents forcing wives on their sons? Not in this community. Some couples, though, were kept apart by their parents. It was probably around the end of the Meiji period that families first took in a girl they didn't personally know to become their son's wife. Around that time, the marrying off of brides to distant villages started. People became particular about a family's social status and their means. Weddings became more showy. Wasn't it the same everywhere?

In this community my family was among those who were better off, but even so my grandmother came to this house only with a wicker trunk and a cloth bundle. Later she brought a dresser and chest, but the dresser was a crude piece made from pine. And she didn't even have a coat to wear over her kimono at her wedding.

Probably the only time anyone wore a long-sleeved kimono was when Mayor Harada's daughter got married. Among the regular folk, the first time was when Dr. Tōgendō's son was married and his bride wore a long wedding coat that was the talk of the village. Then, on the third day, when they rode in a rickshaw to visit the bride's parents, they created a sensation. Over time, beginning in the Taishō period, everyone came to imitate them.

There's a box in this house with the family register in it. Various details about the past are written there, but I can't read them. When I asked Sawada Hisao to read them, he told me there was stuff in there about living in poverty. Probably that was all the more reason why we got along so well.

Chapter 5

Women's Society

[Ōshima Island, Yamaguchi Prefecture, late 1950s]

Women acted as an important bond that held the community together, but before being members of the greater community they had their own society in which they conversed and helped one another.

* * * * *

Only recently have people begun to gather rice seedlings while sitting on a stool. After the war, when I returned home and started farming, my back and arms would hurt when I crouched in the seed bed gathering rice seedlings. [Seed beds were a slightly raised area in the paddy where rice was densely planted and nurtured before being transferred into other paddies where it was grown.] So I took a plain stool from in front of the oven, one that was used when tending the fire, and tried sitting on it while pulling the seedlings up. It was quite comfortable. A woman passing by said, "Well now, it's like you're resting while you work . . ." and laughed as she went on her way. But that following year I saw people all over seated as they gathered rice seedlings, and it's gone so far now that it's taken for granted that a person sits down while they do this work. But my aunt, who is well over eighty, says the work does not move as quickly when she is sitting down. So she kneels in the water on one knee and gathers the seedlings.

"The way we've done it since the old days is the best."

"It doesn't bother you to get your knee and your butt wet?"
"This way I get into a rhythm and can gather them quickly."

"It's good to be quick, but wouldn't it be nice if it were easy?"
"In the old days, everything to do with planting rice was competition. I can't give up the habits instilled in me then. Back then we'd get up in the dark, go to where the seedlings were planted, and after everyone had pulled up enough seedlings to plant for a while, we'd take them to the paddy and start planting. After that, the men would gather the seedlings for us and we'd plant them. We women planters enjoyed pushing the seedling pullers, and if there was a break in their bringing of the seedlings, we'd yell, 'You good-for-nothing!' The seedling gatherers had to look sharp and when it appeared that they'd fall behind, they called men over from a neighboring paddy to help out."

"And you were never pushed by the men?"
"Are you kidding? Women were superior during the rice planting. It was entertaining to push the men. When the men were incompetent and their seedling gathering didn't move along, if they got too much help from others, the women planters would take mud and throw it at the men who were helping, and finally they'd shove them into the paddy."

"But the men wouldn't have lost!"
"That's not true. Three women together could drag most any man into the paddy and douse him in mud."

"Aunt, did you do things like that too?"
"I was of weak constitution, so I didn't tease the men, but my friends did a lot of playing around. Unlike now,

whatever it was we were doing, there was lots of confusion. In the old days, we didn't lay out a rope to plant like they do now. We planted haphazardly and the fastest among us would plant at quite a pace. And the slower people had to try to keep up so they wouldn't come in last. Once in a while a man would try to join in and the women would compete with one another, and usually he'd end up bringing up the rear. So a man would have to be awfully good or he wouldn't plant. The men fixed the furrows, smoothed out the paddies, got the rice seedlings. . . . There was a guy from Hamagami, a quiet guy who the young women always used to tease. But he was a fast worker, and sometimes he'd join the women and plant with them. The fastest would move beside him and try to make him fall behind, but being skilled and quick he didn't come in last. By the end, the women were no longer planting the seedlings but just laying them out on top of the mud. Later when it rained, the seedlings all floated. That was trouble."

"Long ago, people sure sang a lot of rice planting songs."
"My great grandfather was a funny man who sang well, and when it came time for the rice planting, he'd go here and there carrying only a *taiko* drum. He'd stand on a furrow alongside a paddy that was being planted, bang on his drum, and sing. My grandfather used to tell of it. When I was young, few people were interesting like that, but some sang well and we'd have them stand on the furrow and sing. Then we'd sing along, and singing, our hands would find a rhythm and the work would move along well."

"And weren't there times way back when lots of taiko drummers, singers, and women planters came out for the rice planting?"
"Yes, that kind of thing happened from time to time. Once every three or four years, to celebrate someone's recovery from a long illness, or the building of a house, or some other auspicious occasion, a person of means would hire all

Miyamoto's aunt. Ōshima Island,
Yamaguchi Prefecture.
May 1957.

the women in the village and get
all the cows to come out. They'd
put dozens of cows in the family's
largest paddy and turn the soil.
After that, they'd plant the rice. The rice-planting women
wore splashed-pattern kimonos with their sleeves tied up,
and braided hats. The lead singer would keep time and it
was a splendid thing. And when word got out that a 'big
rice planting' would take place, people came from all over
to watch. Unlike now, there were few pleasures in the old
days. So when people got together, whether it was for work
or not, there was lots of singing and dancing. At the time
of the rice planting we were busy, but because everyone got
together to do the work, we were spurred on."

"I've always liked the rice planting. That's why I come back
every year to plant. I've heard enough stories from the old
women to fill a book. You sure told me a lot of stories too,
Auntie."

"You listen to our silly stories, and before we know it we're
telling you more. Now your grandfather, he was a talker, and

I grew up listening to his stories. Since I don't know much about the world, I don't know many stories."

"Just the same, you took one or two long trips didn't you?"
"In the old days, no one would marry a girl who didn't know the world. Someone who wasn't worldly—someone who 'only knew how to behave in front of an oven'—was inevitably narrow-minded. In my eighteenth year I'd suffered from a long illness. When I finally became well again, I was encouraged to go on a pilgrimage around Shikoku for my health. So when I was nineteen, I traveled around Shikoku with two girlfriends. [Shikoku—literally "Four Domains"—is one of Japan's main islands, lying to the east across the Inland Sea.]

"In those days there was a boat for hire that often went to Iyo, so we got a ride up to Mitsugahama in Iyo and visited the Ōyama Temple and walked from there all the way to the border of the Tosa Domain. I don't remember well, but a lot of poor people lived in the mountains back behind Uwajima. Their houses all had thatched roofs. Most lived on straw mats spread out on a dirt floor. Even in the homes with floorboards, none had tatami. Everywhere we were put up we were fed only sweet potatoes, but just the same the people were all nice. We were never wanting for a place to stay. I imagine you've walked around those parts too. They were farming in paddies and fields on the tops of frightfully high cliffs. Even now, when I think of the pains they went to, I get the chills. It made me realize how people suffer because of the place where they were born.

"We didn't go to the back end of Tosa. They said Tosa was a land of demons, a frightful place, and that few families put people up. So instead of visiting the four countries of Shikoku, we left out Tosa and visited three. We went to the border of Tosa, walked straight back to Mitsugahama, and then went round to the east. It was like paradise.

"We weren't the only group of girls. Lots were on

pilgrimages and many were from the Bungo Domain [now Oita Prefecture, across the water to the south]. We met up with groups of girls from Bungo everywhere. We'd fall into company with one another, and when we asked where they were from, they'd say 'from Hime Island in Bungo' or from someplace or other in Bungo. Then we'd introduce ourselves and walk together for two or three days. In time, for some reason or other, we'd part and join up with another group, and so on. Because we had no money, we couldn't take a boat, so we walked to the border of the Awa and Tosa domains and back again. But as long as we were walking, we didn't lack for a place to stay. There were 'charity houses' everywhere that readily put us up. And because it was spring, people brought offerings from all over and there was plenty to eat.

"People made offerings when their next of kin had died. They'd bring food to feed the pilgrims as alms in memory of the deceased. They came to Uwajima from all over. Many came from Bungo. They'd place their offerings on top of a bench on the temple grounds and say 'I'm from such and such a place in the Bungo Domain. Please receive my offering,' and then they would give it all to us pilgrims. Many of us from the Suō Domain went to the area around Mitsugahama. If we ran out of food, we'd sing a Buddhist hymn or a pilgrim's hymn and be given something. We left home with two yen and came back with five more."

"So it wasn't just things to eat . . . "
"Yes, they gave us many things. Deep in the mountains of Iyo someone asked us to take their daughter with us. They said, 'You can use her any way you like, as long as you feed her until she's big.' They were really bad off. Many of the pilgrims had a child in tow, and it seems that most were adopted. In these parts too, there were lots of children who'd been brought back from Iyo in the old days. At one time there were as many as ten or twenty of them. Some

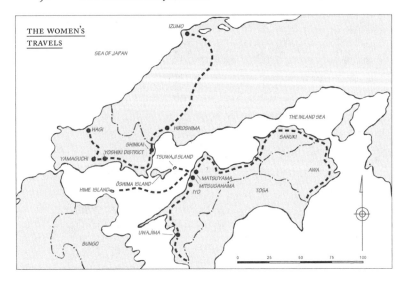

THE WOMEN'S
TRAVELS

had been bought, but in most cases the parents were unable to raise them and just asked that they be taken in."

"Auntie, did most of your friends travel around Shikoku?"
"Yes, and those that didn't went to Izumo [to the west, on Honshu, and the location of a major shrine]. That was a trip of about ten days so it wasn't too long, and along the way a person from the Ōshima District had a place where everyone stayed."

"Just the same, wasn't travel filled with hardships?"
"Well, it was rough compared to now, but we traveled because we had to, so it wasn't that bad. Travel these days is paradise."

"What did you enjoy about travel in the old days?"
"Travel companions, probably. You'd be walking along, and before you knew it you'd have company, and the travel would become that much easier."

"And did anyone get married?"
"Yes, they did. You probably know them. West of here, there's a family called Ninomiya. The daughter met her

husband when she was traveling. Said he was from Miyazu, in Tango. They became intimate on a pilgrimage to Izumo."

"**Were most women's travels pilgrimages?**"

"No. We also went for work. I went to work in a brick factory in the Shiki District. Grandpa just couldn't seem to pay off his debts, so I went along with my older brother to work in the Shiki District. It was hard work. My brother was very strict with me. We quit after we'd only been there a year. Those who were healthy and strong went to Shinkai, in Iwakuni, to pick cotton in the summer, and to the back side of Yamaguchi to harvest rice in the fall. They went in twos and threes, with others they got along with. I never went there, so I don't know much about it, but they'd walk from here to Kuka, take a ferry across to Jikata, and walk from there.

"If they asked, 'Need a harvest hand?' they'd usually get hired. Even if they didn't say anything, walking along in work clothes—an apron, leggings, and a towel or a straw hat on their head—people generally knew they were workers and asked, 'Will you harvest my fields?' and they'd find a place to work in no time. When work for one family was done, they'd go to the next, and so on. 'Harvest help' was forty days of labor, so they'd work for forty days and come back. They were given food to eat, and the pay was a little over three pounds of rice a day, so a hard-working girl could work for forty days and bring back a 130-pound sack of rice. With an extra bag of rice, families could easily make it through New Year's, so young women worked in this way until they got married. Because my family grew enough rice to eat, I didn't do harvest help and neither did my daughter. The daughters these days live in paradise."

"**What was cotton-picking like?**"

"I've never picked cotton either, so I don't know much about it. From around here, Kaichi's mother went. When she was young, she was strong-minded and beautiful. When she was picking with her friends, the young men would come along and tease them. Most girls kept quiet regardless of what was said, but she would talk right back, even joke with them, and soon become friends. She'd even have them help out with the cotton picking. At night the young men would come to play. They'd dote on her, calling her 'Miss Okane, Miss Okane.' It seems that while talking, I've gathered most of the rice seedlings."

As ever, my aunt was on one knee in the seedbed, gathering the rice seedlings.

* * * * *

In the old days, young girls often ran away. They usually left home having made arrangements with their mothers, unbeknownst to their fathers, and relying on friends who had left before them. Many girls came home for *Bon* and New Year's, and it was then that plans were made. In the feudal period, many went to the castle town of Hagi, and not a few others took a sailing vessel to Matsuyama in the Iyo Domain.

There was a girl who fled in this way. She arranged for a boat and left home without a hitch. The boat traveled to Tsuwaji Island, just east of the island of Ōshima, but met with a headwind there and was unable to cross over to Iyo. The girl spent a whole month waiting, and finally the decision was made that the boat would go back. So the girl had to return as well. She was utterly disappointed, having wanted so badly to work as a housemaid in Iyo. She'd learned a tiny bit of the Iyo dialect and speaking in the Iyo accent she brought everyone to laughter, saying, "Thirty days in Iyo and I've utterly forgotten our own island dialect." But she couldn't say anything more. And the story is told of how she then went to the home of a woman in the neighborhood and said, "Thirty days in Iyo and I've utterly forgotten the island dialect. Could you cook me some rice gruel?" The latter half was spoken in the island dialect.

Travel was an opportunity for girls to learn, and gaining knowledge the islanders did not have was a source of pride. One example of this was the learning of other dialects. Here's another story:

There was a girl who was thinking she wanted to travel. Just then, a girl who'd been in Matsuyama came back home. The girl who'd just returned encouraged her to leave, saying, "I won't be going back, but the family where I was in domestic service is a fine family, so if you're interested in going, you should give it a try." Hearing this, and with the help of the girl who had just come back, the girl gladly fled. Her father was quite angry that she had run off, and he asked people to search for her in every direction. Running away did not mean jumping on just any boat that came ashore. One would look for an opportunity to leave home unobserved by the father, generally hiding with a friend until a boat could be arranged. That's why, when a parent realizes their child has run away, they ask people to look all over. And at times they find them. This girl's father tried everything too, but was unable to find her. Ultimately he became ill, and the girl's mother, no longer able to ignore the situation, asked the girl who'd induced the flight to bring her daughter back home. So, the "temptation" girl sailed all the way to Matsuyama to bring back the "runaway" girl. She arrived to find runaway girl depressed and not yet comfortable with the family where she was working. Temptation girl explained the situation to the master of the family and obtained permission for a discharge. The two girls, travelling together, came as far as Mitsugahama and, growing hungry, entered a tea shop where they ate sushi. Temptation girl, using the language of the place (the city language), said *oishii ne* [Delicious isn't it?]. Not knowing that *oishii* had the same meaning as the word *umai* did back home, runaway girl answered *ha-koishii ne* [Yes, I'm homesick.] It seems she was missing her home.

In each of these stories, the girls' names were explicitly used and people in the next generation knew who they were. But as these proper names are forgotten, the stories become ordinary small talk. Stories of this type were told by many of the women during rice planting. They picked out the foolish among them and made them the butt of their jokes, but they also appear to have made helpful lessons out of the stories. The main focus of their humor was the use of language. When they went out into the world, the women had to be able to speak properly wherever they went. This was a measure of competence. So I will introduce a few humorous stories of this sort.

The village neighboring my own had a reputation for its coarse language. Discouraged by the fact that they were being slighted for this, in a village meeting it was decided that they would attach an "o" to their words ["o" being a formalizing prefix]. But this was disastrous. On one occasion one of the villagers said: "The o-Jōnen Temple o-now has o-twenty and o-two o-initiatives." Everyone burst into laughter because "twenty-two initiatives" had become "ten demon initiatives." Attaching too many o's being problematic, they apparently returned to speaking as they had before.

But it happened that a girl from this same village went into domestic service and because she spoke entirely in her native dialect the woman of the house said, "It would probably be nice if you were to attach a few more o's when you speak." Then one day the girl went into the wardrobe and showed no sign of coming out. When the mistress of the house went to look in on her, she found the housemaid attaching hemp string to everything in the wardrobe. She had mistaken the honorific "o" for the "o" meaning hemp.

When she had been taught that "o" was the honorific "o," she attached the letter "o" to everything she said. "O-wife, shall I o-wash the o-rice in the o-rice bin?" or "O-wife, the o-rice is o-cooked," and so on, to the point that she was quite annoying. So she was cautioned, "Perhaps it would be best to reduce the number of o's a little." But this too led to trouble. When the mistress called the housemaid, she answered, "What is it *kusama*?" having removed the letter "o" from the proper word *okusama* used to address a married woman. "What is *kusama*? Oh, you've taken the "o" off of *okusama*. You do not need to remove that. By the way, where have you put the beans?" To which the girl answered, "The beans are in the *ke* [*oke* = wooden bucket, *ke* = hair]." This story was a favorite among the women. At the rice planting it wasn't told by one person but in dialogue form by several. And it came with a comic twist at the end. Until the beginning of the Taishō period, for the most part words like *okusama* (wife) and *ojōsama* (daughter) were not commonly used in the local dialect. The wife of someone of high status, such as a member of the warrior class, was called *o-urakata*. The wife of a village headman, a Shinto priest, or a lower-ranked warrior was called *o-katasama*. Wives in the wealthy families in the village were called *o-gōsama*. And all of the daughters from families in these classes were called *gōsama*.

Early in the Taishō period, the son from a long line of village heads became governor of the prefecture and returned home with his wife. This was an honor, and the entire village gathered to meet him. Someone from the village had to formally greet the governor, but they did not know what to say so they drew lots to decide who would speak. A farmer who had become a representative in the village assembly drew the winning lot. He was a man of staunch character, a member of the righteous faction in the village assembly, and had a reputation in the village for being clever, but he had no idea what to call the governor or how to address his wife. Calling them "*Danna-sama, o-urakata*" [husband, wife], being old-fashioned, was not good. As he had heard the expression "His Excellency the Governor," he decided he would call the governor "His Excellency," but he was perplexed as to what to call his wife. Because young women were being called *o-jōsama* of late, he decided it would probably be best to call her that. So, standing before the two of them in a formal half coat and holding a fan, he began his speech "On this occasion, we welcome back His Excellency the Prefectural Governor and *o-jōsama*." To which she retorted, "I'm not his daughter. I'm his *sai* (wife)."

At this the village assemblyman hurriedly added "Yes, greetings to the *o-sai-sama*." To the villagers an *o-sai* is a side dish, so when the story reaches this point everyone bursts into laughter. This was the talk of the village for a long time.

Here is another story from that same day when the governor visited the village. An educated member of the village who subscribed to the newspaper, seeing that this same governor [of Yamaguchi Prefecture, or *ken*] was always referred to there as *Yama-ken-kun*, had made up his mind that he would call him that. So the man addressed him, saying, "By the way Yama-ken-kun ... " Proud to be the governor, thinking inwardly that he was of a higher social status than the people of the village, and having been addressed as if he were a friend, the governor said, "Isn't that rude?" That was the whole story. It did not gain much popularity as a joke, probably because it was short on humor.

In the old days the planting of rice was sloppy. But planting in straight rows has become popular since. A rope, tied here and there with red or blue knots, is stretched across the paddy and rice seedlings are planted where the knots are located. This method seemed quite inefficient to me, so I made a ruler and tried using it for planting. This way there was no need to stand up between rows, so efficiency was greatly improved. I used it when I planted with my family, but the technique never did come into general use. For one, there were few paddies in the village, so there was no need to rush with the planting. And people were not interested in a planting method that did not leave enough time for talking. People did not tire as much when planting with a rope, because every time the rope was moved they could stretch their backs, and they had time to rest their hands and to talk as well.

In the last two or three years rice planting has grown more efficient. The women have formed planting groups and are now planting by contract, at a rate of one thousand yen per quarter acre. If the owner of a paddy reserves approximate planting dates with the planting group, they will come to plant. Housewives no longer have to prepare meals for the rice planters, and owners

Miyamoto family planting rice. Ōshima Island, Yamaguchi Prefecture. May 1957.

don't have to look for individual planters. In exchange, the paddy owner is obliged to participate in the planting for one or two days. This system was devised by the women. With increased efficiency, their earnings grow, so talk while planting has gradually decreased. And their stories have become fragmentary, rather than creating a flow.

Meanwhile, with the spread of radio and television, housewives have grown accustomed to standard Japanese and have learned the art of using it as well.

"We still bend over when we plant rice like we used to in the old days, but it's changed quite a bit. Everyone wears work pants when they plant. Braided hats have become wood-chip hats. Though it used to be that rice planting was women's work, the men are also helping now. Rice planting is no longer something to look forward to." An old woman shared this with me while planting rice.

In fact, women have begun to dread this kind of work. Probably one reason for this is that their lives have changed, as reflected in one of the rice-planting women's exchanges:

"These days there are fewer interesting women . . ."

"That's for sure. Before, there were lots of interesting women. Teasing men, joking . . . things like that have disappeared."

"That reminds me of Kannon-sama [The Goddess of Mercy] (a woman who lived in a neighboring village). She was an interesting woman."

"Why did they call her Kannon-sama?"

"You don't know?"

"I don't. Did she have a shrine to the Goddess of Mercy?"

"You mean worship the Buddha? This was a woman who lived her whole life alone. She had no use for Shinto gods or Buddha."

"So what's Kannon-sama?"

"*That's* Kannon-sama."

"That?"

"You've got one too."

"No, really?"

"She must have been a little over thirty at the time. Kannon-sama was crouching, wearing only a loincloth. It was long ago. She wasn't wearing underwear or work pants. So even though she had a waistcloth on, when she squatted, you could see everything from the front, you know."

"No, not a story like that!"

"Yes. A young man from the neighborhood was squatting in front of her and while he was talking, he was glancing down there. When Kannon-sama scolded him in her usual manner, saying, 'What are you looking at?' the young man said, 'The Goddess of Mercy's been unveiled, so I'm praying to her.' To which she said, 'If you want to worship Kannon-sama so much, then worship her,' and she opened her loincloth and thrust herself right in his face. No matter how much the guy might have liked the thing, having it thrust under his nose weakened him, and it's said he ran off in a real hurry. After that, she was called Kannon-sama. And when the young boys even thought of going there to play she'd say 'You want to pray to Kannon-sama?' and chase them off."

* * * * *

"I have big feet, you see. I wear a size 11 . . ."
"They say that when the feet are big, the hole is big too . . ."
"Really? I'm not that big."
"What? I'm talking about the hole made by a footprint."
"When the hole's big it's bone-breaking work to fill it."
"Has to be a pretty healthy man to fill it up . . ."
"Now you're talking about those things again . . ."

This too is the talk of the women while they plant rice. When people started using a rope to plant in a straight line, they stopped singing rice-planting songs. But just because they have stopped singing does not mean that they plant in silence. They talk incessantly. And almost all of their talk is of this sort.

"Things must be pretty dull these days for the rice-paddy god."
"Why's that?"
"Because everyone wears pants when they plant."
"What?"
"Rice planting was wretched work and progress was slow, so we humored the paddy god and got him to help out with the planting."
"Is that so?"
"Yes, it is. Without work pants, and wearing only a loincloth, you could see everything from below, so the paddy god smiled in satisfaction."
"Probably hard for him to get much work done."
"I hear he looked here and there to see whose was good."
"Could that be true?"
"They say so. There's the good looking and the bad, different from a pretty or an ugly face though."
"That's probably true. Would a man show his affections even to the ugly?"

"You can tell right away if a face is pretty or not but it's not so easy to tell with Kannon-sama."

"That's why they say you don't know a horse 'til you try riding it."

Talk like this continues without end.

"Look! In no time we've planted two and a half acres."

"That was quick."

"That's because the god is pleased."

"I'm going to head home and please my husband."

There is a particularly large amount of this kind of talk when the women are planting rice. And a lot of the rice-planting songs they sang were about sex as well. It has long been the custom to connect the production of crops with human reproduction.

Sexual gestures are quite commonly found at rice planting ceremonies at New Year's, and erotic talk during rice planting can be seen as carrying over from such events. During the rice planting and at other times, spirited women of about forty years of age are most often at the center of this talk. And though it may be a little too strong for the younger women, the talk is wholesome. When young girls were among the women planting rice, it was common for talk to turn to the first night.

"Long ago, a girl got married but she came back crying."

"What?"

"Her parents asked why she'd come back. She said that when night fell her husband had tried to drill her stomach with a large drill. It had hurt more than she could bear, so she'd come home."

"Well?"

"'You're a fool,' they said. 'If it hurt, why didn't you put spit on it. You know how the pain goes away if you say "Parent's spit, parent's spit" when you put saliva on an open wound? You know that much, don't you?'"

"How was it for you?"

"I broke my bowl when a young man visited my house one night."

"I wonder how it is these days? What was it we used to say in the old days? On the first night we talked about a persimmon tree . . ."

"What kind of talk would that be?"

"The husband would say, 'there's a big persimmon tree out behind the house and it's bearing good fruit.' And he'd ask his wife, 'Do you mind if I climb it?' If she said, 'Climb it,' the husband would ask, 'Can I take the fruit?' and the wife would say, 'Take it.' That's how it was done . . ."

Every year, I look forward to the rice planting. Some of the stories are repeated from the year before, but many are not. At times a person must talk in a subdued voice, but when two people are side-by-side talking in whispers, someone will call out, "Whispering is the way to vice." Only those erotic stories that can be shared openly are told in places like this. That is how wholesome they are. And one's own experiences are mixed in as well.

Stories of this sort were told before and after the war, without change. Even when talk of sex was prohibited [probably a reference to government censures], farmers—especially the society of women—continued to share these stories, and in an entirely natural manner. This talk was repeated not only while planting rice, but also during other work performed by women. Of late, mandarin-orange sorting stations have become a good place for such talk. An abundance of wit apparently moves the work along.

Of course, it took a long time for talk of sex to come this far. And it was through such talk that women acquired the power to be critical of men. Interestingly, most of the women who are skilled at erotic talk are in love with their husbands, and this cheerful world is an expression of their happiness. In listening to women talk, I have increasingly come to think that there is nothing wrong with their eroticism. If there is a problem, it lies with those who distort its meaning.

Chapter 6

===

Tosa Genji

[Kōchi Prefecture, formerly the Tosa Domain, January–February 1941]

Where are you from? Chōshū, is that so? Lots of people from Chōshū have come to these parts. They've always been hard workers. Woodsmen and carpenters came to work around here. The carpenters were skilled. They all did good work.

And what kind of business are you in? You say you're a farmer. You're no farmer. You don't talk like one. You're not a merchant. Well fine then, you're a farmer. You tell me you want to hear my story, but I know nothing. Nothing at all. I was a cow trader, so if it's something to do with cows or horses, I know it. But if it's anything else, I don't know a thing.

So you want to know how I came to be blind? My blindness, I've been blind coming on thirty years. Punishment for all the debauching I did. I did a lot of bad things. So many that I never made an honest living.

Do you have a wife? You must take good care of your wife. Even if you become blind, your wife's the one thing you shouldn't abandon.

A fire sputters in the fire pit. A tiny old man, well over eighty, sits cross-legged by the fire. His face is the shape of a fig, he does not have a single tooth left, and his cheeks are sunken. His torn kimono is so dirty it's hard to make out the stripe design.

This is Yusuhara Village, in the mountains of Tosa. And this old man's dwelling is nothing more than a beggar's shed—whatever wood was on hand has been bound together by straw rope and the outside covered over with mats of woven straw. Straw mats are stretched across the ceiling as well. The mats are pitch black from the smoke. Above the roof is a bridge. This is to say, he is camping out under a bridge. He is living on mats laid out on top of rice husks strewn on the ground. The entrance is a mat that has been left hanging.

Every now and then one can hear the sound of footsteps passing above the ceiling. Their quick pace suggests the walker is cold.

You must be quite an oddity yourself, to come along wanting to hear the stories of a beggar. Who brought you here, to my place? Oh, Nasu's husband? Nasu's husband, now that's a fine man, a saint of a man. It was thanks to him that I came to live here. Grandma led me by the hand, traveling here and there, and when we'd come this far that man said, "If you're blind it's all the same where you live. As long as you don't impose on people, you won't be allowed to go hungry." Because of his kindness to me, I came to live here under this bridge. I'm given people's leftovers and I eat them, and I've been under this bridge near on thirty years now.

In all my eighty years, this is the first time I've met an eccentric like you. I never thought I'd meet someone who'd come along and want to hear the stories of an old man of eighty. I haven't done anything in eighty years. The time went by deceiving people and meddling with women.

You say I might at least remember the girls I cared for? The girls I loved? That was a long time ago.

I was a fatherless child. My mother became pregnant on the seed of a man who came calling in the night, and that seed became me. Wanting to miscarry, she got into a river and chilled her loins but that didn't work. She rammed her stomach into a rock wall but I didn't come down. She even jumped down out of a tree but I didn't come out. When she'd finally given up, I was born prematurely. Once I was born, it was too pitiful to kill me so my grandma and grandpa took me in and raised me. After that, my mother was married. Then one night, in her husband's home, when she was feeding mulberry to the silkworms, she knocked over a lamp and the oil spilled all over her body. It caught fire and she was badly burned. She died a brutal death. So I don't remember my father's face or my mother's. When I first became aware of the world around me, I was playing with a nursemaid. The nursemaid wasn't for me. She was taking care of another child and I just followed them around and played.

In the old days, the girls in poor families were all hired out as nursemaids. They made a towel into a headband and chased after the children. They went in packs to the forest by the shrine or to a dry riverbed on the edge of town and played house and fought and sang together. Us boys with no nursemaids somehow just joined those groups. They say, "Children raise themselves, even without parents," and that's true.

When it came time for everyone to go to school, I didn't go. Playing with the nursemaids was better. Lots of the nursemaids didn't go to school. When I was a kid, people weren't so strict about going to school. I preferred playing with girls.

And besides, a lot of boys turned ten and still didn't go to school. I played with the nursemaids and they took a liking to me. Even though there were other boys who didn't go to school, the children from poor families all helped out at home. But being an illegitimate child and raised by my grandparents, I wasn't told to go work on the mountain or in the paddy.

Around that time, I started to learn bad things. There was no place to play on a rainy day. Three or four nursemaids would gather in a barn somewhere and the children would play. When the children fell asleep, they'd lay them down on straw mats and the nursemaids would play among themselves. "Playing" wasn't anything in particular. They'd burrow into the piles of straw, sometimes bare their fronts, compare the size of their thighs and the size of their sex, and put their fingers in one another and scream and make a fuss. They'd tell me to pull mine out, and they'd make me pull it out, and they were amused by it. In time, an older nursemaid said, "to have sex, you put a boy's in here. The other day I saw my older sister with a young boy, in the shade of the tall reeds behind the house. Why don't you try putting it in me." And saying that, she put mine in. That was my first knowledge of women. I didn't think it was particularly good and the nursemaid said, "well that was nothing." She was suspicious because her older sister had seemed so happy.

Just the same, from then on there was one more way to play and the nursemaids said "put it in me," and "put it in me," and because I was the only boy I put it in all of them. So, mostly just on rainy days we played that way in the barn. I didn't think it was that good, but all in all it was the most interesting way to play.

If you walked here from the direction of the Kita District, you must have a good idea what the villages are like in those parts. There are places, you may recall, where the valley is wider and as many as ten houses are clustered together. Otherwise the houses are mostly scattered on the hillsides, in ones and twos. There are maybe fifty houses, but spread over quite a wide area. When it didn't rain, the children would yell to one another to meet in the forest by the shrine or in the dry riverbed. When it rained, it was

*A small village
in rural Shikoku.
March 1963.*

all we could do to get the kids together from the closest four or five houses. So when I speak of the girls I was close to, there were only three or four. When I was sleeping with the oldest among them, we were startled when a lot of blood came out and the girl went home crying. I thought she'd die, and in my dread I couldn't eat anything that night. When I went to the riverbed the next day, that girl came along and she was fine. I asked, "What happened?" and she said, "I'm an adult now. That was the touch of the moon, a sign I've become an adult, so I'll not be a nursemaid much longer." She'd suddenly become quite full of herself. And she told me, "I won't be playing with you anymore." When I asked her why, she said, "because I'm an adult now and in the next two or three days my aunt (the mother in the house where she was working) said she would cook *sekihan* [rice with adzuki beans] to celebrate. After I eat the *sekihan*, the young men will try to sneak into the house under the cover of night, so I must be careful." And I wondered if that was all there was to it. I asked, "You can't do it with me?" and she said, "You're not a young man." So I came to think that I wanted to quickly become a young man.

* * * * *

The year I turned fifteen, my grandpa died suddenly from palsy. My uncle (my mother's older brother) said, "You're an adult now and your grandpa's dead. You can go work for a farmer or help out in our house, but because your grandpa let you play, you're lazy and unable to do anything. You should go work for a cow trader." So I entered the service of a cow trader located some seven miles from home. Following the boss' orders, my work was to drive cows to the auction grounds, and to take cows that were to be traded to the homes of farmers. I drove cows every day, all over the place. It was a different cow every day. I'd bring that cow here and take this cow there. The boss was a smooth talker who told only lies. He'd say, "This is a good cow," and leave a bad cow with a farmer, and take the good cow the farmer had and lead it off elsewhere. He'd take a calf to a village back in the mountains and move the big cow that was there to a place a bit farther down the mountain. And move the cow that was there down a bit farther still. In that way, he'd move the bigger, better cows farther and farther downhill. The cows for slaughter were generally taken to Uwajima.

The cows in these parts were all large. Cow *sumo* [cow fighting] was big in Uwajima since way back, so the cow traders searched desperately for good cows. When they found a good cow, they'd fasten their eyes upon it and work hard to get a farmer to raise it, and then they'd sell it for a good price to one of the big cow traders.

Cow traders stayed in places called "cow trader lodgings" located where the houses were a bit clumped together, and most often these were the homes of slightly pretty widows. The cow traders didn't just sleep there. Sometimes they'd drink together or gamble, and what's more, the

widow was usually sleeping with one of the cow traders.
My boss had a woman like that in every direction. They had
relations with other men and at times a serious problem
would result. That kind of thing happened all the time.
I was always seeing that kind of thing, so naturally I
picked up the same habits. My boss was quite lecherous.
We'd pass in front of the home of a woman he was intimate
with, and even in broad daylight he'd enter the house and
take a roll with her. I'd take the cow somewhere nearby and
wait, and after tying the cow to a tree thereabouts, sometimes I'd go and take a peek.

All these lewd stories. I'm not being very hospitable.
But there's nothing I know better than women and cows.
Cow traders wear clothes and we have balls and at a glance
we look like other men, but society doesn't see us as equals.
Because we make a profit by fooling people, the expression
for telling a lie is "cow trader's mouth." Society didn't trust
us and we were looked down upon. But even so, people
were deceived by the cow traders into exchanging their
cows. We'd take them a bad, helpless cow and, saying, "This
is a good cow," we'd leave it behind. And when no more
than half a year had passed, we'd go back and the farmer
would've made that bad cow into a good one. A good farmer was like a god, having the power to turn even a stone into
gold. From the perspective of a person like that, we were the
dregs of humanity. Our only redeeming feature was that we
didn't steal from people.

Life was always hard here in these mountains and there
were lots of thieves who'd force themselves into the homes
of people with possessions or a bit of money. Do you know
Kamegorō Ikeda? Kame the Robber? He was probably the
top among the thieves. No one could lay a hand on him.
That man could walk right in front of a policeman and not
get caught. He'd go into any house and steal from it. They'd
go after him and he wouldn't budge.

He came down with leprosy and went to Nagasaki to

treat it, but it just wouldn't heal. Hearing that eating the raw livers of children would cure him, he came back to these parts and did inhuman things. There were a number of children who fell into his clutches. Finally, his actions became so bad that they couldn't be ignored and he was seized at a temple where he was staying. When he wasn't doing those atrocious things he'd done a lot to help the weak. So there were those who feared him and those who looked on him as a saint.

Kame the Robber wasn't the only thief. There were lots of them, and they had their places to stay too, called "thieves' houses" or "trap houses." Most of them were houses that stood alone on the side of a mountain. The owners of these houses would take in thieves or sell the things they'd stolen. Of the wealthy who lived in the mountains, many were the owners of these thieves' houses. When compared with such thieves and thieves' dwellings, cow traders were one rank higher.

As for a cow trader's lies, they were accepted. We'd take a useless cow that was being raised by a somewhat lazy farmer and pull it along to the home of a hard-working farmer and push it off on him. And since he'd then turn it into a beautiful cow, the farmer wouldn't feel that he'd been fooled all that much. So there is a world in which lies can be taken for the truth.

And we wouldn't take them a cow that was bad to the core. It wasn't as if we were lying completely. So even if the lies had the upper hand, there was still a 30 percent truth. And the farmer would turn this into an 80 or 90 percent truth. In this way, liars were also able to make their way in the world.

There were times when we couldn't lie. If you took a cow to auction, anyone knew a bad cow. People couldn't be fooled. And there was competitive showing and we were no match for them. Ten out of ten people can recognize a cow that can win in cow *sumo*. So us small traders did our best not to go to those places and did all our walking deep in the mountains.

* * * * *

When I was twenty, my boss died and I started to work on my own. My boss, a good-looking man with a fine build, had died young. He'd had a lot of women and it seems he'd made some enemies. He was killed while sleeping with a widow in one of the cow trader houses. The house was set on fire and as it was windy that day, the house burned to the ground. It was said that the fire in the foot warmer had been poorly tended and that they died in the fire, but it was odd that their two badly burned bodies were lying side by side. It seems unlikely that such a man would sleep undisturbed while the house burned down around him. Because it was out in the mountains, the matter was left at that, but I had a theory. That widow had a fine body and the men were in constant competition for her. In the end, my boss had made her his own, and there was a cow trader who resented him for it. If this had been between members of the village, it would have come out right away, but we traders weren't from the village so the people weren't all that aware of what we were up to. And even if they had noticed, getting involved would've been a nuisance, so when there was nothing to be gained, they kept their mouths shut and didn't say anything.

I took on my boss' clients and became an independent cow trader. After that, things became interesting. I didn't have a home to speak of. As for my childhood home, my grandmother had died and only my uncle was left, so even if I returned, there wasn't a place there for me. So I traveled here and there, from one home to another of the widows my boss had been intimate with. They treated me well and in this way the time passed.

Those of us who didn't really have a home or family in

the village weren't able to join in with the young men. And not being one of them, we weren't allowed to steal into the women's houses at night. If they found out one of us was calling on a young woman's house at night, we'd have taken a crippling beating. They were strict. So while I had a lot of sex with nursemaids when I was young, I hadn't slept with a young woman since becoming an adult. For the most part I slept with widows. If the widow was living on her own, no one complained even if I went in through the front door.

There are a lot of widows in these parts, though I have no idea why that is. Most of the cute ones are mistresses to the married men. Yes, there are lots of mistresses. Most of the married men have one. You said you went to the house of a Shinto priest. Which one did you go to, the one below? Was there a fair-skinned woman a little over forty there? She's that priest's mistress. I'm unable to see what she looks like, but in the village it seems she's known for her beauty. She and her husband went to live in Osaka and when her husband died, she came back. After that, the priest began visiting. He's an old man in his mid-sixties. He built her a house, and every other day he goes back and forth between the main house above and the lower house where his mistress is. In this village, four or five of the husbands have mistresses. Resourceful men corral women in this manner. Unresourceful men play with widows and steal other people's wives. But as for farmers, they're upright. During the day they work together and at night husband and wife sleep together in the storeroom. In a life like that, for there to be any infidelity the man has to really like women or the woman has to really like men. Most of the people like us who chase after women are not farmers. They called us libertines.

If you live in a village, there are the rules of the village, and you have to submit to them. Village rules are strict and if you do something out of line, you'll be ostracized. But someone like me, who wasn't a member of the village, didn't have to participate in it. In turn, society didn't look me straight in the face, because I wasn't doing anything straight. So I ended up playing with widows because that wasn't an imposition on anyone. A lot of these were inherited from my boss. It's hard to start a new intimacy. Unlike my boss, I wasn't able to lord over women. First of all, I was of small build and didn't have his physique or dignity. And I was not as well off as he was, either. So I had no alternative but to enjoy myself on the sly, in the shadow of others.

So you ask how it was that women would take an interest? If you know how to please a woman, she'll come along. Look at Grandma, my wife. She's been with this piece of trash of a man for sixty years.

My wife was a daughter in one of the houses where the cow traders stayed. Her mother was intimate with my boss. After my boss died, she looked after me too. In the beginning, the mother was often angry with me. She'd say, "Your boss was good. He pleased me. You're unreliable. You're small." So, thinking to please her, I worked hard and did all sorts of things. But whatever I did I could never keep up with a spirited woman. What is more, she was almost twenty years older and always treated me like a child.

When I was following my boss around and we first began staying with that woman, her daughter was a child of not even ten. But by the time I came to have relations with the mother, her daughter had come of age and the men of the village had begun to take notice. Despite being wanton herself, the mother feared her daughter's falling into the hands of one of the young men and always had her daughter sleep beside her at night. So naturally, the daughter saw us doing it. And I came to know everything about the daughter. While the mother was sleeping I made her mine. And then I took the daughter with me and fled. Crossing over the mountains in the falling snow, I came from Iyo to the village neighboring this one for the first time. I too wanted to become an upright person, to have relations with neighbors, to start a home and have children. But since childhood I'd never done any real work and I'd never entered the society of young men. When I tried joining in the life of the village, I found I was not the type of person who could hold up any of its rules. And yet I rented a small shed there, and together with my wife started a home. I went to work for a paper wholesaler, traveling from place to place to buy paper mulberry trees. That was for three years, and that was when my life was the most decent.

* * * * *

It would have been good if I'd stayed like that, but in spite of myself I fell victim to temptation. Among the paper mulberry trees there were also *ganpi* trees [winter daphne], from which paper money is made. There were a lot of these ganpi trees in the government forests and the farmers would buy the trees from the government and cut them down. Officials from the government office for the Kobayashi District were responsible for looking after the government forest, and as a buyer of paper mulberry trees I often met the official in charge. The official had a fine house built for him and he lived there with his wife. His wife was from a home near the castle in Kōchi and she was a fine person. Being from Tosa, she was not all that fair-skinned, but she had thick eyebrows and large black eyes, and a straight nose. And she was a gentle person. She always served me tea when I went there.

At first I went to visit the husband on mulberry business, but before I knew it I was going out of my attraction for the wife. It started innocently enough. When I called upon the husband he was away and his wife was out in back doing the wash. I thought I'd leave right away but she served me tea and while I watched her do the wash we fell deep into conversation. To say we conversed—all I know is cows, so I told her stories about fooling people and getting them to buy or sell cows. She was wringing out the wash and since she was going to draw more water up from the well, I drew it for her. And I helped her pour out the water that was in the washtub. That was all I did, but she thanked me, saying, "You are truly kind." It was the first time I'd ever been treated like a real person and thanked by someone of such social standing. Until then, people like me who were up to no good feared government officials more than anyone else. The government officials of the Kobayashi District, when they were doing their rounds in the mountains, wore clothes like the policemen and had sabers hanging from their belts. One look at them and my sphincter would tighten. So I can't tell you how happy I was to be thanked by that wife.

After that I went there frequently, timing my visits to when the husband would be out. The house was in the back and somewhat high up, so I could visit without being seen much. I'd buy cheap sweets and take them, and when I was in town I'd buy something unusual and bring it along. And I did this in a way that my wife wouldn't notice. I'd go and we'd talk of silly things, but being an outsider, she had no one to talk to, and her husband was often away. And since I was there, I'd help out in little ways.

I'd thought that because she was a woman of standing I was not the kind of person she would give herself to. But when I was helping her hang the wash our hands would touch, or I'd squeeze her hand, and she didn't shake me off.

It was fall. I came to want, by whatever means, to sleep with her. When I went to her house she was doing the wash. I called out to her and she smiled. I told her, "I'll be waiting up above, at the Daishi [Great Teacher's] Temple," and left quickly, climbing up a path leading up from the side of the house. Just above the house, a steep path passed through a grove of young pine trees and climbed for about one hundred yards to the temple, a square hall under a large pine tree. On the twenty-first of every month people

Winter in Shikoku.
January–February 1941.

came to pay their respects, but on other days no one came here to pray. Out of breath, I climbed up to the temple thinking, "What have I said now?" With a feeling half of regret, I leaned up against the pine and looked down below. It was a busy time in the fall, and in the paddies in the valley, visible through the young pines, everyone appeared to be engaged in the rice harvest. And there I was trying to steal someone else's wife. I cannot say how I felt. I thought of running off, but I stayed and waited.

I waited for half an hour. It was evening. The evening sun fell down through the young pine trees and the wife came up from below. Wearing a kimono with a splashed pattern and wiping her hands on her apron, she came up slowly. I watched intently from above. How I struggled with my resolve. What truly unpardonable things I do, I thought, but . . .

When she'd come nearly halfway she looked up, and when I smiled, she smiled too. When she arrived at the top I took her hand, led her to the hall, and sat down on the stairs there. Saying that it would not be good to be seen, she entered the hall and I entered too. I asked her, "How is that you've come to listen to a person like me?" And she said, "You're a kindhearted person. Women want that more than anything else." This woman of high social status was the first person who had treated me like a real person.

After that, we probably met another four or five times. Not wanting to cause her any trouble, without telling her, and without saying anything to my wife, I returned to Iyo alone in the falling snow. Four years had passed.

* * * * *

In all my life there was never a time that took more out of me. I don't remember how I lived those six months. I was out of my mind. I don't know how many times I went to the top of the pass. Not wanting to see my wife, I hid for that half year. And when that time had passed, I was finally able to bear it.

After that I became a cow trader again. And I went after every woman that caught my eye. But I never met a person like that wife. Well, there was one. Can I tell you? Have you ever been totally in love with a woman? Have you licked their front? I've never told anyone this story before. I thought I'd die without telling it. It being inexcusable to that person. . . . You ask if I have the kind of story in me that can't be told? Well, I do. But if I were to die no one would know, and for a blind man over eighty to tell it, there's no longer anyone who'll be the worse for it.

I laid my hands on the wife of a village official. Her husband was a member of the prefectural assembly and theirs was the biggest house in the back end of Iyo. When we had the occasion to meet along the road, he called down to me from atop a rickshaw, saying, "Cow trader, provide me with a good cow. A quiet cow would be good. If you go to my house, my wife will be there. Talk it over with her."

He was on his way to Uwajima. I had often met him on the road and I always bowed my head to him respectfully, but he'd never spoken to me. As I lived far from his village, we had no connection. And in that area there were a number of excellent cow traders, but for some reason, he asked me.

I went there fearfully. Long ago the home of a feudal lord and now that of a village official, his house had a tall stone wall in front and stone stairs. It was like a castle. Climb the stairs and there was a gate, a gate with housing built in. I went to the kitchen door and said, "I just met the master and he told me such and such and told me to discuss it with the lady." The lady came out. I'd never met such a woman. She'd probably not turned forty yet. Her skin was white, and she was well-rounded and refined, like the Goddess Kannon [the Goddess of Mercy]. In that kind of house, I figured they left everything to the maidservants and manservants, but that wasn't the case. She herself went to the barn and explained that they'd kept the bull for a long time and that he was a good worker but that being a bull he was rough-tempered and they wanted to trade him for a cow. I told her, "If you plan to use it in the paddies, it should be a bull. Because men will be working the animal, a bull is best. And there probably isn't a better animal than the one you have here." But she said, "My husband's most often away and since managing the house is such back-breaking work for a woman, we've decided to loan the land out to tenants. So we don't need a large animal. But since I like cows, I'd like to continue to care for one." I said, "Oh, is that so," and departed. I'd never met anyone who spoke so gently. Since she was always at home, I'd never seen or met her before. I'd only heard rumors that she was a beautiful and quiet lady.

So I went all out, searched for a cow she would truly take a liking to, and led it there. She was delighted. And would you believe, when I went to take out the bull that had been there, she fed it rice cooked with adzuki beans, gave it *sake* to drink, treating it no different from a human being. I thought, "so this is what upper class people are like," and was a bit taken aback. It was too much. A regular farmer wouldn't go that far. When it finally came time to take the bull away, the lady spilled lots of tears saying, "May you go someplace good where you will be well cared for." Then I thought, what kind people there are. So different from a person like me who makes things up as I go. It was all so astonishing.

After that I visited the master's house every now and then to see the cow. But the master was rarely there. The couple seemed to get along well, but they didn't have any children, so she was lonely. The master kept a mistress in Uwajima and it was said that he had three children by her. The husband was also pretty carefree so you could say they were well suited to one another.

It so happened that . . . when was it? Probably about 3:30 in the afternoon that I went to the house and the maidservants and manservants weren't there. Thinking it strange, I called out, "Excuse me," and the lady appeared from around back with her sleeves rolled up. When I asked what she was doing, she said that she was tending to the cow. And once again I was astonished. I didn't think that such a graceful person who never raised her voice and who spent most of her time indoors would do such a thing. I went to take a look in the barn, and she had scrubbed the cow clean. When I told her, "You should have the men do such things. This is not the kind of thing for a lady like yourself," she said, "I like cows, so at 3:30 I have the maid-servants take tea out to the manservants working in the fields and during that time I tend to the cow in this way." Once again I was surprised. And I'd learned that if I went at 3:30, I'd find the lady alone.

While I knew it was wrong, in spite of myself I began to visit at that time. Not knowing much of the world, we had nothing in common to talk about other than cows, but it felt good just to be at the lady's side. We were always together and I helped out. I explained things to her and she listened to it all with interest. Sadly, as I haven't had an education, I was unable to say a thing properly, but when I made a mistake she laughed and taught me.

You ask if at times like that I remembered she was the wife of an elected official? You're bad yourself, thinking of this as an infidelity. Not for a moment did I forget my wife. And at the same time I fell in love with the lady. Thinking that it would be wrong to lay my hands on her, I generally visited her after being with another woman but that didn't work either, because I felt I'd wronged my wife. Over time, and by degrees, I laid a trap for the lady. I said, "Lady, after all since you have such a fine cow, we should arrange for it to have a calf," and in time the decision was made to impregnate her. So I borrowed a fine bull and led him there. The lady cleaned the barn, changed the straw that was spread there and scrubbed the cow to the point of shining. Farmer's cows all sleep in their own shit and it's all stuck to their asses. I said, "Lady, I've never seen anyone who took such good care of their cow. You made it so clean, it's utterly possible to lick its ass." Thinking this was funny, she said, "You say that, but no matter how clean it is, can one lick an ass?" "Yes they can, yes they can. Even cows lick one another. If it's the ass of a woman I like, even I could lick it." At this she turned bright red and turned away. I thought I'd said too much and I led the bull to the cow. When I did this the bull got large and mounted the cow. I was so involved in it that I didn't take notice of the lady, but when the bull had finished and I looked over at her she was watching intently. After the bull had finished, he licked the cow's ass, so I said, "well look at that," and the lady said, "perhaps cows are more loving." In that moment I suddenly understood that she was not happy. I said, "Lady, people are no different. If it were me, for you I'd . . . " She didn't say anything. She squeezed my hand firmly and her eyes filled with tears. There in the barn, in the straw, I slept with the lady.

After that I thought that whatever happened I had to protect her. I wanted to become a good person. I told her of my villainous behavior and of my wife. When I told her, "I'm the dregs, but even as the dregs if there's anything I can do, please make use of me," she cried out of happiness.

It was hard to avoid being seen, so I didn't visit as much as before. I no longer took the initiative. But being who I am, I was happy to be treated with affection and respect. The first time we were together was in the spring. Then fall came and winter approached. The lady caught a cold that became pneumonia and she died suddenly. I took to my bed and cried and cried for three nights and three days.

Whoever the woman may be, if you are nice to her, she will give herself to you. And I pursued women until I finally lost my sight. In the end, after my eyes had been hurting for three nights and three days, I became blind. It was punishment for being a scoundrel. There wasn't a single productive thing I did. Real men didn't trust me. And for whatever reason, only women did as I asked.

I really don't understand. Men all treat women with neglect. So if you're even a little bit kind, women are compelled to follow. Come to think of it, I didn't do anything a woman wouldn't like. I did as they asked. I did what would please them.

You ask about my wife? When I fled to Iyo, she came after me. But I wasn't living in any one place and my wife returned to her mother's. Sometimes I'd just stop by. The mother had a new man and I no longer had any relations with her.

As my wife, Grandma did well to put up with a man like me. We only lived together for the first three years. After that, until I lost my sight, I didn't return home to speak of. When I lost my eyes and had no place to go, I went to Grandma. She said, "So you've finally returned," and she cried and was happy. Then, saying it would help me to regain my sight, she took me on a pilgrimage to the eighty-eight temples in Shikoku. She took good care of me, pulling the hand of one who'd suddenly gone blind.

But after all that I didn't regain my sight, and I fell to being a beggar. I've come to the end of my life without ever owning a real house. You ask if with all my philandering I've ever had a child? I may have for all I know, or I may not have. I didn't become a member of the village and live by its rules. When I had relations with a woman, I wouldn't allow for something to happen that would cause her to lose her position in society. So before others knew about it, I withdrew. I couldn't allow it to be a hindrance to my business either.

Only Grandma lasted to the end. You too have played with women, haven't you? Women are pitiful creatures. They put themselves in the place of men and sympathize with them, but it's rare for a man to put himself in the place of a woman and care for her. In any event, if nothing else, you should be sympathetic to women. The affection you give will not be forgotten.

I fooled a lot of people, but the cows were never fooled. Cows remember well. Five years pass, ten years pass, and if you meet again the cow will always call out with longing. Only the cows could see through the lies. Women were the same. I may have slept with them, but I didn't deceive them.

But, after all, it's best to do everything like other people do. If I had done like others, I wouldn't need to beg. It's about time for Grandma to return, so let's call an end to this talk of women. After they've finished their dinner, Grandma goes to the homes of farmers for leftovers. Even if it rains or if a wind blows, that's her job. All I do is just sit here like this. The only walking I do is down to the riverbed to the toilet or to bathe in the water. Thirty years of blindness were long and they were short. I think back on the women I was with. They were all gentle, good women.

Chapter 7

My Grandfather

[Miyamoto Ichigorō: 1846–1927; Ōshima Island, Yamaguchi Prefecture]

When all is said and done, my grandfather Miyamoto Ichigorō left the strongest impression on me, though to those around him, he was exceedingly ordinary and has already been forgotten by most. Born on the island of Ōshima, Yamaguchi Prefecture, in 1846, he died there in 1927. The second son of a medium-scale farmer, he stayed home and farmed because his older brother had left home at a young age to become a carpenter. Ichigorō had also thought to become a carpenter at first, but shortly into his apprenticeship his teacher struck him on the head with a hammer. Thinking that carpentry was not worth such suffering, he returned home.

In this area, it was common to become a carpenter regardless of whether one's family was wealthy or poor. And when a son became a carpenter he almost never succeeded his father as the head of the family. Generally the quietest son remained at home and farmed. Accordingly, it was not uncommon for the youngest son to inherit his father's role as the head of the family. In my family too, generation after generation, the eldest son established a branch family, and it was into one such branch family that my grandfather was born. My grandfather had a younger brother who also became a carpenter, so although my grandfather was not the youngest son, because he became a farmer, he succeeded his father as the family head.

Paddies and fields combined, the family owned about three acres of farmland. This is plenty for an independent farmer to live on, but from time to time my grandfather's older brother would come home and, without notice to his father or younger brother, sell a portion of the land, so it was diminished little by little. When properly documented, the purchase and sale of farmland is quite difficult, but apparently it was handled quite loosely. Though many stories about this have been handed down, I will omit them here. With such an older brother on his hands, my grandfather grew poorer and poorer. To make things worse, my grandfather's younger brother came home with dysentery in 1866, having contracted it while traveling. It spread to his father and he died.

My grandfather's father, Zenbei, had been a very hard worker. Though a total amateur, he was skilled at building stone walls, which remain here and there to this day. It is said that when he cleared land in the mountains and found that the soil was full of pebbles, he sieved it all. Having to work the paddies and fields in the daytime, he performed this work at night, by the light of a torch. The loss of his hardworking father hit Ichigorō hard. And to make matters worse, the dysentery spread throughout the village, killing many and causing a great imposition. That was the same year, 1866, that a punitive expedition came to Chōshū, and at such times of war everyone went into the mountains to stay out of harm's way. My family, too, lived for a time in a hut beside their rice paddy in the mountains. They washed clothing that had been soiled by the sick in the river, and when people downstream used that water, they became infected.

Ichigorō was gone at the time, working as a military porter in the war, and when the war was over he became the head of the family. He was still in his twenty-first year. So gentle he would not even kill a bug, my grandfather had been dragged into training as an agrarian soldier before the war started and had practiced fencing every day. It seems he became quite confident in his technique. During a break in the fighting he was walking along with several friends. Having left Yashiro, a village on the west side of the island, they came across two samurai warriors. The path being narrow, Ichigorō inadvertently bumped the tip of the warrior's scabbard. At this the warrior abruptly rebuked him, calling him "insolent." He apologized, but the warrior complained that his apology had been poorly made. Saying, "In that case I take you up on your challenge," Ichigorō unsheathed his short sword. Apparently the two warriors were taken aback by this. They were left with no choice but to draw their swords and fight. Astonished, Ichigorō's farmer friends looked on helplessly. It was two against one. Swords held pointed at one another's faces, no one moved. Just then a somewhat imposing warrior came along and, after hearing what had happened, made them sheath their swords.

I did not hear this story from my grandfather. When he was more than seventy years old and fencing matches had become popular in the village, someone encouraged him, saying, "Grandpa, would you like to give it a try?" Enduring his physical disabilities, he competed. These were rural folk, so there was no one of great skill, but my grandfather defeated all who came up against him beautifully. I felt invigorated watching. When he had finished the last match he said, "I seem to be short of breath," and showed no interest in fighting thereafter. All who were there were struck with wonder. It was during a match that day that an old man told me of the time, long before, when Ichigorō had been ready to cross swords with a samurai warrior. They had been in the war together as military porters.

When he was seventeen or eighteen, there was a girl that Ichigorō liked. She was pretty, even a bit showy, but also in the possession of a coldness that kept young men from approaching her recklessly. Saying that such women did not make good housewives, his father Zenbei was against a marriage. Then, when Zenbei died, her parents refused their consent, saying they did not want their daughter to marry into a poor family. But the girl showed no interest in marrying anyone else. They were the same age and, still single, they both entered their twenties. In time, there was a smallpox epidemic. The girl came down with it and became a bit pockmarked as a result. The story goes that the girl's parents asked Ichigorō, "Do you like her even now that she's pockmarked?" He responded, "I do." So they allowed the couple to marry. That was 1873, and they were both twenty-eight at the time. After that, they lived together for fifty years.

People said, "Marry a woman like that and you'll suffer your whole life through," but apparently Ichigorō thought that was fine. No matter how busy her husband was, Ichigorō's wife rarely helped with the farm work, and she was not the only one. Spinning and weaving were popular in these parts, so women seldom set foot in the fields. The only exception was when the husband was a carpenter and he had gone off to work somewhere.

Ichigorō worked hard but without accumulating a fortune. Now that he was married, his older brother no longer came back for money, but after he had split his property with his younger brother, my grandfather had only one acre of farmland. This meant he had to rent land in order to have enough to eat. What is more, their house was burned down. A child in the neighborhood was playing with fire, and it spread to the house. Three homes burned down, and the cow died in the fire as well. Though it was caused by a child, because the fire had spread from my grandfather's house to the other two, his position in the village was compromised. From then until the time of his death he generally kept a low profile.

Using clay tiles, my grandfather built a small shrine to the cow that had died. He worshipped it as a cow deity, making offerings of grass tied in small bundles. Word got out that it had the power to cure skin disease, so many came to pay homage to the shrine. Before long it was no longer in the care of my family but was being worshipped by the villagers as they pleased. But now, with the development of medicines for the treatment of skin disease, the incidence of this ailment has decreased considerably, and with it the number of worshippers of the deity as well.

Small shrine on Ōshima Island,
Yamaguchi Prefecture.
June 1955.

Ichigorō always awoke at four in the morning. He went to the mountain, did some work, and came back for a breakfast of rice gruel. He then set out to work in his paddies and fields. He worked solidly until noon and after eating lunch, in the summer months, he napped until three o'clock. After a bite to eat he returned to his paddies and fields and worked until dark. On rainy days he made rope, mats, and sandals out of straw, and at night he worked for a while as well. Even on festival days he worked during the morning. And when he had time to spare, he hired himself out as a day laborer. When he had finished the day's work, he prayed to the Shinto gods and to the Buddha and went to sleep. He worked so hard, it was impressive he was able to keep going.

He was neither displeased with nor questioning of this life, only grateful to live each day without mishap. Ichigorō enjoyed singing while he worked. He had apparently learned his songs from his own grandfather, who taught him when he was a child. In addition to the work songs for rice planting, grass cutting, weed pulling, and milling, he had also mastered a variety of songs that accompany dancing at the *Bon* and other festivals. Though my grandfather's grandfather was the eldest son, he had been adopted into his uncle's family. Apparently he was an easygoing man who went through life without ever marrying, singing the songs he liked and leisurely going about his work. When it came time for the rice planting, he took a *taiko* drum and traveled here and there singing rice-planting songs. And when it came time for the *Bon* festival he went where there was dancing and sang to keep time. He took in travelers and, since he had no children of his own, he adopted his younger brother's eldest son. That was Zenbei. Zenbei worked hard and they continued to take in travelers, though they were never paid anything for it. Travelers ate whatever the family was eating, said a word of thanks the following morning, and were on their way.

No matter how much time passed, their lives did not improve.

Ichigorō and his wife had four children, two boys and two girls. Having suffered as a carpenter's apprentice, he did not want his sons to become carpenters. He tried to make his eldest son [Miyamoto's father] a farmer, but the son said that as a farmer he would not be able to hold his head up in life, and he began willowing cotton. Then foreign cotton came along and his business hit a dead-end overnight. After that he apprenticed with a dyer, but he failed at this as well. So, at twenty-one, he went to work in Fiji, but that fell through and he came back in a little over a year.

During that time Ichigorō's wife visited the local tutelary deity every morning, as did all the families that had someone working away from home. And every several days people would place a bowl of rice on top of their roofs as an offering. The rice was for the crows, which were thought to be the bearers of news. If the crow called in a good voice, came along, ate the rice, and departed, the distant family member was safe. As it would happen, one day the crow's call was dreadfully bad and it ate very little of the rice. At that time their son had fallen ill in Fiji. I was told that of the 350 people who made the voyage, only 105 returned to Kobe the following year. Somehow, their son had come back alive.

When Ichigorō's wife was visiting the shrine, she found a black puppy crying under the floor of the worship hall. Taking pity on it she carried it home, gave it food, and tamed it. After that the dog grew quickly, but the neighborhood children tormented it. Their abuse became so pathetic that one evening Ichigorō took the dog into the mountains, to the boundary of the village. Abandoning the dog there, he spoke to it as if he were reasoning with a person, saying, "I want to take care of you but I can't bear to see you so abused. Ahead, there's probably a family that will treat you kindly, so go along and see what you find there." But Kuro [Black] stayed put. Ichigorō came down from the mountain, worried all the while, but the dog did not follow him.

Some years later, Ichigorō went to a village on the west side of the island. When he was on his way back home it grew dark. This was long ago, so the path was narrow and he somehow lost his way. At a loss, he squatted in the path, resting, when a black dog appeared. It bore a strong resemblance to Kuro. After he had followed the dog for a spell, the light from a farmhouse came into view. He breathed a sigh of relief and then realized that Kuro was no longer there. Ichigorō told me this story from time to time. All things have a spirit, so we must honor them. That was Ichigorō's credo.

I was probably not more than five or six at the time when a baby turtle was living in a small well beside a rice paddy deep in the mountains. I looked forward to gazing into the well at this turtle whenever I went to the mountains. Thinking it pitiful for the turtle to be forever confined to such a small place, I asked my grandfather to take it out of the well. I then tied the turtle up with a rope, determined to take it home with me and care for it there. I started back on my own in high spirits, but as I walked along the turtle became more and more pitiful. I thought of how lonely the turtle would be if I took it to an unfamiliar place. And, still carrying the turtle, I began to bawl. When a woman who happened along asked what was wrong, all I could say was "the turtle's miserable." I walked back, crying, in the direction of the paddy in the mountains and the woman kindly came along. When I arrived at the paddy my grandfather consoled me and returned the turtle to its well. To this day I remember him saying, "This turtle has his own world, so it's probably best we put him here." The turtle lived in the well until around the time I finished elementary school. It had become quite large. Then one day, an old man from the adjacent paddy said, "This turtle's grown quite large. The world's probably pretty narrow in there." Saying this, he took the turtle out of the well and placed it in the mountain stream that ran beside it. From then until around the time I turned thirty, when my grandfather was walking back along this mountain path in the evening he would sometimes come upon the turtle plodding along. And when he did, he never failed to tell me about it.

People from my grandfather's time interacted with animals and humans in much the same way, and they imparted these feelings to us as well. Until I was eight or nine, I slept in my grandfather's arms. During this time he told me many old tales. At first he sang something that resembled nursery rhymes. When I think back on it now, these were *haya monogatari*, stories told quickly and rhythmically, in a manner that made them easy to learn.

Not only did my grandfather sleep with me at night, he took me to the mountains with him. He would put a large bamboo basket on top of his wood-framed backpack and carry me in that. I enjoyed swinging along as we went. Once in the mountains, I played alone, gathering rocks and stacking them or collecting leaves. At times, I went deep into the mountains. When I became lonely, I yelled, "Grandpa!" and hearing him respond "Ho-y," I was put at ease. When I turned about five or six, I began pulling up weeds in the fields. My grandfather would tell me, "You pull one weed and it becomes that much easier for me," and before I knew it I was enticed by his words. In the beginning I tired after pulling up one furrow's worth, but out of happiness at being praised, I came by degrees to have more staying power. My rewards for pulling weeds were the ears of cogon grass, sorrel, knotweed, strawberries, wild grapes, and oleaster berries that grew wild on the ridges and levees between the fields and paddies, and I was quite contented with these. When I was lonely and wanted to go home, my grandfather sang to me in a beautiful voice.

One day, as it grew dark, I saw something glittering brightly in a field across the valley. When I asked my grandfather what it might be he said, "The *mameda* have lit their lanterns." A *mameda* is a tiny raccoon dog. These are charming, harmless creatures. He told me that when people become lonely in the mountains, the *mameda* come out and strike up a friendship. In fact, this was the evening sun reflecting brightly off broken pieces of mirror hung over a field of foxtail millet to scare off the birds. My father told me that much later.

For a time every evening, the glittering light from the tiny raccoon dogs' lanterns was a big comfort to me. And thereafter, when I heard the sound of an axe cutting trees deep in the mountain or the sound beyond the mountains of a chisel splitting stone, I came to think that these were all the work of the tiny raccoon dogs. And in thinking this, I was drawn to the depths of the mountains and beyond.

"Wherever you are, whatever you are doing, as long as it isn't bad they will all come to your aid. At nightfall, when you return alone on the mountain path, the mountain god will generally follow along and protect you, uttering a cry something like *hoi, hoi.*" I believed these words my grandfather had spoken to me since I was little, and thereafter, no matter how late at night I walked a mountain path, I suffered no anxiety.

When I was about six, my grandfather climbed to the top of a cliff to cut some tree branches. When he was carrying the branches down with him, he caught his foot on a vine, and falling, was seriously injured. He had fallen into a rice paddy and, after crawling up out of it, had called out to a man passing on a path up on the ridgeline. The man had come and carried him on his back out to where there was a road, and from there my grandfather was carried on a shutter door. Fortunately there was a good doctor who dressed the wound well and saved his life, but my grandfather was hospitalized for a long time. For quite some time thereafter, the person who had saved him said, "He may be a timid old man who won't even kill a bug, but he sure was courageous." It seems that deep down, farmers all shared this strength of spirit. After the wound healed my grandfather had a bit of a limp, but even so he did not stop working in the mountains.

When I turned ten, I no longer slept with my grandfather. There was no particular reason for this, but, as a child will, I started to feel like a grown-up and probably became shy about such things. Thereafter, when night came, my grandfather sang alone, and continued to do so until he died.

My grandfather told me a countless number of old tales, but because I heard them all before I was ten, I have forgotten most of the longer ones. Some of the stories took two or three nights to tell, and they were not of the kind that grandfathers usually tell their grandchildren. The stories that were not long were all related to daily life, and he told them to me not only when we were going to sleep but on a variety of occasions.

When I was little, for some reason the end of my penis became swollen. When this happened my grandfather said, "You've peed on a worm." He then dug a worm up from the field, and after washing it carefully, put it back. He told me, "Whenever you pee out in the open, you should say, 'Please get out of the way,' before you pee." Up until I graduated from elementary school, whenever I peed outdoors these words inadvertently escaped my mouth. And I developed the habit of peeing in places like ditches.

My grandfather often told me, "Unfortunately, worms are unable to see. Because they brought unhappiness to their parents they were sent away to live naked in the soil but because they love to be clean, they find it the hardest to bear when they

Even the mountains were cultivated. Ōshima Island, Yamaguchi Prefecture. March 1957.

are peed on. When night falls and they cry '*jeee*' they are telling you where they are." In the spring and summer one can hear "*jeee*" coming out of the twilight, from nowhere in particular. I did not learn until much later that this was the call of the mole cricket. And until then I felt a deep compassion for these unfortunate creatures.

Around the time that spring turned to summer, crabs often came up out of the holes in the gutters. I would rumple up a Japanese mugwort leaf, tie it up in string, and dangle it by the entrance to a hole. When I moved it, a crab would come out and grab it with its claws and I pulled it up. This was one way for a child to have fun. My grandfather approved of this "fishing" but often warned, "Don't harass the crabs or they'll come and pinch your ears at night." When I tore the pincher off a crab he admonished me, saying, "The pincher is a crab's hand. Without a hand, he can't eat. So don't pull them off." He also suggested, "After you've played with the crabs, put them back where they were, otherwise they'll stop playing with you." In this way he taught me to treat crabs as friends.

My grandfather retired from his role as head of the family when he was sixty. Handing down debts that only grew no matter how much he worked, my grandfather moved into a four-and-a-half-mat [9 x 9 ft.] room with my grandmother and though they ate with everyone else, he left the management of all household affairs to his son.

Thinking there was no chance of paying these debts growing only rice and barley, Ichigorō's son (my father) began to raise silkworms. Though my grandfather was not opposed to silkworms, he was against the planting of mulberry trees on farmland that had been handed down for generations. For that reason, before my father could grow mulberry trees, he had to rent land in the mountains that belonged to the village and to buy forest land and clear it. This was hard work, but my father weathered it and after clearing more than one and a half acres of land, he began to raise silkworms. I do not recall my grandfather collaborating in this land-clearing work. My father did not attempt to lure my grandfather into it, either. Sericulture was entirely my father's and mother's responsibility.

But my grandfather did manage the fields and paddies. Year after year, he grew barley, planted sweet potatoes, and sowed millet. And he took on all of the straw work. In other words, he continued to live as he had all along.

My grandfather believed that "One mustn't act against their convictions." So, although he could see the importance of raising silkworms for a profit, he was against the reduction of land used to grow rice and barley toward that end. While he preserved the old, he did not compel others to do so. He just wanted to live his life in a way that he could accept.

This was not true only of my grandfather. Rather, it appears to have been the general thinking of the people in this area. When a mother-in-law and her daughter were different in character, and when the daughter was not as reliable as her mother-in-law, the mother-in-law took every opportunity to entreat the family's ancestors for forgiveness, saying, "In my generation I will work fully for the family. Please forgive my daughter-in-law even if she is slack in hers." I often heard such talk from the elderly women.

My grandfather reliably fulfilled the obligations that were required of him. Visits to the family altars during *Bon* and to the homes of relatives at New Year's were my grandfather's work, and he would set out in the morning, taking me with him. Visits to the family altars were also referred to as "bowing to the ancestors," and we would enter the home of a relative and, without saying anything to those who lived there, sit in front of the family altar and pray. Then we addressed the person whose house it was with, "It's a good *Bon*." If it were New Year's, we would enter saying, "It's a good spring," and, bowing before the family altar, offer the ancestors a New Year's greeting.

When my grandfather died, old relatives from several families came to our house and suggested, "Seeing as how Grandpa's dead, let's call an end to associating as relatives." And with that, we were no longer related. One's relatives came with the household through the head of the family and his wife, but the elderly largely determined who they were. Association with relatives usually extended as far as cousins, but if one had a strong sense of duty it included second cousins as well. This was decided in discussions with the other families.

In my family my mother now makes the rounds, greeting relatives at New Year's and our ancestors at the time of the *Bon* festival. But my wife goes almost nowhere. In this way, the performance of family duties changes with every generation.

As for social relations or what might be called "society," it appears to have been most important not to impose on others. More than it did in my family, finding fault with local society or splitting hairs over one's social status occurred one social rung above us, among the village's leading families. And this phenomenon was certainly not limited to my birthplace. When I read the autobiography of Hasunuma Monzō, who had been raised in a poor farming family in a remote location in the Aizu Valley, I saw that life in his family was virtually no different from my own. Almost no writings about the everyday affairs of poor farming families exist, and only recently have books like *Silent Farmers* and *Creators of Folktales* begun to come out. To date, most books about farming villages have focused either on people who are well off or on something unique about the less fortunate. And from the beginning, readers have not shown an interest in works that do not have conflict and pathos.

When my grandparents had been married for fifty years, their children celebrated their seventy-seventh birthdays and golden wedding anniversary. Although they had been poor, my grandparents were content with the life they lived. Early one evening in March of that year, my grandmother went to the house across the way to use their bath, talked there for a while, returned home, and when she was about to enter her room, died from a stroke. My grandfather, preparing to sleep, went out into the corridor on his way to the bathroom and found my grandmother lying face down. He spoke to her, but she did not respond. He shook her but she did not move, at which point he called out to my mother. My mother went to look, but my grandmother had already died. The villagers said my grandmother could not have been more fortunate, for she had died without troubling her daughter-in-law and without suffering herself. They said it was a reflection of her character, and they were envious.

No matter how busy the time, my grandmother had rarely set foot in field or paddy, and she had always kept herself well groomed. Up until the time of her death, she had prettied her hair with oils and pomade, and she had almost no white hair mixed in. She had lived her whole life as she pleased. People were also impressed that she had not put aside any money when she died. In these parts, a family's wealth protects and supports the lives of its members, but individuals have their own secret savings so they can do the things they want to do. At times family members will receive money from the head of the household, but generally they earn this money on their own. Meanwhile, the head of the household and his wife are so busy with the work of the house that it is quite difficult for them to earn money on the side. So the housewife will often receive money from her own mother, who is usually living in retirement and can use the money she earns as she pleases. This money is often given to daughters who are married. Because my grandmother worked very little she didn't have much money stashed away, but she did receive money from my father and his younger brother, and she also sold family possessions at times. The money she accumulated in this way went to support her married daughters and grandchildren. I often received such endowments through my mother and from my grandmother on my mother's side. In this way, traces of the matrilineal could be found through the time of my childhood.

In these parts, it is customary for a person to leave some money behind when they die. This is called "death money," and with this money a person pays for his or her own funeral. My grandmother did not even have this money. This was not from being poor, but because she knew that those she left behind would give her a proper funeral.

Thereafter my grandfather often prayed before a stone Jizō in the center of the village. When people asked what he was praying for, he said, "I want to die suddenly like Grandma, so that's what I'm asking for."

My grandfather lived for five more years after my grandmother died. He continued to work the whole time. With no one to talk to, it seemed his only pleasure was the singing of folk ballads.

In my village, *Bon* was still practiced in keeping with the old lunar calendar until early in the Shōwa period [around 1930]. On the seventeenth [of July], though others were taking time off, my grandfather was out working in his fields. Early in the morning he put rice gruel left over from breakfast and pickled vegetables in a bowl and attached it to his wood-framed pack. Saying he would not be back for lunch, he departed. He worked in his fields in the morning and repaired places where the mountain path had grown worn in the afternoon. Someone who passed by on the path and saw my grandfather repairing it alone said, "It's *Bon*, you should be taking a break." To this he apparently responded, "After *Bon*, lots of people will pass this way, so it should be repaired during the holidays."

That evening my grandfather came back from the mountains and after eating dinner he went to where the people were dancing to sing ballads. Over eighty and without a single tooth, whether he was calling out a beat or singing a ballad, his voice was practiced and had the power to pull the dancers together in perfect unison. He sang floridly to keep time, but when it came to ballads his voice was melancholy, and aside from his voice and the sound of the *taiko* drums, a hush would come over the dancers and they danced quietly, as if in a dream. My grandfather was particularly skilled at singing *Bon* ballads. Up until around that time the convention was to sing to maintain a beat during the twilight hours and to save the ballads for late at night.

On that night my grandfather sang ballads until late. He came back just before midnight and, upon entering his room, collapsed. Hearing a groan, my mother spoke to him but he did not respond, and she ran for a doctor. The doctor came and examined him and diagnosed my grandfather with encephalitis. Though he was unconscious, his hands and feet moved and at times he kicked and struggled. His condition was quite serious, and he grew weaker and weaker. Three days after the first outbreak of the illness, Ichigorō died. As he had wished, he died without suffering and without inconveniencing his daughter-in-law.

The day after my grandfather died, an old man from the neighborhood brought a bank deposit book with my grandfather's name on it. This was to pay for his funeral. The old man who had been entrusted with this deposit book was the young boy who had burned down my family's house long before. When, in his youth, he had become mentally agitated, my grandfather had looked after him. As a young man he went on a pilgrimage around Shikoku and did not return for a long time. When he did return, however, he was completely well. He started a small business. Honest and kind, he was a good friend to the poor.

Although he had brought misfortune to my grandfather's family, my grandfather had trusted him and though this man was much younger, my grandfather had apparently conferred with him on all matters.

After my grandfather died, the *Bon* dances began to fall into disorder. The villagers were no longer able to dance in a state of rapture when following other singers' leads. They even tried changing to something new, but that did not work either.

I did not sufficiently inherit my grandfather's abundance of old stories. He was not one for small talk, but it can be said that his life was itself a folktale.

Chapter 8

The Worldly (I): Masuda Itarō

[1851–1930; Ōshima Island, Yamaguchi Prefecture]

Walking the villages of Japan, I have encountered a surprising number of people who traveled freely when they were young, people their fellow villagers refer to as the "worldly." Apparently such travel was already common late in feudal times, though this practice seems to have grown even more popular in the Meiji period. I have often heard it said that the villagers of old lacked individuality. Yet when compared with people in the present day who speak of their own individuality while tending to resemble one another, many among the elderly are highly active and in the possession of a certain intensity. But they are dismissed as stubborn.

While my grandfather and Masuda Itarō were neighbors and in-laws, the two were neither constrained by this relation nor did they intervene in one another's lives, and accordingly, they did not strongly influence one another. Watching them in their later years, I saw that each followed his own path and neither was ever the slightest bit critical of the other.

Late in the Edo period, the population of my own village grew, and by the 1830s, the village had become saturated. And yet, because people were able to support themselves with work other than farming, branch families were created in great numbers.

From the beginning, this work was not available in the village; it was outside. Countless jobs as carpenters, sawyers, stonemasons, mariners, salt workers, and the like awaited the second and third sons who left the village to do such work. It is fair to say that almost every old person I know went away to work, and Masuda Itarō was among them.

In 1866, at the time of the Chōshū expedition [when the shogunate attempted to restrain this part of Japan], Itarō was fourteen years old. In those days boys entered the local youth group at fifteen, and in so doing, they were recognized as adults. But Itarō's father was ill, so although he was a child of fourteen and still had a child's bangs, he set off to become a military porter. He wore a dark-blue kimono, a short sword at his side, and carried a bamboo spear. Still being a child, he followed a neighbor by the name of Shōkichi, who was a sensible man and one of the worldly villagers. Shōkichi often went to Iyo for work, and when the war began he was pulled into it.

Men like this delighted in going to war. They knew the world, they had a reckless streak, and they were looking for trouble. So when the war started, they really exerted themselves. In a sense, this was a war to defend their own homes, and samurai and farmers were engaged without discrimination. What is more, many of the shock troops who were at the center of the battle [to defend this area against the shogun's army], were fellow carpenters and the second and third sons of farmers.

Old man Kika was from the same village and, as a young man, had gone in the direction of Hagi to work as a carpenter. When he was passing through Yamaguchi, the shock troops were enlisting men, and he casually joined up. He was a big boaster who sometimes even believed his own talk. Once he came out with: "Go to the top of Mt. Shiraki (a 1,200-ft mountain south of the village), and you can see the mouth of the river in Osaka." To which another man said, "I've never heard anything so foolish," and the two got into an argument with neither backing down. Finally, it was decided that they would confirm matters by climbing to the top of the mountain. Well, they climbed the mountain, but were unable to see anything that looked like the mouth of a river. Kika was reproached with, "Can't see it, can you?" To which he responded, "That island is in the way. Remove that, and you can see it."

Well, when Kika had grown old, he came upon a large group of people talking idly about how terribly poisonous blowfish are. Hearing this, he said, "That's not true." To which one of them drew close and said,

"In that case, try eating it, old man."

"I'll eat plenty. I'll show you. But if I eat blowfish and don't die, how much will you give me?"

"I'll give you five yen."

So it came to pass that the old man had to eat blowfish. There being many stories in these parts of people eating blowfish and dying, no one had eaten blowfish of late. So the ocean was full of blowfish.

When they're caught they're usually thrown back, and they are exceedingly easy to hook. Because the old man had said he would eat blowfish, he had to catch one. Using hermit crabs as bait, he dropped his line in from the top of a stone wall, and he caught any number of blowfish from six to ten inches long. A curious man, wanting to see the old man eat the blowfish, followed Kika home. The old man called his cat and, as a trial, gave it a fish, and the cat went off somewhere with the fish in his mouth. Seeing this, the old man was put at ease and said, "Look at that, even a cat will eat it." With a feeling of triumph, he skinned the blowfish, gutted it, and after removing its head, he cooked it. Then he ate it in front of everyone. At this moment, the man who had followed Kika said, "Grandpa, cats don't eat blowfish," and brought out the fish the cat had taken earlier. As might be expected, the old man was shocked, but putting on a bold face he said, "To eat something that even a cat won't eat, that's remarkable. And I'll be one step ahead of you on the way to paradise. Paradise is fine you know." As it would happen, he didn't die. And he became utterly fond of blowfish. Thereafter he caught blowfish every day and ate them all.

"Grandpa, when are you going to paradise?"

"Well, they haven't come for me yet but it'll probably be around the time I've eaten most of the blowfish in the ocean."

The old man didn't eat all the blowfish in the ocean, but he did live quite a bit longer.

Many others joined the shock troops, and there was a man among them who resembled old man Kika in character. He didn't know how to read or write but had committed the troop's orders to memory perfectly. One could not help but be amazed at the length of the statement he had memorized. Then, on one occasion, he was handed a document and, not being able to read it, he held it upside down, studying it with a knowing expression. When the man who had brought the document said, "That's upside down," he responded casually, "I'm showing it to you."

This same soldier, when he had grown old, was walking along a path when he came upon a young man, and the young man asked,

"Grandpa, where are you going?"

"Where my feet are pointed."

To which the young man responded,

"Really? Your feet are pointed north and south. It looks like you're headed for both the mountains and the ocean."

The old man, who was quite splay-footed, said,

"Oh, no. I'm not going to the mountains or the ocean. I'm following my nose."

Anyway, these guys were all cranky, obstinate, and a bit soft in the head, which may have been a trait the people of the island shared at that time. And that gave birth to an endless number of funny stories.

But their character also led to fatal problems. Shortly before the Chōshū expedition, two shock troopers passing through a village in the Iwakuni Domain on their way back to their headquarters on Mt. Iwaki asked a farmer on the side of the road, "What time is it now?" The farmer responded, "About the same as this time yesterday." Jokes of this sort were commonly told amongst close friends, but one of the shock troopers became angry, saying this was an affront. The other soldier calmed him down, and finally they returned to headquarters where the angry soldier reported this matter to Tateishi Magoichirō, the head of the rifle corps. Tateishi suggested to his superiors that the farmer should be punished for insulting a samurai warrior. But the secretary, Narasaki Gōjūrō, was against this. Narasaki was originally from a farming family and was quite familiar with the character of the farmers in these parts. Tateishi was from Kurashiki, in the Bitchū Domain, and was a wandering and masterless samurai who was recognized for his skill as a swordsman. Upon joining the shock troops he had been promoted to head the rifle corps. Well, Narasaki won the argument, but Tateishi took offense. He ambushed Narasaki on his way home that night and cut him down. Tateishi then deserted the unit, gathered his companions, and attacked the governor's office in Kurashiki.

Soldier or not, the kind of person who could not understand a joke like this was not welcome in these parts. And it was amidst an overflowing of this mood that the Chōshū expedition began.

* * * * *

Masuda Itarō grew up in these times, and participated in this war. Being young, he worked in the rear of the war, and apparently did nothing that made him stand out. For a time, the island of Ōshima was occupied by the shogun's military, but the local shock troops came to the rescue and within several days the military had withdrawn completely. A number of prisoners were tied up in a farmer's cow stable in Yashiro, and curious people came in droves to see them. Itarō was one of the crowd. "They all looked like nice guys. We'd tell them they were going to be beheaded and they'd begin to wail....We knew that prisoners weren't killed, so we teased them. They were all from somewhere around Matsuyama. We'd say, 'You're the guys who burned the houses here on this island,' and they'd put their hands together and say, 'No, that's not true, no, that's not true.'" Itarō told this story often, until he grew old.

Later the prisoners were given travel money and even clothing to wear, and sent back to Iyo. "After that, we were told that many warriors from Iyo were surely still hiding on the island and to look for them, so I followed Shōkichi and we traveled the mountains looking for them. He'd scare me by saying, 'There they are!' and my balls would shrink for a moment. But there was no one there or anywhere. So we decided to head home, and when we were on our way down Ushimarugi Slope (west of the village), a warrior in a torn kimono came up from the bottom. His hair was in a mess, and he appeared to be from Iyo. He was a warrior, and we were farmers, so if we were to cross swords, it was certain we'd lose. The hair on my head was standing on end. Shōkichi too was silent and, unable to pull back, we finally went forward. After we'd passed the warrior, Shōkichi looked back and said, 'Where are you going?' At this the warrior looked back as well, and staring steadily at us, said, 'I am going to pray at the Hachiman Shrine [to the God of War].' Shōkichi, putting on airs, said, 'You have my permission. Go.' I thought, this guy sure talks big, and when we'd headed down a bit farther, I said, 'Uncle, you're really something. My hair's standing on end.' To this Shōkichi responded, 'Me too. But when I passed the warrior, I tried touching my balls ever so slightly and they were hanging freely. They say that if your balls are loose, you won't lose to your opponent, so I took courage.' Since then, whenever there's trouble, I check my balls."

* * * * *

After the war, Itarō became a woodsman and went from Iyo to the mountains of Tosa to work. [Hereafter, as told by Itarō:]

Everywhere we went, people were living harsh lives. There were big trees though, and we cut them down and turned them into boards, mostly for building boats. Life in the mountains, day in and day out, wasn't easy.

What ill fortune made you a woodsman,
young man deep in the mountains?
The woodsman eats three pounds of rice
and the stump of the pine tree sheds a tear.

We sang songs like this while cutting down trees. I did well if I could make one *ryō* [a silver coin that preceded the use of the yen] in half a year. I was fifteen when I first entered the mountains in Tosa, and at the end of that year, to celebrate the New Year, I returned home. I decided to travel alone, separate from my fellow woodsmen, and when it was finally time to go, I missed home more than I could bear. With a bundle slung over my shoulder, I walked day and night to Mitsugahama. Along the way, I crossed over several mountain passes, one of which I had been told was infested with bandits. It had already grown dark when I arrived at the bottom of that pass. When I asked the way at a farmhouse beside the path, they warned me that I could easily become lost crossing the mountains at night, and that there were bandits as well. They offered to put me up for the night, but I refused and went on, pulling up a suitably sized stake from beside the farmer's field. I had a short sword and with the stake this made a pair. Though it was pitch dark, my eyes grew accustomed, and I could vaguely see. When I neared the top of the pass, I saw someone coming from above. They didn't have a lantern either, so without a doubt, they were suspicious. Thinking I'd finally run into a bandit, I tried clutching my balls and found that they hung loose. If I spoke out, they'd know I was a child, so I decided not to respond even if I was spoken to. The other saw that I had two swords and, perhaps out of fear, stepped off the path, allowing me to pass. When I had climbed a bit farther, I heard voices behind me.

"Who was it that just passed?"

"A warrior."

It sounded like a conversation between two bandits, and when I had crossed over the pass I ran for my life.

I arrived in Mitsugahama on the evening of the following day. I asked if there was a boat to my home and was told that one would leave in the morning. It would have cost me to stay in a lodging so I slept on the beach, using my bundle as a pillow and curling up into a ball. I awoke at dawn having rolled down to the water's edge. Surprised, I looked around. My bundle was gone! Thinking it had surely been stolen, I searched frantically and found it far up the beach, just as I had left it.

In this way my first work trip came to an end, and I returned home.

* * * * *

A woodsman's work was truly wretched. Originally, those who felled and cut trees were called sawyers. Our work was divided into cutting down large trees, or "first mountain," and cutting these felled trees into shorter logs, then slicing them into boards, which was called "last mountain." Saws weren't used in first mountain. No matter how large the tree, we cut it down with a single axe, which was hard work. Once the tree had fallen, we removed its branches, leaving only the trunk. Because we couldn't carry such a large tree, we cut it into lengths that could be moved to a river and floated downstream. But deep in the mountains, we boarded the trees and carried them out on our backs.

When cutting down trees we had to be particularly careful of the trees the *tengu* [long-nosed goblins] liked to stand on. Most often these were trees with big branches sticking out up high, and if you didn't ask permission of the *tengu* before cutting one down, in all likelihood you would be sent flying or be pinned under the tree. Your bones would be crushed, and there were times when a person's skull was split in two.

Mt. Ishizuchi was home to a *tengu*, and he would sometimes wander there. Even in the absence of a wind, the treetops would make a commotion as if they were caught in a gale. Or in the middle of the night it would sound as if the mountain was being torn in two, or a tree had fallen. These were called "trees toppled by the *tengu*," and when morning came, nothing had happened.

When we built a small hut and worked in the mountains, we had to keep a fire going in the indoor fire pit all night long. You never knew when an evil spirit might come along. First of all, wolves would come. Back then there were lots of wolves. The sound of them crying "uo-uo-" on mountain ridges was something terrible. Without fail they would come down around the hut in the small hours of the morning. Wolves liked pee, and they'd come to drink it. So we would generally remove the bottom of the wooden pee pail to keep them from drinking it. Just the same, at times they would come to lick what was left on the rim of the pail.

Wolves are said to travel in packs of a thousand, and they always did. When you crossed over a mountain, they would follow. And if you were to trip on a rock or the root of a tree and fall, they would pounce on you and eat you bones and all. And if you spoke ill of the wolves, they would curse you and, at times, a thousand of them would hide behind the frame of the *shōji* [sliding paper doors], their ears straining to hear you.

When you walked the mountain path back to your hut, you had to turn around and thank the wolves, saying, "Thanks for your trouble." On the other hand, if you didn't speak disparagingly of wolves or do anything to cross them, they would protect you. If you bathed at night, you always had to say "please step aside" before throwing out your bath-water, because it should not be allowed to splash on a wolf.

It was rare for raccoon dogs to do a person harm, but they were a nuisance because they played practical jokes. When you could see a fire flickering on a mountain across the valley, it was usually the work of a raccoon dog. What appeared to be a fire in the distance was actually a trick being played right before your eyes, and if you took a stick and suddenly struck the ground at your feet it was pretty effective at putting an end to their trickery. Raccoon dogs often came to the hut in the middle of the night to do mischief. They'd knock on the door but if you went outside, generally there was no one there. If you hide in the shadow of a tree and watch, I've heard it said that you can see them doing a handstand and striking the door with their tail.

The worst of their mischief is in the middle of the night, when the fire in the indoor pit burns out, and they come into the hut and paw at your face, lick you, and sometimes climb up on your chest.

When the day's work was done and we were back in the hut, talk was mostly ghost stories of wolves, raccoon dogs, *tengu*, and the like. These stories continued every night, without end, while we drank unrefined *sake* that had been bought in a nearby village. The production of this unrefined *sake* was quite popular in Tosa. In this way, if nothing else, I became able to hold my liquor.

When we worked near a village, we'd all go to play in the young girls' houses. Unlike the domestic servants, we woodsmen didn't work for the master of the house or have to bow our heads to him. If a woodsman didn't like the work, or if the employer was arrogant, we'd quickly change workplaces. This made us all the more straightforward and vital, and popular with the girls. So there were lots of times when someone married into a family in the mountains and settled down there.

Itarō continued to work as a woodsman for seven or eight years, but life in the mountains was dreary. Wanting to be around other people, he became a carpenter's apprentice after he turned twenty. Generally a carpenter's apprentice trains for five to seven years but Itarō was old, and after working under a teacher for two years, he became an independent carpenter.

It was at this time that the Saigō uprising [when samurai, frustrated to have lost their social status and led by Saigō Takamori, fought the new Meiji government] occurred, and the city of Kumamoto was destroyed by fire. When rumors spread that a lot of carpenters and other laborers were needed for the city's revival, groups of carpenters, plasterers, and stonemasons headed south, one after another. Itarō was among them.

The restoration of Kumamoto was so fast, it happened right before their eyes. Itarō rented a shed beside the house of a village head in the suburbs and traveled to work from there. The village head adored Saigō and was a big supporter of his argument that Korea should be attacked. If Saigō had had his way, the village head would have carried a spear and made the crossing to Korea. Whether they should be called followers or subjects, it was said that there were nearly a thousand people devoted to him. One would expect the village head to have joined in the Saigō uprising but he did not, fearing that if he was not careful he would get himself killed and would not be able to participate in the conquest of Korea. Itarō liked the village head's boasting from the bottom of his heart. And it seems that Itarō, the arrogant itinerant artisan that he was, was loved by the village head as well.

Itarō worked together with a number of friends. They were

all young, so when night came, they went to play at the young girls' houses. And on their way home they would steal into another house and take a chicken. Most farmers in these parts kept chickens and used them in place of clocks. They ranged free during the daytime, pecking at whatever grains they could find. When night fell, they returned to the house and slept on a perch above the dirt floor in the entrance. So, in the middle of the night, on their way back from playing at a young girl's house, the carpenters would open the front door, sneak in, and steal one of the chickens from its roost. Then they would pluck its feathers and boil it in a pot.

The people in these parts did not eat chicken and generally had an aversion to beef and other meats as well. So, for a time, no one noticed that the chickens were being taken and eaten. If a chicken was missing, they figured it was late coming home and was off sleeping somewhere. In time, dozens of the village's chickens had disappeared. Then, for the first time, people took notice. Some among them complained, "It would appear that the carpenters from Chōshū are stealing them and eating them. How rude!" But no one reproached them or made them pay. The problem was that people were more careful to close their doors, so the carpenters were no longer able to visit the young girls at night. With nothing to amuse them, the carpenters gradually left, and only Itarō remained. Unable to visit young women at night, and with the village head as a go-between, he married into the family of a fine young woman.

But Itarō had a wife he had just married back home. Quiet and a hard worker, Itarō had been told she was too good for him, and regardless of all that he had gotten himself adopted into another family far from home. He was living a carefree life. Two years had passed without his coming home to his family, so his wife sent someone to check on him, and they found him in this state. Saying that what he was doing was wrong, they took him back home.

"You shouldn't be meddling in my affairs. Here I was finally living well in Higo [the feudal domain which, in 1876, became

Kumamoto Prefecture] ... " This is how Itarō railed at his wife when he returned home. He didn't dislike his wife, but he didn't feel that he had wronged her either.

After returning home and taking it easy for a while, Itarō joined his teacher, a carpenter by the name of Hara, in Kagoshima. Hara had been contracted to build a temple in Kagoshima for the Shinshū sect. Their work on the temple was quite good, and the locals watched with interest. The homes in Kagoshima were generally crude. Carpenters in the employ of feudal lords were about the only ones doing quality work, and the carpenters from Chōshū gained a reputation for doing good work as well.

Many government officials and military men were from Kagoshima, and most of them moved to Tokyo. When one of these men returned to Kagoshima and saw the quality of Itarō's and the other carpenters' work, he invited them to Tokyo. That sounded interesting, so the carpenters decided to go.

Hara had worked in Kagoshima before, around the time of the Saigō uprising. When the fighting started he had left Kagoshima without being paid, and when he returned, he made no effort to collect his debts. Impressed by this generous behavior, the people of Kagoshima, with their strong sense of honor, showed Hara respect and saw him as more than just a carpenter. Accordingly, in Tokyo, Hara and the others mostly built homes for naval officers from Kagoshima, and there were many such homes in Mita, Takanawa, and Shinagawa.

In 1891, while they were working in Tokyo, a large earthquake [the Mino-Owari earthquake] struck the nearby Nōbi region. Some four thousand died, and many homes collapsed, so carpenters came from all over to work there. Itarō arrived in Mino even before the ground had stopped shaking. People were hanging mosquito netting in bamboo thickets to sleep under.

Itarō found the work in Mino more interesting than in Tokyo, and he was not the only one who felt that way. In Tokyo,

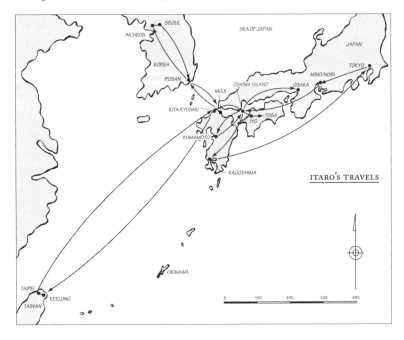

ITARO'S TRAVELS

the money was good but the homes were all crammed together. He was always having to bow and scrape to those around him. When he worked on Yamamoto Gonbei's house, Gonbei was so dour that he scarcely spoke with the carpenters. Itarō thought, "This damn fool!" and was surprised later when Gonbei became the head of the Navy. Thinking, "How a man like that could ever ... " Itarō could not stand it, but then, with the Siemens Incident [a bribery scandal involving naval officers], Gonbei fell from grace. Itarō often told this story, concluding with, "well, that's all the man he was."

Carpenters were well cared for in Mino. People were friendly, and since the carpenters were in the possession of a skill, they didn't have to bow all the time. And when there was a party, they were generally invited. Being a talented singer, an adept entertainer, and socially knowledgeable, Itarō was good company. So he was out drinking almost every night. He had a girlfriend and didn't lack for anything.

But his work wrapped up in a year or two, and Itarō returned home once again. His wife had been living the life of a widow. The next time he set out, she said she was going with him. She could no longer endure him not sending any money home and doing whatever he pleased. Fortunately, there was work in Yamaguchi, so he went there and took his family along. That was at the time of the Sino-Japanese War [1894–95]. Japan won a big victory and made Taiwan a territory. Itarō's fellow carpenters suggested they go to Taiwan, so he sent his wife back home and made the crossing. They took a boat from Moji. It was full of passengers going to Taiwan to seek their fortunes.

In those days performers didn't have to pay boat fare as long as they performed while they were on board. There were a lot of roving performance troops because not only were the boats free, but generally the flophouses were as well. So, if a person had some knowledge of the arts, they were able to subsist even if they were not otherwise able to make a living. That's why people used to say, "the arts are lifesaving." If only you knew how to entertain, you wouldn't starve or be left behind. On the boat crossing over to Taiwan such performers sang, danced, and performed magic. Not only did the carpenters not suffer from boredom, they didn't even know when they had arrived in Keelung.

From Keelung, the carpenters went on to Taipei. There was any amount of work to be done. Government offices had to be built, so they started by doing that work. They also built barracks for the military. Around that time Itarō became a master carpenter and had his own crew of five or six carpenters. They received work from a contractor, formed a crew, and were entrusted with a portion of the job. Itarō was an exceedingly arrogant man who made things up as he went along, but he did good work and shouldered the responsibility. Quick to gain people's favor, he was trusted and well taken care of. He never suffered from a lack of work, but he did suffer from the absence of a woman. He was a stranger to the ways of Taiwanese women and had no interest in meddling with the shameless prostitutes from Japan. He liked Japanese farmers' daughters best; they put him at ease and looked after his every need. Before he knew it, being with them felt like being married. But there was none of that in Taiwan, so Itarō was bored.

He decided to leave Taiwan, and when he had gone as far as Shimonoseki [at the southern tip of Honshu] he ran into carpenter friends on their way to Korea. At that time Japan was extending her influence on the Korean Peninsula, and many had crossed over to Pusan and Incheon. Hearing about Korea from his fellow workers, Itarō decided then and there that he too would go. He and his friends nearly died in rough seas at Genkainada, but they were somehow saved and finally made it to Pusan. From there they went to Incheon and on to Keijō [Seoul]. Itarō had finally come to Korea, after hearing so much about it in Higo [Kumamoto] after the Saigō uprising. But it was not what he had imagined it would be, and in a little over a year he left.

For a time he tried working in Osaka and Kitakyūshū, but by then fewer and fewer artisans found the work irresistibly interesting. People just wanted to make money and rather than roam the countryside, they were moving to the cities to work. But that world was of no interest to Itarō.

Around this time, the Russo-Japanese War [1904–05] broke out. Itarō's eldest son went to war and was killed there. Though he had generally neglected his son, Itarō's love for him was without limit. His death hit Itarō hard, and though he was still of a working age, he stopped traveling and sat by the charcoal brazier all day long, smoking his pipe. When someone came along who was willing to listen, he talked, without tiring, of days past. He lived that way, without change, for all of thirty years, and died in his eighties.

Chapter 9

The Worldly (II): Sakon Kumata

[1853–1943; Osaka Prefecture, first met in February 1936]

I first met Grandpa Sakon Kumata of Takihata in Takō Village (in what was once the Kawachi Domain and is now Kawachi-nagano City), on February 11, 1936. I wrote of this meeting in *Stories of Things Past: Grandpa Sakon Kumata of Takihata, Kawachi Domain.*

Takihata is a mountain village up the Hachiri [literally the "twenty-mile"] Branch Road, near the border of the Kishū Domain. This road begins in Nagano and follows the Saijo River, and if one continues up it and over the Zaō Pass, one comes out at Myōji, in the Kishū Domain.

Up until the war, many old customs were still practiced in these parts, and it was here, by chance, that I met Sakon, an eighty-three-year-old man. Thereafter we met some thirteen times, and I listened to stories that would fill three hundred pages and become two books. The first half, primarily related to folk customs, I arranged and published in the aforementioned *Stories of Things Past*. The second half was with regard to forests, land, and various social frameworks in a village community.

While this man's stories did have incongruities and dogmatisms, I don't think there is any material that is more valuable to an understanding of the environment that one old man

Grandpa Sakon Kumata.
Osaka Prefecture, 1936.
Photograph by Sudo Isao.

lived in, the kind of knowledge he brought with him, and how he is living now. When I first listened to Sakon's stories, I was only interested in phenomena related to folk customs, old social organizations, and the like. But when I looked back and reconsidered, I came to want to tell this old man's story as an expression of how people's characters evolved from the time of clan government [during the Edo period] to Meiji and on into Taishō.

The family name "Sakon" is a bit unusual. It comes from the fact that his family lived in a place called Sakontono. At first, they called themselves the Sakontonos but, since *tono* [lord] is only used when addressing someone else, they changed their name to Sakon. In Meiji, when everyone came to have a last name, most people in the village took the name they had been addressed by and made it their family name. Before that, there were about ten families that had family names.

This mountain village was a peaceful place. There had been famine, storms, and floods, but the villagers had somehow scraped their way through each year. No one lived in the three-mile ravine between Hino, at the valley's entrance, and Takihata, so it was as if the village had been misplaced there in the back of the valley. Sefuku Temple was located atop Mt. Makio, at the back of the valley, on its west side. As this temple was on the Saigoku 33 circuit [a pilgrimage to the Goddess of Mercy statues in 33 temples in Kansai and on the Kii Peninsula], pilgrims were given amulets when they visited. To pass from Mt. Makio into Kishū, most travelers came up the Takihata Valley and crossed over the

Zaō Pass, so although this village was in the mountains, many people passed through it. Most of them were pilgrims and *yamabushi* [mountain ascetics].

Grandpa Sakon grew up in these mountains and his first distinct memory is of the battles of Toba and Fushimi. He was only twelve at the time.

I was in the forest when I heard a sound so loud it shook the mountains around Takihata. I'd never heard such a large noise, and I came tumbling down the mountain back home. Doors and *shōji* [sliding paper doors] had been knocked right out of their grooves, and the villagers gossiped about what the sound could possibly have been. One of the villagers thought to climb a tall mountain and from there he could see black smoke rising in the sky above Osaka.

People were saying that surely something out of the ordinary had happened in Osaka when a man who'd been there on business returned. He said the Chōshū soldiers and the Tokugawa soldiers had fought at Toba and Fushimi. The Tokugawa had lost and set fire to their gunpowder storehouse at Osaka Castle. The man added, "Before long, the *rōnin* [lordless samurai] will flee in this direction, so it's best you all hide," so we all built huts deep in the mountains. Those who remained in the village were rounded up as laborers. People from the Tokugawa side were looking for laborers and they said, "refuse to come out, and we'll kill you . . ."

A lot of the land in the surrounding area was retained by the Tokugawa shogun, but Takihata was a possession of the Hōjō Domain, based in Kawachi Sayama.

Two or three days after the burning of the gunpowder storehouse, many *rōnin* fled in this direction. They sought refuge in the farmers' homes and dressed themselves in the farmers' clothes. Then, leaving their samurai clothes, swords, and guns behind, they crossed the Zaō Pass and headed home. The farmers cooked rice and fed them, and gave

them rice balls to take along. Many of these samurai warriors were from the east.

Even in the fields of Izumi, the Tokugawan loss was so
bad it was hard to look at. The shogun Yoshinobu was the
first to flee Osaka Castle. Three or four well-dressed samurai came bustling down to where a small boat was moored
on the side of the Aji River and asked to be taken offshore
from Tenbōzan. Their behavior was arrogant but when the
captain responded defiantly, they said, "This is an emergency so we earnestly implore you."He took them on board
reluctantly and headed downstream. When they had arrived
off the coast of Tenbōzan, they directed him to go to where
a warship was waiting. Thinking he'd be killed, the captain
hesitated, but they told him they'd do him no harm. When,
with great effort, he had brought them to the warship, one
of the samurai who boarded it said "Thank you, captain. I
am Tokugawa Yoshinobu." Surprised, the captain said, "Oh,
Honorable Shogun," and got on his hands and knees on the
deck.

Because the shogun had fled first, those who remained
behind ran off by degrees, and in no particular order. A
lord by the name of Shimizu Chūnagon, whose domain
was in Izumi, ran in that direction. Because the people of
his domain were being rounded up for labor, he hid [to-
gether with his retinue] in the home of a village headman
during the day, and at night, moved on to the next village
headman's house. Unable to travel on the main road, they
took the paths between the paddies. Because they couldn't
light a lantern, they often lost their footing and fell into the
ditches there. Just the same, without once being challenged
along the way, Chūnagon arrived at the home of the Takahashis, in the village of Kitaikeda in Izumi. Figuring he was
probably safe there, he waited for things to calm down.

Thinking that Chūnagon was probably bored confined
to the house all day long, the farmers sang and danced to
entertain him. The Takahashis had a large garden and the

farmers performed a variety of acts there while Chūnagon watched from inside the house. There was a poor community in the domain called Tonogi that had faithfully borne Chūnagon's palanquin when he fled. Remembering them, Chūnagon said, "Have someone from Tonogi do something." Well, they couldn't say, "Tonogi has no arts," so they decided to wrestle *sumo* for him. This being a collection of rough types, they broke into fistfights in the *sumo* ring. Chūnagon was delighted, saying, "I've never seen such interesting *sumo*."

Tokugawa had lost the war but wasn't fretting over it. Chōshū had won, but wasn't wreaking havoc. One after another rumors of this sort reached places even as remote as Takihata, and those who'd been hiding in the mountains came out and returned to their former lives.

It was also around that time that amulets from the Ise Shrine fell from the sky, and the people danced in the streets saying, "Who cares?" And it was shortly thereafter, in the first year of Meiji [1868], that people misinterpreted one of the Five Articles of the Imperial Oath which said, "follow your heart to attain your goals," and went all over the place stealing other people's wives.

Until then, in these parts there had only been one day a year when you could do as you pleased. This was on the day of a Buddhist celebration at a shrine to Prince Shotoku in Shiki Village, also located in the South Kawachi District. The celebration was held on April 22, on the old calendar, and on this night, anyone could sleep with anyone else. Around here this was called the Prince's All-Night Orgy, and a lot of people went.

Tall lanterns were placed in front of the temple and the worshippers gathered there. They called out in rhythm and pounded stones together, singing:

"Bring it out, bring it out, if you don't bring out the *sake*, *yo-ho-hoi*."

In the middle of the excitement, a man would rest his

hand on the shoulder of a woman, and she would squeeze it. You'd put your hand on someone you liked, and if they didn't shake you off this meant an understanding had been reached. The girls were all prettily dressed and holding a boy's hand they would go off somewhere into the forest nearby and sleep together there. They said that this was to get good sperm, and it was limited to that one night. Long ago, most of the girls at the celebration were from good families, but later a lot of vulgar women came as well. The children conceived at this time, though they didn't have fathers, were well cared for.

When I turned fifteen, I went to the all-night orgy and slept with a woman for the first time. After that I always went to the festival, although around the end of Meiji it was no longer observed.

But in that first year of Meiji, anyone could sleep with anyone at any time. In the middle of the day, at home, in the woods, it was the rage to sleep with any woman you liked. Until then, unmarried men and women met at night, but there was no sleeping with married women. But those restrictions disappeared. People said life is good and played together, but then the police started to complain, saying it was wrong to do such things.

When I was twenty-one, I took the conscription exam and passed. At twenty-two I fought in the Seinan War [against Saigō Takamori and other samurai frustrated by their loss of status during the Meiji Restoration]. This area was called Sakai Prefecture, and the prefectural office was here. In those days when a farmer appeared before a prefectural governor, we had to crawl about as we once had before feudal lords.

Saigō had started a war in Kyushu, so Grandpa Sakon and the others went to suppress him. They took a boat from Osaka to Kokura, and walked from there to Tabaruzaka. Saigō and Kirino had led the enemy army, and the saying went:

Who made the soil black in Kumamoto of the Higo Domain?
Saigō Takamori and Kirino, it was the treason of these two.

Grandpa and two hundred and fifty others were in the first battalion. They advanced rapidly and came upon bamboo that had been placed on either side of the road. Thinking it was strange to see bamboo, they walked on. The enemy had left this bamboo behind with mines planted inside. The mines went off and most of Grandpa's battalion died. Only eighteen were uninjured. Grandpa's face was badly burned and he was sent back to Osaka, where he spent one hundred and fifty days in an army hospital. Even so, his face was scarred and half of one eye was destroyed.

My face became quite difficult to look at and my health was not good, so after I got out of the army hospital I went to Yu Village in Tajima for a hot spring cure.

Many in Takihata had learned to make Kōya tofu at Mt. Kōya, and a lot of these people were originally from Tajima. Having lived in comfort, the people of Takihata were generally unable to do this work in the cold of winter and without respect to day or night. So people from Muraoka, in Tajima, came and made tofu. Among them was a man from Yu Village, and because he had said the hot springs were good for a person's health, I went there.

When I got well, because my family was also making Kōya tofu, I went to Awa to buy soybeans, from which tofu is made. Awa was a soybean-growing area. I also often went to a place called Kitagaichi on the banks of the Yoshino River. In the course of going I fell in love with a girl and she ran away with me. We stayed in Yasaka Yahama for a time, and when her older brother came for her, we moved on. After that, I married her and we settled down. From then until my wife left me at fifty-two, we were busy with work and raising children, and the time passed in the blink of an eye.

I grew up in a poor family. I started babysitting when I was seven, and when I was ten I went to work at a charcoal kiln. Since way back, a lot of charcoal was made in this area. I didn't know how to read or write a single character before I went to the Seinan War. People from families in the village who were of some means went to a writing teacher in Yokoyama and Niwadani, in the Senboku District to learn penmanship, but that was about it.

In 1875, there was a land tax reform. We were told that land taxes that had been paid in rice would now be paid in cash, and the government checked the land and everything else. No one knew at the time that the untaxed land—reclaimed and otherwise—had become government-owned forest. It's hard to know just how much we lost because almost no one in the village knew how to read or write.

Before people knew it, what had once been their own forest land was owned by the government or by a village headman. Grandpa came to understand that there was this thing called the law and that something could be done if he understood it. So he diligently visited a lawyer in Osaka by the name of Mori.

I knew that if I didn't first learn to read, I wouldn't get anywhere. The law wasn't something you could grasp only by hearing it described.

Late in the 1870s, a school opened in the village. In the middle of the village there was a hall we called the "large hall" where village meetings were held. That came to be used by the school, and there was a teacher by the name of Danzaemon who was from Kagoshima. That teacher taught me my ABCs, and then I learned how to write my name, the village name, all the domain names, and words like "receipt," "invoice," "purchase document," "loan agreement," and "agreement." It wasn't easy to get a hold of a notebook like it is now, so I learned to write the basic characters on the palm of my hand. And I learned other characters by writing on dirt walls. When I'd learned such things, the teacher read me textbooks that contained the twenty-three admonishments, Buddhist moral teachings for children, Buddhist life teachings for children, and the Four Chinese Classics. I studied these things until around the time I was thirty. I didn't learn the meaning of the texts, I just wanted to learn how to read and write the characters.

Elementary schools in the old days were peculiar and easygoing places. At New Year's—as a New Year greeting—the children took a gift of money to the teacher. The teacher would feed them sweet adzuki bean soup with rice cakes and give them *sake* to drink. The children got drunk and ran around in the large hall.

Well, because I'd learned to read and write, I could understand the law, and I helped with purchases of government-owned forestland. But this cost a lot of money and those who didn't have the money to buy their land back saw their forest lands go to people from other villages right before their eyes.

Up until late in the 1890s, time passed in this way, without people knowing what was going on. It was the same in all the villages. Because people didn't know how to read or write, they were pushed around. And I came to think there was nothing more important than being able to read and write and knowing the law.

In those days, lawyers were called "swindlers." They hid behind the law, told lies, and cheated people. But the lawyer Mori taught me many things.

Around this time, I'd finally begun to understand the world. The villagers had become utterly poor, and only those who knew how to read and write were making money and doing good things. Those who didn't know how to read were easy to fool, because they believed everything people said. In the case of a person who always lied, they could say, "He's a liar," and there was no need to believe him. But as for anything anyone else said, they had to believe it was the truth even if it was a lie, because they couldn't tell truth from lies.

Around the beginning of the Taishō period, a blacksmith by the name of Tsujiri from Arita, in the Kishū Domain, was living in Yokotani, in Takihata. Rumor had it he'd killed someone and been put in prison for ten years. He boasted of having traveled throughout Japan but didn't know how to read a word. His stories were all outrageous, and though he was exceedingly poor, because he could do the work of a blacksmith people said he was reliable and, trusting him, they mistook his lies for the truth.

I don't know where that man had heard it, but he said that if you gave fried food to a fox, the fox would make you rich. Reach out your hand and without fail it would be filled with money. Around that time there'd been a lot of gossip that a fox was taking the form of a woman and appearing on the plateau at Mt. Shinoda in Izumi. Tsujiri entreated the farmers who came to have their tools repaired, saying, "Go to Uenohara (the southern portion of Mt. Shinoda) and catch a fox. If it's in a woman's form, you can make money by selling her, too. You've got nothing to lose either way."

Hearing this, there were those who said, "Like there would be such a ridiculous thing nowadays." But one among them remembered, "When I was coming back down the south slope of Uenohara, I suddenly felt a weight on my back. Thinking it strange I looked back, but no one was there. When I'd gone down as far as Kawanaka, I suddenly felt light again. That's when I noticed that the fried bean curd I'd bought in the town of Tori and tied to my waist was gone."

There were two men who agreed with what Tsujiri said. But when one of them went home and told his wife, she said, "What idiocy," so he came back to tell them he had to drop out. So Tsujiri and the other man got a hold of two mice. That night they deep-fried one of them, and just when they were putting the second mouse in the pan someone knocked on the door. They thought the fox had already come, but then heard the voice of their friend who'd dropped out, saying "I've come!" Thinking the fox had made quite a transformation, they hid the mouse and opened the door. A man stood there draped in a woman's undergarments. They felt his butt, but there was no tail. The man who'd dropped out said he was sleeping with his wife when it occurred to him there might be money to be made so, after making sure his wife had fallen asleep, he'd come along.

Well, the three of them put the two deep-fried mice in a wire net, left Yokotani that night, and walked to Uenohara. One wore his wife's clothes, another wore a wool coat, and the third was dressed in a suit of armor. They waited at Uenohara, but nothing came. They decided to walk around in the forest a bit, but found nothing there either. In time, day broke and they saw that their clothes had caught on trees and were torn all over. They were quite a sight and couldn't just go out and walk nonchalantly on the main road so they hid in a graveyard. When someone came along to visit a grave, they saw these suspicious characters and reported them to the police. Lots of police came, seized the three men, and when they investigated the matter they learned what I've just described. Apparently the police couldn't close their gaping mouths.

No one among these three men knew how to read or write. And in a world without writing, there was this kind of shared inanity. Grandpa Sakon had also grown up surrounded by such talk. But a person couldn't live their life doubting others because, if you started doubting, there was no end to it. If you were fooled once, you could no longer trust anyone. So, in that life without writing, people were fatuously easygoing and truthful, but careful not to trust anyone from a world they weren't familiar with.

Similarly, when Grandpa was young and left home, he was not trusted. People rarely put him up for the night so he slept under the floors of shrines. But when they came to understand what he had been through, people were good to him.

After my wife left me and took the children with her, I didn't remarry. I wanted to live in a carefree manner, and when I was fifty-six I decided to travel. Living in the mountains we all suffered a lot, and nothing would come of leaving things as they were. I figured that if I took a good look at how other people in the world were living, it might be of some use to the village.

I'd been to Yu Village long before, and thinking to go in that direction, I went to Kyoto and walked on to Kinosaki. In Kyoto, I met a man by the name of Ōkawa. He was a fortune-teller. Realizing that fortune-telling not only benefited others but was also a way to pay one's travel expenses, I decided to follow this man. Even when there was a train we rarely rode one. We traveled with our kimonos pulled up, wore close-fitting drawers and straw sandals, and carried a satchel and a walking stick. Most often we tied the satchel to our other belongings with a string, slinging them to the front and back. After spending some time at the hot springs in Kinosaki, we walked to Tomioka, in Yu Village, and on to Daisen Temple. On May 8 every year, people living at the base of the mountain dress their cows beautifully and climb up to Daisen Temple. Then they make offerings of beautiful splashed-pattern cloth to the temple and hold a large cow fair right there in front of the temple. With these donations of cloth, the temple was able to support itself for a whole year, for many came to buy it. From there we went to pray at the Grand Shrine of Izumo, and then we walked from Iwami to Chōshū, and on to Akamagaseki [Shimonoseki]. A boat was leaving for Otaru, Hokkaido, and I took it alone to visit my middle son, who'd become a priest and was living there.

With no particular need to return home, I traveled here and there visiting one old friend after another. The man

Ōkawa, while traveling as a fortune-teller, carefully studied the customs and manners of each place and wrote them down in his notebook. Everywhere he went, he shared what he had learned but he didn't save money.

"Sakon-san, there are many people in this world who are in trouble or in pain. Sometimes they can be saved by one or two things, I say. Lots of people are enduring hardships they can't share with others. If there isn't someone, somewhere, who is kind to them, there's no hope for this world. I'm not interested in working out in the open, but in the shadows I must help these people." He often talked like this at night, when we were lying side by side, going to sleep.

"Sakon-san, when you spend the night in a lodging, you must be friendliest to the housemaids because they work constantly, without rest. So you should try your best not to ask anything of them, to give them time and make it easier for them."

This man Ōkawa's way of talking was always a little different from other people. And he faithfully kept his word.

When Grandpa Sakon traveled alone, he often made advances to women.

Without even really making advances, one thing led to another. There are truly a lot of people in the world who are in trouble or are suffering, especially among those who go to see a fortune-teller. There were times when, before you knew it, the conversation would become deep. The strange thing was, here I was, ugly and a traveler, not the kind of person you'd want to marry, but women were cheered up by what they knew was just a single sexual encounter, and they usually felt better after.

Just once, Grandpa was chased after by a woman. On his travels, he had become intimate with a maiden from the Shinanō Shrine, and she didn't want to let him go. She threatened to place a curse on Grandpa and kill him if he left her, and she wore him down completely. She had a special ability to find him, a sixth sense of sorts. He fled from one place to the next, but wherever he ran, she found him.

Sleeping with a woman was one of the refinements, and one who did not understand refinements made a mess of things when he slept with a woman. But Grandpa was a refined person. The court nobles of old wrote poems to women. When they did this the women were generally waiting for them at night. When men didn't come, the women also expressed their feelings in poems, and that would bring the men along. Grandpa also had an experience of this kind.

There were many elegant and refined women in and around Kyoto. Once, at my lodging, I met a graceful housemaid, so I wrote a poem and placed it on my dinner tray. When she came to take it away, she glanced at it and inserted it in her *obi*. She said nothing, but when I was sleeping that night, she came quietly. Write a poem and give it to a refined woman and she'll usually do as you please. But that wasn't true outside the capital.

Grandpa's first trip was so long that his son's wife reproached him, saying, "You may be single and all but you shouldn't be on the road for years at a time. You're already sixty. What'll happen if you die on your travels?" So he said, "OK, I won't travel alone any more, but please allow me to travel if I'm with someone else," and he waited for a companion. When the priest at Kōtaki Temple (an old temple in Takihata) said he was going on a pilgrimage, Grandpa went with him to Narita and on to Nikkō, although they traveled by train so it wasn't all that interesting.

So I asked Ōkawa-san, and whenever possible I traveled with him. When I was sixty-six, we made a circuit around Kyushu. Kyushu was a fascinating place, so we decided to go again. We took a boat to Beppu and were idle there for a while, then went on to Unzen, Shimabara, and Nagasaki, before crossing over to the Gotō Islands. We were both dressed like beggars, and we were put in with the cargo. Ōkawa-san was a man of character but he was unconcerned, saying, "places like this are fine too."

A lot of people were in trouble on those islands, and they wanted to have their fortunes told. And there were a lot of cunning people. When a gentleman came along, for example, they were slow to provide a boat so that he would spend money on a place to stay. They were after a person's money. Customs and manners vary from place to place, and where the soil is barren and life is hard, people are unkind.

On our way back from Kyushu we walked around Shikoku as well and went on a pilgrimage to Yashima. When a fortune-teller sets out on a trip, it usually lasts for two years. You travel where you're asked to go, and if you gain a reputation as a talented fortune-teller, you end up staying in each place for ten, even twenty, days. People ask anything and everything. Half of it is for advice regarding personal affairs, farming, fishing, and the like. Ōkawa-san was a man of great experience who wrote everything down, and he'd tell people stories from his travels. Most left satisfied. After staying in one village for a time, we were called to the next. We never took much money. We were filthily dressed, so anyone could easily come along for advice.

Grandpa traveled with this fortune-teller until he was seventy and Ōkawa was over eighty. Saying he could no longer take long trips, Ōkawa returned to Kyoto and died shortly thereafter. Grandpa Sakon hasn't taken a long trip since. He was never able to tell a fortune as well as Ōkawa-san.

One had to have great knowledge to tell a farmer or fisherman his fortune to his satisfaction. A fortune told at a crossroads at night is not a fortune. Whether good or bad, a fortune must be something that gives direction to the life of the person who hears it. It must not be mere flattery. And if the fortune-teller gets rich, he is acting out of selfishness and is not genuine. A true fortune-teller is poor but does not lack for something to eat. Ōkawa-san taught me these things. When I finally came to understand the ways of the world, I was already seventy. I don't know what I've done with my life.

Saying this, Grandpa sighed. Here in Takihata, ninety years have now passed since the Meiji Restoration. Early on, a car road was built. Before that, the forests in this area had all but become a possession of, and had been planted by, people from other villages. The people of Takihata were late to realize that money could be made planting trees, and they mainly supported themselves making charcoal.

As there was an abundance of forestland, speculators came and bought up gold mines and forests suited to the making of charcoal. They weren't serious about this work; they just wanted to cheat people out of their money. Most of the people who came to the village were brokers of this sort. The villagers had been deceived continuously by these people since the beginning of Meiji. Meanwhile, people said there was no profit to be made in Kōya tofu, and they left. Sericulture was popular as well for a time, but that too fell into decay.

Grandpa Sakon was the liaison for these new and varied stimuli from the outside world, and he was an unyielding negotiator. But he didn't earn a cent, and the village didn't grow rich, either. When Grandpa was over seventy, it was difficult for him to travel far, so he built a six-mat room next to the main house and confined himself to it.

Here and there along the way, this old man had learned what he needed to know to live. And in this way he had come through life. But, in the end, when he had the knowledge that came from having seen so much of the world, and when that knowledge was most needed by the village, Grandpa had already grown old and was no longer able to take a leadership role in the village. The villagers asked him to be their guide when they went to Kōshien to see the Grand Expo of Japan's Rapid Progress [in 1936] and when they went on a pilgrimage to Mt. Kōya, but this was all Grandpa's broad knowledge of the world was used for, and he became a person of the past.

I visited Grandpa Sakon frequently until I moved to Tokyo in 1939. Before I left, the book *Stories of Things Past* came out, and I took it to him. Delighted, he wiped the tears from his eyes. On that occasion he asked me to visit him if he became fatally ill. When we parted, I said, "I will most certainly come," but I have not had the opportunity to return to Takihata since. During that time there was a major war, but if I had compelled myself to go, it seems I could have found the time to visit. I regret that I did not.

When I look at the life of this man, he definitely was sensitive to the times, and he made a concerted effort to accommodate changes in the world. This effort to accommodate change was not his alone, but could be observed in the other villagers as well. Just the same, most of their efforts brought little in the way of results and are being forgotten.

From Meiji to Taishō and into the first half of the Shōwa period, though few in number, such worldly persons were to be found in every village. And the modest directional guidance they provided in bringing their villages up to date cannot be overlooked. These people all acted out of their own volition in taking on this role; it was not something that was directed by the government or the schools.

It can also be said that with the existence of such people, the villages were able to keep up, though belatedly, with changes in the world. This being the case, I think we would benefit from digging further into the lives of these worldly persons.

Chapter 10

Literate Transmitters (I): Tanaka Umeji

[1867–1941; Shimane Prefecture, November 1939]

A large, distinct gap can be found between those who were literate and those who were not. Those who didn't know how to read or write took what they had heard at face value and attempted to pass it on without much thought of changing its content. But those who could read and who had access to the written word were able to mix in and pass along knowledge they had acquired through reading in addition to what they had heard. And corrections could be made to information that had been passed down verbally. People had a tendency to believe that "What they are saying came from something they read, so it's reliable." But if it contradicted what had been transmitted in the village to date, it was rarely adopted by the entire village. As long as a literate individual did not put new information in writing, only those who heard it directly or indirectly from them believed it. Meanwhile the other villagers just remembered the individual as someone who was accomplished.

The literate were extremely sensitive to written stimuli from the outside world. While living the village life, they were forever concerned about the world beyond and were strongly compelled to conform to it. My impressions of one such man, Grandpa Tanaka Umeji, remain vivid to this day.

As I recall, I first learned of Grandpa Tanaka in the spring of 1939, when Kuriyama Kazuo [an ethnologist] showed me a glossary of rice farming in the Ōchi District of Shimane Prefecture. Entitled *Grains of Hardship*, it was written with a brush and in a beautiful hand. Leafing through a few pages I came upon a rice-seedling pulling song.

One person begins to sing:	*Shall we sing a song?*
And everyone else responds:	*ha-do- nara do- nara*
The first person sings:	*I hesitate to say, but . . .*
Then, all together, they sing:	*I don't know the words to this song . . .*
Another person sings:	*Take that back . . .*
The first person responds:	*I hesitate to say, but . . .*
Then, all together, they sing:	*I don't know the words to this song. . .*

In this way, and without stopping, they sing on. A woman with a beautiful voice takes the lead and the others respond.

Thinking, "goodness, they had big rice planting here," I read on with great interest. And when I asked Kuriyama-san what kind of person had written this book, he knew only that the author was an old farmer living in the mountains of Shimane. At the time, even in the field of folklore, no study of rice-growing customs was this meticulous. In those days, if you wrote about something in fine detail, you were laughed at and told, "But aren't those things already completely understood?" For example, an entry in the glossary under the title "Oil Peddler" read: "At the time of the big rice planting there are plenty of people, so some men loaf considerably. They stand here and there doing nothing. This is called 'peddling oil.' It can be taken to mean a person is slippery like oil or that they are idle." In 1935, the expression "oil peddler," meaning "an idle person," was commonly used and known to everyone. So, at the time, it was not common for someone to go so far as to write it down.

Anyone who had been alive one generation earlier, at the end of the Meiji period [the early 1900s], would have actually seen an oil peddler. Oil peddlers sold camellia oil that women applied to their hair, and rapeseed oil used for cooking and to light altars and shrines. They carried these oils in oblong wooden boxes hung from either end of a pole that rested on their shoulder. If someone asked for camellia oil, for example, the peddler would set down his load and insert a tiny funnel in the little bottle the buyer had brought along. Then, using a three-ounce ladle, he would scoop the oil out of the box and pour it into the bottle. Because the buyer wanted every drop they could get, they fixed their gaze on the ladle until all the oil had dripped from it and waited once again for every drop to fall from the funnel. This was indeed a time-consuming and tranquil scene. Peddling oil probably became synonymous with idleness because of the very nature of oil and of this ritual, but with the disappearance of the oil peddlers of old, this expression has already fallen partially out of use.

Such information had been recorded in Grandpa Tanaka's glossary, and Kuriyama-san wanted to know if there was some way of getting this work into print. I too was moved, but I was nothing more than a poor elementary school teacher. When I thought of my acquaintances, no one came to mind. But I had, owing to the warm friendship of Shibusawa Keizō, published two books through his research facility, the Attic Museum (now the Japan Folk Culture Research Institute). The first was a book entitled *A Record of Life with the Ocean, Centered in Suō Ōshima*, about life in my own birthplace, a coastal village [on an island in the Inland Sea]. The second was *Stories of Things Past: Grandpa Sakon Kumata of Takihata, Kawachi Domain*. So, thinking to ask Shibusawa-sensei for his help, I wrote to him to explain the situation. He responded saying that he wanted to know more about the location described in the glossary and about Grandpa Tanaka himself.

That summer a short course on language instruction was held

on Okino Island, and I set out to attend it. I had made the crossing to Okino Island once before, but had not had adequate time to study the fields there that were used alternately for growing crops and as pasture land for cattle. So I hoped to examine these fields as closely as possible.

On this trip I met Moriwaki Taichi for the first time. He had also come for the course and had a frightful amount of energy. Around that time Moriwaki-san had published *A Record of the Ōchi District*, a book that was more than a thousand pages long. Moriwaki-san had only graduated from elementary school, but he loved to study. He had taught himself, passed the teachers' certification exam, and become an elementary school teacher. Later he had been adopted into a merchant family by the name of Moriwaki but he was a farmer's child at heart, and he farmed while he taught. He was a simple man with an unquenchable thirst for knowledge, and he put everything into his studies. Because he had not had a real education, Moriwaki-san wanted to find a way to study under good teachers and to acquire practical knowledge. In order that this knowledge would be of use to him and to his students, rather than attend study sessions and the like, he decided that he would invite teachers and receive instruction directly from them. By farming, Moriwaki-san removed any worries about having something to eat, and he saved his salary. In this way he was able to invite one teacher at a time from the Shimane Teacher's College and, by walking around the Ōchi District with that teacher, to receive practical, onsite instruction. They looked at natural and cultural phenomena in the district—its geography, history, plant and animal life, and so on—and Moriwaki-san learned how to look at these things. He carefully documented everything he was taught. He paid for this study entirely out of the money he had saved. Moriwaki-san's manuscript reached several thousand pages and, using his savings and a small subsidy from the education committee, he published *A Record of the Ōchi District*. This was how he had occupied himself during his twenties.

Moriwaki-san was not driven by ambition. Rather, he took

great pleasure expending his energy in this way. Once when I saw him after the war he explained, "I'm thinking of quitting my job as a teacher and becoming a mail carrier." He asked me quite seriously, "What do you think?" He was interested in place names and family names at the time and did not feel he could research them adequately as a school teacher. As a letter carrier, if he could get himself assigned to a remote area, he could probably conduct research that delved deeply into such matters. This being a time of rapid inflation, I asked if he would be able to get by. Moriwaki-san said that he would be able to find a way, though he did not go through with it. He also collected a large number of old stories. I was told that he had gathered nine hundred. Whatever he did, he was not content unless he had done it thoroughly. And he was bright and carefree.

Well, I met Moriwaki-san on Okino Island and had the opportunity to ask about Grandpa Tanaka in some detail. Grandpa Tanaka had been the largest contributor to Moriwaki-san's account on the Ōchi district.

"He's an interesting old man," Moriwaki-san told me. "If you were to meet him, you'd like him at once. I've never met anyone so generous with their knowledge. You really should meet him. You'd probably talk day and night for two or three days. He's a good and uncomplicated man." In his introduction to *Grains of Hardship*, Moriwaki-san described Grandpa Tanaka as follows:

Tanaka-san is more than seventy years old, but he has strength and spirit in reserve. When conversation turns to his birthplace, there is nothing he does not know. He will talk animatedly through the night leaving those who have come to see him with no choice but to wonder at his ardor and erudition. For this reason he is respected as a walking encyclopedia. In his introduction to *A Catalogue of Things to be Preserved Eternally*, under the title "Tedious Talk to be Recorded," he writes, "I have had the habit of preserving everything since I was little. And since my school days I have liked things related to history. . . . When I look now at what I wrote when I was young, none of it is of any use to me. But when I look at it in historic terms, I know what happened at that time. And it helps me to understand how things were when I was a certain age. . . . Something that appears to be of no use, when viewed historically, seems to become more interesting as it grows older."

Walking in rural areas I often meet old literate farmers like Grandpa Tanaka. Many are passionate about their birthplace, and they are not boastful. Aware of both the good and the bad, they love their native land.

I wanted to meet Grandpa Tanaka and, with Moriwaki-san's permission, I sent *Grains of Hardship* to Tokyo. That fall, I quit my job as an elementary school teacher and went to Tokyo to join the Attic Museum. Then, at the encouragement of Shibusawa-sensei [its founder], I set out to walk the entire country. My first trip was to Western Honshu. I walked the Shimane Peninsula and visited the annex school in Seimi, Nagatani Village, Ōchi District, where Moriwaki-san was teaching. It was a tiny, one-room schoolhouse. Moriwaki-san taught the first through the fourth graders all together in one class. Before *A Record of the Ōchi District*, Moriwaki-san had written *A Record of Nagatani Village*. The school was closed when I visited, and no one was there. Learning from a nearby farmer that Moriwaki-san was ill and had taken time off, I walked to his house in Atoichi. It was about three miles straight down a wide road that, for many years, Moriwaki-san had traveled to teach at the annex school.

Moriwaki-san told me he had been sick since eating something that disagreed with him on Okino Island that summer. He had been lingering between life and death ever since his return, but he was feeling better lately. After suggesting that Ushio Michio take me to see Grandpa Tanaka, he called him. Ushio-san was from Shiyama, more than seven miles from Atoichi, and he came early the following morning. Ushio-san was intently researching "big rice planting" and was intimate with both Moriwaki-san and Tanaka-san.

Grandpa Tanaka Umeji.
Photographer unknown.

Many people like this, with a love of learning, live out in the country. They communicate with one another and travel back and forth, but within their own villages they are most often intellectually isolated. They do things for the village, and they excel as leaders and pioneers yet rarely do they seek out companions in their own area of study within the village. Rather, their studies are a window on the outside world, and it was through these studies that I was connected to them as well.

Ushio-san and I went from Atoichi to Tsunozu and took a train back up the Gō River from Gōzu. We got off the train in Kawamoto and took a bus to Izuha. We walked from there to Grandpa Tanaka's home in Masubuchi, Tadokoro Village. When we arrived, night had already come. I have also written of this time in my book *Village Travels*, and even now I can recall how eager I was. I bought *sake* and fish and took them along with me. Sliding my legs under Grandpa Tanaka's *kotatsu* foot warmer, we fell deep into conversation.

The talk was far-ranging. Grandpa Tanaka said that he wanted me to hear some folksongs and went to wake an old man who lived nearby and had a beautiful voice. So, that night I heard many old folksongs, rice-planting songs, dance songs, packhorse-driver songs, and Kodaiji dance songs. I found it interesting that packhorse songs had long been sung in these parts and that Kodaiji dance songs, sung [at *Bon* festivals] throughout the Hokuriku districts in the north of Japan, were sung here as well.

The following day Ushio-san set out in a light rain to visit an acquaintance in Asuna Village, and I spent the entire day with my legs under the *kotatsu*, listening to Grandpa Tanaka. I wrote of this in *A Record of Folkways in Western Honshu*, a work that has yet to see the light of day.

Grandpa Tanaka talked continuously from morning until late into the night. I listened without moving except for meals and trips to the bathroom. Until then I had only met a few learned old men who liked to talk this much, Ishitetsushiro Fujinosuke of Ishitetsushiro Village in the Ōno District of Fukui Prefecture, and Igashira Danshō of Tenkawa Village in the Yoshino District of Nara Prefecture among them. These men were quite different from other old men I had met who made little or no use of the written word.

Those who had little relation to written language looked out for themselves, faithfully did what they had to do, loved their neighbors, were in the possession of a limitless cheer, and lacked any concept of time. If they were talking or if you were doing something together, it rarely came to an end. They never asked, "What time is it now?" If their wives said "Dinner" they responded with "Is that so?" and then proceeded to eat. When the sun went down, about all they might say was "It's grown dark." But when morning came, they were extremely early to rise.

Those who can read, on the other hand, often look at clocks or ask what time it is. At noon, they call into the kitchen. They think in terms of the twenty-four-hour day, and live their lives accordingly. They have begun, somehow, to live in the grip of time. These people are always comparing their own village with the world at large. But they share in a deep sense of responsibility when they attempt to take knowledge from the outside and introduce it into the village. Before thinking of the good, they think of any bad influences it might bring with it.

"Just because it works somewhere else doesn't mean it will work here. I don't want to put people in a difficult position . . ." For Grandpa Tanaka, the development of an industrial guild was a lifelong undertaking. In 1909, he established a credit union, predecessor to the industrial guild, making a transition from high-interest private financing—where a person who went into debt lost his land—to low-interest, credit-union financing. When, during the depression in the early 1930s, the credit union's loans became irrecoverable, Grandpa took responsibility for this and sold his house and land to get the credit union out of the red. Then, after apologizing to his fellow villagers for the inconvenience, he resigned.

With the redistribution of farmland, production increased threefold. A large cattle market was built, and motor roads were constructed running the length and breadth of the village. As a result, productivity rose village-wide and life became more stable. When I visited in 1939, they had survived the financial crisis and the village was one of the wealthiest in Shimane Prefecture. Grandpa, however, was poor.

While Grandpa was forever ushering in the new, his own life was dreadfully old-fashioned. When one looks at the history of his public service, he became a handyman at the local government office when he was sixteen [in 1883], a clerk at the Izuha Post Office at eighteen, and a scribe at the local government office at twenty-one. In that year he was also adopted into the Tanaka family. At twenty-six he quit his job at the local government office and at twenty-eight became the proxy head of his ward. When he was twenty-nine he established a village agricultural association and became its executive secretary. He became a member of the village assembly at thirty-one, a member of the board of education at thirty-two, and an interim member of the civil engineering board at thirty-three. At thirty-seven [in 1914] Tanaka-san became the assistant manager of the Wartime Agricultural Incentive Department in Tadokoro, Ōchi District, and he produced extraordinary results. They encouraged farmers to submerge rice seeds in salt water and remove those that floated, introduced regular interval planting, exterminated insects that were harmful to rice plants, protected barley against black stem rust, improved compost production, and so on. Activities of this sort were taking place throughout the country at the request of the national government. Every time Japan went to war, rice production increased by fifty million bushels. It can be said that Tadokoro Village was typical in this respect. At forty-two Tanaka-san established the credit union. At forty-three he became the secretary of the village government office, and at fifty-two he was appointed deputy mayor of Tadokoro Village. He became manager of the animal husbandry union for the Ōchi District at fifty-three and standing director of the industrial guild at fifty-six. At fifty-seven he became an arbitrator of land tenancy disputes. When he turned seventy, Tanaka-san retired from all public service.

Discerning progress in the world, Tanaka-san established various organs to accommodate it. In his capacity as a public servant, he put the national government's demands into practice and contributed to the improvement of living conditions. He was confident that the raising of individual living standards would lead to a strengthening of the country as a whole.

At twenty-five Tanaka-san began writing poetry, and in his early thirties he became a subscriber to and member of *Hototogisu* [Cuckoo], receiving instruction from Masaoka Shiki [a famous Japanese *haiku* poet] and Naitō Meisetsu. He encouraged many others in the village to join and created the Oil and Miso Poetry Association. Late in life he published a book of poetry entitled *Sweeping up Persimmon Leaves*.

The above was taken from Grandpa's curriculum vitae, not from Grandpa himself. He handed me the resume when I asked him about such things, explaining, "Talk of this sort has a tendency to become boastful, so take a look at this." In the prologue he had written:

In 1909, for reasons of my own, I retired from my position as village assemblyman. Though intending only to continue with the agricultural association and the union, I also became the secretary, the treasurer, and the deputy mayor. There are those who at a glance would think that the deputy mayor was something I had been working toward, but that was not the case. Until that time, the mayor and deputy mayor were extraordinary and honored posts, and one had to be a gentleman to occupy them. There was no hope for the child from a family such as Tanaka Fuchi's (the name of the main Tanaka family) and, in keeping with this, I harbored no such hopes. From beginning to end, I have worked in every way I could for the autonomy of this village and for the development and expansion of industry. I was neither driven by vanity nor looking for my own pleasure.

These were Grandpa's feelings. That is why he took on the roles of representative at the local temple, bookkeeper at the shrine, and member of the committee of household heads. He did these things for the village and farmed diligently in his spare time.

In his later years this strong love for his village made him a new kind of transmitter of knowledge. After retiring from public service he farmed when the weather was good and read books when it was not, ever with a notebook tucked into his bosom. Even when he was turning his paddy, if he thought of something, he would set down his hoe, sit down on a nearby ridge, and write it down.

"I'd lick my pencil and remember how one thing was or another. I'd look at the soil or at the sky while I wrote, and a white cloud would float by, and I'd want to write a poem." He passed his time in that way. And when he organized what he had written it became *Grains of Suffering*.

We talked all day on the twenty-second and he suggested we continue on the twenty-third, but I departed Tadokoro to visit a friend in Ōasa in Hiroshima Prefecture, across the mountains to the south. Before leaving I suggested that, since he had written an account of activities related to the growing of rice, he also write something with regard to dry-field cultivation. Grandpa agreed to take this on, and in April of the following year he sent me a manuscript with regard to dry-field cultivation entitled *A Drop of Sweat*. This title probably came from Masaoka Shiki's *A*

Drop of Ink. A student and admirer of Shiki's, he owned every issue of *Hototogisu.*

A Drop of Sweat was published by the Attic Museum in September 1941. But Grandpa Tanaka had already died. In September 1940, when the galleys for the book had just come out, I visited Grandpa Tanaka one more time, together with Shibusawa-sensei. On that occasion we were joined by Ishida Haruaki, Ōniwa Yoshimi, Moriwaki Taichi, and Ushio Michio, making it a lively trip. As there were many of us, we stayed at a lodging in Shimotadokoro. This was once a lonely place, but after it became the intersection for two motor roads, a post office was built, followed by an inn and stores until it had become a tiny urban center. In *How Things Change* Grandpa Tanaka recorded in great detail how it was that this urban area had come into existence, where the people had come from, and how the village was evolving.

When we had made ourselves comfortable in the parlor at our lodging, Grandpa Tanaka came before Shibusawa-sensei and greeted him once again, formally. I was heedless of what had happened, but when Grandpa had gone downstairs to his room, Shibusawa-sensei observed, "Tanaka-san is truly old-fashioned. Just now, when he greeted me—an ordinary person would probably place their palms on the *tatami* when addressing someone— well, he squeezed my hand lightly and placed his palms on the *tatami* facing inward, a sign of his sincerity and his adherence to old ways. That man's knowledge of the old is precise, and his mind is filled with it. It is something I want to pull out and record. He is really something." Once again I was surprised by the keenness of my teacher's eye.

Shibusawa-sensei added, "That man is remarkable. He doesn't wear his knowledge on his sleeve. Walking the countryside, you come across guys with learning who take pride in what they know and are arrogant about it, but he has none of that. He's not a boss but a true farmer."

Some time passed, and Grandpa came back up to the second floor. There was a cattle fair in Izuha, and he wanted to know if we might like to go. The Izuha market was once said to be the largest in Western Honshu with cows brought in from all over. It sounded interesting, so we all filed out and went, but there were fewer cows than we had expected. The cows had come from all over, however. Grandpa was the kind of person who knew, at a glance, where a cow was from, how old it was, and even to whom it would most likely be sold. Cows from places that were famous for their cattle, places like Chiya, Iishi, Hiwa, and Jinseki came and went, or were tied up and sat or stood in the open lots between the houses. The cow traders were going this way and that, sticking their hand up people's sleeves to negotiate a price [a silent negotiating technique, unique to this trade, involving the squeezing of fingers in a number equal to the price being offered]. Those who had concluded their bargaining were closing deals. Weaving our way through this commotion, we were given an education on how to look at cows. Grandpa knew everything.

Laughing, Shibusawa-sensei said, "One could write a whole book just about how to look at cows. There is no record to date of how knowledge related to the raising and breeding of cows has been passed down. And no one has written about the history of cattle grazing in this area either. Maybe we should ask Tanaka-san."

That was an enjoyable time, and I have had a deep interest in cows ever since. On our way to and from the fair, Grandpa Tanaka talked without end about the use of cows in the big rice planting, the foot bellows commonly used in these parts for iron-sand smelting, related folksongs and the like. But big rice planting was no longer practiced here, and foot bellows were no longer used in smelting. Being things of the past, they were rapidly disappearing from the collective memory. It is the responsibility of those who do remember, and who are literate, to write such things down.

At the lodging that evening, after Grandpa Tanaka had returned home, a consensus was reached that we should ask him to write down everything he could remember while he was still in good health. The following morning when we parted I suggested, "Tanaka-san, you're full of energy so how about if you write down everything you've seen and heard, things you've done, whether old or new, everything you can think of. When you need help, I'll come. And you've got Moriwaki-san and Ushio-san too. Even if something seems insignificant, if it touched you, write it down." Hearing this, Grandpa narrowed his eyes and laughed. "I had thought that the elderly were of little use, but it seems in fact we are."

On October 12, less than a month after we parted, Grandpa died suddenly. He was seventy-three years old. He had suffered a heart attack. In the middle of the night on October 10, he complained of a stomachache but it turned out to be nothing. On the eleventh he rested and ate very little. Then, on the morning of the twelfth he suffered from chest pains and called a doctor, but as he was feeling better he ate some apple. He was talking with his son when his condition changed suddenly. Within five minutes he was dead.

Grandpa Tanaka was the product of a village that had kept in step with the times as the country moved forward in the Meiji and Taishō periods. If the village could be condensed into one man, it was Grandpa Tanaka. In his postscript to *Grains of Suffering*, he wrote of the village: "Seven hundred households, population thirty-six hundred. Eighty-three acres of paddy land, eighteen acres of fields, and fourteen hundred acres of forests. Land ownership well distributed. No conspicuously large landowners. Most farmers have about .25 acres of their own land or a combination of their own and rented lands. No farmers are working only rented land. Main occupation is rice growing. Auxiliary work includes the production of charcoal in the winter months, and the sale of cows and lumber. Women and girls spin hemp. The ocean is twenty-five miles to the south and twenty-five miles to the north. Fresh fish are hard to come by in the summer months so are supplemented by meat from a storehouse. Rice is stored and that which goes uneaten is sold. Villagers are self-sufficient with regard to other grains and vegetables. Lumber, firewood, and charcoal are virtually unlimited. One large river runs through the middle of the village and is fed by many tributaries so there is no shortage of water for the paddies and fields. As the surrounding mountains are small, there is no fear of large winds or heavy rains. There is great reverence for the god located in the local Hachiman Shrine. All villagers are believers in the Shinshū Buddhist sect and there are five temples. People are deeply religious, making this, for the most part, an ideal village."

It was not an ideal village from the beginning, however. There was a disparity in wealth, and many farmers were in debt. Much of the paddy land was boggy, and the individual ownership of arable land was scattered all over. People worked hard, but production levels remained the same. Starting around 1903 and wanting to improve matters even a little, Grandpa Tanaka made a desperate effort to make adjustments to the ownership of land and to establish a credit union toward the rearrangement of debts. In time, the village became the envy of the surrounding villages and a role model.

Grandpa wanted to make the village a place where people were proud of their work, and he believed that something close to this had been accomplished. He writes:

> While feeling a closeness to the beauty of nature and while turning their own soil, farmers make food that is important to the people of this country. Is any work this pleasant and interesting? Though he must work in the fields even if it rains all year, does anyone have more freedom than the farmer? Is it not the farmer who, after scattering seeds in the seed bed, can go to the hot springs, and visit the Honzan Shrine and his relatives, all during the two months it takes before the rice is to be planted? Is it not the farmer who, after the seedlings have been planted, and after he has cut the grass to feed his cows, can then take a long nap? Is there anyone but the farmer who, once the harvest is in and the rice has been stored, can spend nearly three carefree months sitting by the indoor fire pit working with straw,

braiding two or three pair of sandals before calling it a day, and going to the temple to brag of all the work he has done?

These were the proud and confident words of a man who had made the village what it was. He wrote of every aspect of the world he lived in with the intention of passing this information on. It was his thinking that not only did knowledge have to be conveyed, but when parents passed something on to their children it had to grow as well.

The country needs educators and government workers. Industry and commerce need laborers. These should come from healthy rural farm families. Do we not have enough second and third sons to meet the demand? Our eldest sons, our heirs, must continue to farm at all costs. We must convey to them that farming—the farmers' grains of suffering—is divine work, the very foundation of Imperial Japan. This I declare.

Grandpa's language was strongly influenced by his time, but in these words one can hear the voice of a man who is living fully in a place and is infatuated with it. This poignant feeling belongs to one who, while an eminent and progressive leader in the village, also worked hard to pass on something splendid to his own children and grandchildren, not just in his capacity as a transmitter of knowledge. Grandpa represents the birth of a new type of transmitter, one who because he is literate is able to convey knowledge not only from his grandfather's, father's, and his own experience but is also able, through the written word, to understand the world outside and to bring it into the village, receiving it there in as simple a form as possible.

Those who were born before 1890 did not feel compelled to add new interpretations to old knowledge. For them, traditions were traditions and practice was practice. They distinguished between the two. People born after 1890 began to add their own interpretations. And they disowned that which appeared to be irrational.

In this regard, Grandpa Tanaka was a rare, literate transmitter who died just as he was about to put the lives of farmers of old into words. And nearly twenty years have since passed.

Chapter 11

Literate Transmitters (II): Takagi Seiichi

[1887–1955; Fukushima Prefecture, December 1940]

I met Takagi Seiichi in December 1940 as the year was rapidly coming to a close. I had left Tokyo in the beginning of November and set out on foot from Niigata. I headed north up the coast of the Japan Sea to the Shimokita Peninsula and, after spending some time at the north end of the Ōma headland, I traveled south to Ōfunato in Iwate Prefecture. There, for the time being, I had ended my travels and was on my way back to Tokyo for New Year's.

Takagi-san lived in Kitakabeya, Kusano Village, in the Iwaki District of Fukushima Prefecture, in what is now a part of Taira City. I had learned his name from Yamaguchi Yaichirō and Iwasaki Toshio in 1935 at a folklore forum in celebration of Yanagita Kunio's sixtieth birthday. I knew nothing of his station in life, but I was given the impression that he was a man of great learning. With Takagi-san at its center, the Society for the Study of Iwaki Folk Customs had formed shortly thereafter.

It occurred to me to try calling on this man, my senior, on my way home, and I got off the train at Kusano Station, one stop north of Taira. Kusano Station was a rustic place. When I asked the whereabouts of Takagi-san's house out front, an old woman told me in detail. It was a walk of about two miles on a path through the rice paddies. Low hills sloped from the northwest to the southeast; between them were shallow valleys with rice paddies. Multiple folds creased either side of each hill, and in these impressions were groups of three and four houses. One house in each grouping was a little larger, making it the home of the main family. Those around it were the homes of the branch families. It appeared that people from the same family were forming small communities. Collections of such kinfolk groups were probably what made up villages in the past. Where these kinship bonds are strong, old practices remain intact.

When I had walked the path through the fields for more than two miles, I asked a farmer who was cleaning manure out of a stable in front of a large farm house, "Is Takagi Seiichi's house somewhere nearby?" At this, the man who had been working straightened his back and, looking down from atop the pile of manure, paused a moment before saying, "I am Takagi Seiichi." Before knowing it I had shrieked, "I'm Miyamoto Tsuneichi." "Oh, so you're Miyamoto-san? I thought you were a traveling medicine peddler from Toyama. I was thinking, if this guy's from Toyama, I've never seen him before ... " Saying this, he came down off the manure pile and brushed the hem of his kimono. I was surprised by this man. I had seen a photo of him in a magazine in which he was finely dressed in a *hakama* [a formal pleated skirt]. He had looked more like a doctor than a farmer, but the actual Takagi-san was indeed a powerfully built elderly farmer.

The two of us sat on his verandah in the sun and talked of many things. Takagi-san did not appear to be at all put off by my destitute appearance. I was wearing a rayon jacket, corduroy pants, gaiters, canvas duck shoes, and a black fedora. I carried a dirty rucksack with an umbrella dangling from the shoulder belt. I certainly did look like a medicine peddler, though my attire was a bit too worn to be one. After more than two months of continuous walking, my canvas shoes had begun to tear. I didn't mind looking poor, though, because I felt at ease, as did the people I met. And

I was most comfortable talking with farmers like Takagi-san be-cause, from the beginning, there was no distance between us. Takagi-san's talk began with farming. He took great pleasure in growing rice, vegetables, and flowers. In fact, it seemed that farming was almost more fun than he could bear. He said that on a hot, sunny day he could feel the rice stalks gulping down the water in the paddy, pointing skyward, growing taller. When fall came and he let the water out of the paddy, he could feel the water flowing, gurgling, pleased to have fulfilled its duty. "It's as if I can hear all their voices."

But Takagi-san was not a simple, rural romanticist. He was a superb realist. He thought earnestly about how to increase pro-duction and make the lives of farmers easier. In a tiny space in front of his house he grew flowers, cut them, and took them into Taira to sell. The persimmons drying on skewers and hanging un-der the eaves of his house looked splendid. This village was full of persimmon trees and when fall came and the fruit began to color, the people picked them. Working at night, they peeled and skew-ered them, creating another source of income for the farmers.

This area had long been a breeding center for horses. But one after another, the horses had been requisitioned for the war ef-fort. People kept horses to do farm work, and Takagi-san found it unbearable that they had been confiscated. It was his thinking that for farmers to increase their efficiency they must not allow the war to influence their production. So he decided to introduce cattle. He looked into the capacity of black cattle to perform farm work, and discovered that cows would more than suffice for the kind of farming in the Kusano area. So how would he go about introducing cows? Takagi-san sent his eldest son to Tottori Pre-fecture to learn how to raise cattle and first tried switching over to black cattle at his own house. This brought good results, so he recommended cows to other farmers and gradually increased the number of cattle in the area. "Right now my eldest son is in Tot-tori buying cattle. He'll probably be back in the morning." Even in the middle of a war, Takagi-san continued to live the life of a farmer.

Regardless of what he talked about, Takagi-san was interesting to listen to. While his life itself was material for the study of folk customs, he was not attached to an old life style.

The lives of farmers of old, in the context of their own time, were the most logical, and they had no alternative but to live in that way at that time. Although this makes it all the more important for us to look closely at their way of life, as times change we must also adopt new ways of living. But we must plan well and experiment. This is an obligation of those in the village who are clearheaded. My family was one of those that had a clarity of vision. I don't know much about it, but apparently they were once *yamabushi* on Mt. Haku, in Kaga. They settled down here, worshipped a shrine to Mt. Haku, and under the protection of this god the village was saved from various misfortunes. Later they put their energies into farming, and the Mt. Haku Shrine that had been the family's god became the village's guardian god. For some reason many of my ancestors were interested in scholarship. Those who farmed were fine, but of the second and third sons who quit farming, none lived to an old age. For that reason we have no branch families.

I too had found this strange. While the communities in this area had one large house in the middle and several other homes clustered around it, Takagi-san's home was not surrounded by other homes. There was a retirement house in front, where his elderly parents lived, and I was told that his father would be turning eighty-eight soon. He is quite healthy and continues to farm. In time, Takagi-san will also have to retire from being head of the household. Then there will be two retirement houses. He said, "the number of branch families doesn't grow, but the number of retired families does."

In this area, it had long been the custom for parents, after retiring from the head of the family, to take their second and third sons with them and establish distinct branch families. That probably gave birth to the communities I had seen along the way.

Even now my family is a bit different from others in the area. We place a high value on old traditions, probably because we housed the shrine and all. That's probably why we take an interest in old things. For me the study of the past has not only helped me to understand the value of old ways, but I've met a large number of fine teachers and elders, received their guidance, and come to know about the wider world. If I hadn't studied folk customs, that probably wouldn't have been the case.

Saying this, he showed me a register with the names of his visitors. Yanagita Kunio's signature was there, and beginning with Ishiguro Tadaatsu and Ono Takeo, many eminent scholars and elders had visited this home. Takagi-san had not invited them. They had come along of their own accord, and a large number indeed. Among them were groups of several dozen that had called on Takagi-san in his capacity as a model farmer. Apparently when a large group of people asked for directions to Takagi-san's house in front of Kusano Station, the people there knew that the group had come to observe farming. When one or two asked the way, this meant that they were related to the study of folkways. Many of the folklorists had read Takagi-san's reports in *Folk Studies* and *Ethnos* and had come to see this place. As a result of these visits, he came to correspond with people from all over.

As for those who were studying folkways, they were good people, easygoing and not driven by ambition. Furthermore, whatever aspect of the village was discussed, no one looked down on the people here or spread exaggerated rumors about them. Takagi-san said that it was reassuring to have like-minded people all around the country with whom he could frankly discuss life here. Though he lived far to the northeast, he did not feel far away. He felt like he was in the center. "This field of study encourages guys like me and teaches us that we don't need to look

Takagi Seiichi (left) and his father (right). Fukushima Prefecture. December 1940.

down on the life we have." Takagi-san spoke with great emotion. "This is a field we farmers must study. If we all looked back on our lives in this way, our lives would probably all improve."

After we had talked on the verandah for quite some time, I was treated to lunch seated at the edge of the kitchen. Then Takagi-san, who was still in his work clothes, took me around the village. He showed me old farmhouses, we prayed at the Mt. Haku Shrine, and we looked at the way people were farming as we walked along. That night I asked him about people's beliefs in these parts. Saying, "Old people know better than I do," he took me to his father's place, and we talked until late into the night. The individual components of life here had not been influenced by Western learning or thought and showed few signs of samurai Confucian morals either. Rather, they appeared to have come from a way of thinking that preceded these things. The importance placed on ties between individuals—within families and the village as a whole—and a commitment not to betray unseen gods are what gave order to these people's lives.

I was deeply moved by the talk of this man who was nearly ninety, while Takagi-san, who sat beside me and drew out his father's stories, was both humble and gentle. Takagi-san confided, "Every time I listen to my father, he teaches me something I had failed to notice before." He also told me that the older he became, the more strongly he felt that even if he lived with his parents for dozens more years, everything they knew could not be transmitted to him.

When I inquired with regard to various things I had seen and heard on my travels in the northeast, Takagi-san talked tirelessly. I found many differences, and some common ground, between the culture of southwest Japan, where I was born, and that of the northeast. There's the "big rice planting" in the mountains of Western Honshu, for example. Dozens of women planters enter a single paddy and, to the rhythm of a flute, *taiko* drums, and a caller, they sing rice-planting songs and plant. Not all of the paddies are planted in this way. Sometimes landowners have these big rice plantings, and at other times cow traders donate their services. When the cow traders are the sponsors, the big rice planting is referred to as a "memorial service for cows" [and is performed in their honor].

Something akin to the big rice planting could be found in these parts as well. Called "*taiko* paddy," it was always performed in the "three *taiko* paddies of Iwaki" that belonged to three landowners. It was quite similar in content except that in this area the benefactor families were fixed. In Western Honshu the families were not decided, and those who wished to became involved. The planting ceremonies long held at Shinto shrines seem to be related to this big rice planting as well. Some scholars trace this practice back to the use of serfs by powerful families when planting rice in ancient times. This may or may not have been the case. The custom of playing instruments and singing while large numbers of people plant rice can also be found in the Philippines and Indonesia. While it would appear that the need to plant in this way did not originate with large landowners, they probably supported its continuation. The three *taiko* paddies of Iwaki may be an example of this.

This is to say that a single folk practice will change in various ways depending on the capacity of those who are transmitting it. For example, *ema* [literally, "picture horses"] are thought to have come from the practice of taking one's horse to a temple or shrine as an offering. When people no longer took live horses but brought drawings of horses as a substitute, the word *ema* was born. Later, in place of drawings of horses, people drew and made an offering of something that was an expression of their own wishes. This progressed yet further to where the number of people who now offer commemorative pictures has increased. Walking in the northeast region, and particularly in the plains of Tsugaru, one often sees *ema* of cats and snakes that have been drawn on wooden plaques and placed at corners and crossroads. The drawings are by amateurs. When female mediums—called *gomiso* or *kamisama*—are asked to divine the reason for an illness or misfortune, they will often find that a cat or a snake has cast an evil spell. It is thought that if one draws a picture of the curser and stands it where a road comes to an end, and if many people pray to it, the curse will be removed. While the general intent of these *ema* is different from that of their predecessors, they have survived in Tsugaru to this day in their capacity as a means of removing a curse.

I talked with Takagi-san about *ema* and the following morning he brought dozens of them down from the second floor of his storehouse and showed them to me. Most had been used to pray for a cure to an illness. Many of these were of crabs, octopuses, abalone, and other aquatic life, subjects that I imagined were unique to this area. When I asked why he was collecting such things, Takagi-san explained that he liked to walk, and that when there was little farm work to do he walked out from his house in all directions. He was a fast walker and covered about fifty miles in a day. He would leave his house in the morning and walk all day, or take a train some distance and walk back from there. He did his best not to take the same road, and he fa-

Oshirasama.
Aomori Prefecture.
March 1964.

vored narrow paths. If there was a shrine, he would always visit, and he called on temples as well. He also talked with farmers along the roadside. He told me that spending his time this way was more pleasurable than anything else; it was on such occasions that he had collected the *ema*.

After breakfast, wanting to see the *shinmei* deities that remain in this area, I asked Takagi-san to take me around. These *shinmei*, attached to the ends of sticks a little less than a foot long, are usually in a pair—the head of a man wearing a tall black hat and the head of a woman with long flowing hair—each wearing a piece of cloth. In Aomori, Akita and Iwate they are called *oshirasama*. They can also still be found in the vicinity of Taira, in Fukushima Prefecture. Takagi-san said that originally female mediums called *waka* carried these with them when they went from door to door for money. These mediums were affiliated with various shrines, Ise, Kumano, and Mt. Haku being common, so the deities were called Ise *shinmei*, Kumano *shinmei*, Mt. Haku *shinmei*, and so on, though nothing about their shape distinguished them. These wooden figures were probably used as idols for various gods.

Most of the women who carried these *shinmei* figures were able to see [though often mediums were blind], and calling them mediums is an overstatement as most were the wives or daughters of farmers. Generally speaking, private citizens could not undertake a specialized profession without support from a large number of people. Only priests at temples and shrines that had been given extensive paddies and fields as donations could devote themselves to their professional duties. When this was not the case, they became homeless wanderers, going door to door to support themselves, or they had another profession with which they supported themselves.

Some among the farming community, either because of their environment or their talents, did other work as well. The female mediums, or *waka*, were one example of this, and consequently many of the *shinmei* figures were to be found in private homes. But, as such women no longer exist, and it was seen as wasteful and improper to have the figures, many have been given to the local shrines. By so doing, many of the beliefs, manners, customs, and traditions attendant to the *shinmei* deities have disappeared. Beliefs related to the *shinmei* deities in this area had also reached that point. Takagi-san was asking private individuals about this disappearing tradition and gathering what he learned. Without someone like him, the knowledge would probably have disappeared entirely from the public memory in this region. Unlike written materials, when something was no longer required in life, it was quickly forgotten and disappeared from the oral tradition. But the *shinmei* deities had not disappeared completely; the object of worship remained although the person managing it had changed.

This loss of knowledge is extremely common when culture is passed down by the people. Most often people do not write anything down until the beliefs have passed the time of their greatest popularity and are in decline. On such occasions the written word was useful for recording culture so that it would not be lost. In this respect Takagi-san played an important role in connecting the knowledge of old transmitters with the present day. He was also a consummate transmitter [a conveyor of knowledge to his own and future generations].

Takagi-san was fleet-footed, too. I am confident in my own ability to walk, but when I was with him I often had to run just to keep up. He wore an inverness coat and carried a stick that he twirled occasionally. He was like a young boy, pointing at things with that stick, and wherever he pointed there was some folk culture that needed to be recorded.

Takagi-san showed me around until early afternoon when I

boarded a train at Kusano Station. My impression of this man can be summed up in one word: thrilling. He was the model of a true farmer, a man whose skills and knowledge were unerring, and one who others could turn to with confidence. People like this always have a central role in farming communities, and they never betray the people's interests.

In rural communities two types of people act as signposts for the people. The first is found among the powerful families or the families of officials, those holding real power. The second comes from among the general farming population. They give direction to the way people think and live their lives. Takagi-san belonged to the latter group. He did not care about titles and was proud to be a farmer beyond all else. Late in the war, at the urging of those around him, he became the deputy mayor of Kusano.

The following is a short biography of Takagi Seiichi by Iwasaki Toshio, in volume 7 of *Outline of Japanese Folklore*:

Born March 17, 1887, the eldest son of Ise Osamu, Kitakabeya, Kusano Village, Iwaki District, Fukushima Prefecture. Entered Iwaki Junior High School in 1901, but his father thought that academic studies would be wasted on the eldest son of a farmer, so he was made to leave school in 1903. Worked briefly as a substitute teacher but retired to devote himself solely to farming. Attended some twenty training courses related to all kinds of agricultural practices and, in particular, received repeated instruction from Yamazaki Nobuyoshi. His knowledge of farming technology grew with every passing year, and he became increasingly known as an exemplary farmer. One after another, individuals visited to observe his farm management in practice. Meanwhile, strongly influenced by agricultural studies scholar Dr. Yokoi Tokiyoshi, he devoted himself to improved farming methods. Early on he also met and came to know Dr. Ono

Takeo and became immersed in the study of the economic history of farming. He attended exhibitions and joined in competitions of all kinds. He was awarded some eighty-seven prizes. Over the next thirty-five years he taught part-time at a school for continuing education in agriculture and at a school for young men. He also held the public offices of district representative, Kusano deputy mayor, and so on. He enjoyed the honor of providing the rice that was offered to the gods at the shrine's harvest festival. He was often commended as a model farmer by the Prefectural Agriculture Committee, The Agricultural Association of Japan, The Imperial Agricultural Association, and the Ministry of Agriculture and Forestry. He studied folkways under Yanagita Kunio, beginning in 1907. In 1935 he established the Society for the Study of Iwaki Folk Customs, was appointed chairman, and focused increasingly on his research work. After the war, for reasons of his own, he resigned from all public duties on behalf of the village and returned to being a simple farmer. He spent the last years of his life farming when the weather was good and reading books when it was not.

Though Takagi-san might appear somewhat pretentious, he probably did not set out to occupy a single public office.

After the war had grown more intense, on occasion Takagi-san came to Tokyo to attend to business, and each time he would stop by. He would show up wearing a black stand-up collar, gaiters, split-toed cloth work shoes, and an old overcoat, contrasting fashions that were, indeed, in perfect accord.

On one of the occasions when he came to Tokyo—Shibusawa-sensei had become vice president of the Bank of Japan, so I think it must have been 1942—I acted as a guide, taking him there. As I recall, Takagi-san said he wanted to report on cormorant fishing in the Iwaki area. When we entered that large building and asked, at reception, to see the vice president, the guard looked suspiciously at this man from the country in his old overcoat. We waited for a while, and a young woman came to get us. When we were walking down the hall, Takagi-san exclaimed, in a voice filled with emotion, "what a fine place!"

When we arrived at the vice president's office he was with another visitor, and we waited for a time. Remarking that "one really sinks down into these chairs," he jumped up and down two or three times to show me. After that we talked with Shibusawa-sensei for almost an hour and headed back outside. Takagi-san looked up at the building; once again he marveled, "what a fine place! Everyone should have a look at a place like this . . . and to think that even in that large room, Shibusawa-sensei didn't look small. He must be quite a great man." I found this comment quite interesting.

I probably saw Takagi-san another four or five times before the war ended, but I left Tokyo in 1944 and did not have the opportunity to see him again until 1946. Wanting to know how friends in the northeast were getting along after the war, I boarded a train in August 1946. Takagi-san was the first person I visited. He seemed relieved the war was over. Although only three years had passed since I had seen him last, he had grown quite old. It seemed his work as the village's deputy mayor had exhausted his energy, though he did not speak much of this.

During the war, the Ministry of Agriculture and Forestry had begun to advance plans for the emancipation of farmland. Research was conducted regarding actual land ownership and management to consider how this would best be done—if, in fact, it were done. Starting around 1944, I had performed research into the status of landowners in Nara and Osaka. Wanting to have a basic understanding of these matters at a national level, I had set out on this trip. The occupation army had taken over the land reform plans made by the Ministry of Agriculture and Forestry during the war, and the plan they announced appeared to be little changed. Now that the execution of land reforms had become a certainty, I thought it necessary to take a look at the state of farmland management.

Takagi-san told me that few landholders in his area owned enough land any more to be emancipated. There were landholding families who had practiced "*taiko* paddy," but many had gone to ruin. Scholars make a fuss about class society, and there is probably some truth in what they say. But, on the other hand, a leveling is also taking place. Traveling throughout the country I am of the impression that there are about as many communities where an averaging has taken place as there are stratified ones, but no one thinks to look at them. Is there not perhaps a new bud to be found in this reality? While it was important to look at the lives of old landowners, I also wanted to see more examples of this material averaging. So I asked Takagi-san about the communities around Kitakabeya.

I learned of a village called Ōura, across low mountains to the north, that had an old landholding family by the name of Watanabe. Takagi-san said it would probably be interesting to compare Kitakabeya, which had no landlords, with Ōura, and he suggested I go there and take a look. His nephew, Wada Fumio, lived in Nagatomo, one of the communities that made up the greater village of Ōura. He was studying folk customs and would be familiar with the state of land ownership.

Takagi-san put three pounds of white rice in a bag, saying, "You won't get stopped for the illegal transport of rice if you have only three pounds, so take this with you. In places where they have nothing to spare, have them cook this. And when you run out, stay with people that look like they have rice."

I crossed the mountains and went to Wada-san's house. With his help I researched the area around Nagatomo. That night, when I was talking with Wada-san, someone called out from the dirt-floored entrance, "Is Miyamoto-san there?" I recognized Takagi-san's voice. When I went out to the kitchen area, he was sitting on the edge of the entrance hall, smiling.

"I came because I wanted to see you one more time. I don't have any business in particular." This man with whom I had parted that morning had, out of a feeling of nostalgia, crossed a mountain to come and see me after eating his dinner. "In this valley they have *jingara* Buddhist dancing, and graves from the Kamakura period, so it would be good to see them both." Saying this, he left. He had not even come up into the house. For one look, he had walked a mountain road at night without a light and returned the same way. For most of us that would have been an ordeal, but for Takagi-san it was nothing at all. It was a matter of course. He may have seemed excessively friendly, but he was not making a conscious effort to be that way.

After Takagi-san had left, Wada-san laughed. "That's the kind of person my uncle is. Everything he does seems quite normal to him." And Takagi-san was undaunted by a crisis. During the war and after, he had only done what he had to in the capacity of a farmer.

Thereafter, I watched some *jingara* dancing, looked at an old monument to the souls of the dead at the temple, visited the Watanabe's house to examine their old family documents, and then walked on farther north. From then until the time of his death in 1955, I did not have the opportunity to meet with Takagi-san again.

Takagi-san made no effort to bring his writings together in book form. When I suggested this to him he simply responded "Well, I'll have to try that," but without showing the slightest enthusiasm. Concerned by this, Wada-san and Iwasaki Toshio organized Takagi-san's writings that had appeared in magazines, making a clean copy on manuscript paper. That was published by the Culture of the Masses Research Institute under the title *Stories from Kitakabeya in Iwaki* in December 1955. Takagi-san died on September 7 when the galley proofs were just coming out. He was sixty-nine.

Two or three years before Takagi-san died, the Committee on Cultural Studies in Commemoration of the 100th Anniversary of the Opening of the Country compiled a *History of Meiji Culture*. We also undertook the writing of a book regarding life in the Meiji period. We focused on the impact that foreign cultures had had on Japanese daily life since long ago and how the Japanese had accommodated this. We sent out a questionnaire to colleagues all around the country. The answers that came back were of substantial volume and superb content. In addition, we hunted down farm families that had kept household accounts in the Meiji period, asked to see their accounts, and analyzed them. Though only a few farmers had kept such accounts in the Meiji period, Takagi-san was one of them. Because his accounts were so precise, they were particularly helpful.

Takagi-san was not particularly interested in speaking out or making appeals. He had done nothing more than write, at the request of others, about things that were a part of his life and about that which was necessary to his own livelihood. In that respect, his life itself was material for the study of folk customs, and Takagi-san was himself an outstanding transmitter of information.

Among Takagi-san's writings, I was most deeply interested in his letters, some of which are included in *Stories from Kitakabeya*. For the most part these are letters sent to him by the folklorists Yanagita Kunio, Nakayama Tarō, Shibusawa Keizō, Sasaki Kizen, Ikegami Hiromasa, and Nevsky. Only a few of his responses are included. His letters are permeated with his character, and nowhere is he the least bit defiant. His friendship with Nevsky was a beautiful thing. A passage from a letter Nevsky wrote in 1921 reads, "I imagine you must be very troubled in these economically hard times, and you have my sympathies. I found it most interesting that, because times are hard, the number of deities has increased." Nevsky was a Russian who had studied oriental languages and come to Japan before World War I. He taught at Otaru Commercial College and at the Osaka College of Foreign Languages. Developing an interest in Japanese folkways, he had researched them deeply. Later, when he returned to the Soviet Union, he was made a political victim and died a tragic death. He had shared a warm friendship with Takagi-san.

When eminent transmitters from among the people are able to write, they do not merely transmit the old and pass it on to the next generation. Their efforts to improve their own lives make them uncommonly strong. In them one finds the simplicity, energy, and brightness that come with being a farmer. Before the war, communities moved forward with such people at their center.

Part Two

Village Stories

Mishima Island,
Yamaguchi Prefecture.
September 1961.

Chapter 12

The Child Hunt

[Ōshima Island, Yamaguchi Prefecture, circa 1959]

There has been a lot of analysis of late with regard to the organization and functioning of villages. But what is life in these villages really like? I would like to insert a small sketch here, set in a small farming community in Suō Ōshima.

A boy in the first grade had asked his parents to buy a television but was told that if he had one he would no longer study, and the neighbors would come to watch and make a mess of the house. For these and various other reasons a television was not bought, and the boy went to a neighbor's house to watch TV.

One evening, when his mother came back from work in the mountains the boy wasn't home, so she sent her daughter to get him. The boy returned in good spirits, probably feeling proud of himself for having come right home without watching a program he'd wanted to see, but his mother scolded him, saying, "a child who doesn't listen no matter how often he's told is no child of mine." Saying nothing, the boy went outside. The boy's grandmother, who was lighting a fire for the bath, saw this. He was so dear to her that she'd do anything he asked, except buy him a television.

It came time for dinner, but the boy hadn't returned. Growing anxious, his grandmother began to search for him, but he

On the road in Shizuoka Prefecture. July 1959.

was nowhere to be found. Flustered, she went about shouting his name. The people of the village took notice, and the boy's mother too. No longer able to ignore the situation, she searched in all the likely places, but to no avail.

Lest something should happen to her son, the mother asked the local civil defense unit [a policing group that existed during and shortly after World War II] to come. Dozens from the unit searched in the forest at a shrine near the house, and the villagers looked in other places as well, but they just couldn't find the boy.

After nine o'clock, the child's father returned home from work. When he heard what had happened, he easily understood his son's motives. Suggesting they search a bit longer, he set out in no particular direction and even tried going to the ocean, but nothing came of it. When he returned home, the boy suddenly came out of the corner of the shutter box, where the storm doors are kept, by the front room. That area had been searched many times, but no one had found him.

The child had hidden to make his family worry a little, but when the commotion grew, he wasn't able to come out. Just when he'd lost all opportunity to reveal himself, he heard his father's voice, and that had brought him out.

The family immediately thanked those who had been looking, and they thanked the whole village over the public address system. When people learned that the child had been found, those who had been out searching came along and expressed their delight to the family.

I was surprised by what they said. One had gone to a shed by a field on the mountain. Another had looked at the edge of the pond and along the river. A third had been to the child's friend's house and a fourth had gone to a neighboring village. They'd all searched in places they thought the child might have gone. No one had directed them to so divide their labors, and they hadn't conferred with one another either. They had heard the announcement and gone looking of their own volition, searching in whatever place came to mind. Thinking about it later, theirs was a truly well planned search.

This was a reflection of the fact that members of the community were completely familiar with the child's family, with their way of life. I had thought village life had become so modernized that the community aspect had been utterly destroyed and lost. But while parents and children, husbands and wives, are now voting for opposing candidates, something like an invisible community mind is still at work. Without taking orders from anyone, their individual actions had coherence.

At the very time these people were earnestly searching, others had gathered in the street and were engrossed in gossip about the missing child. They passed judgment on the child's family, said he'd fallen into the ocean, that he was probably dead, and so on. They too were members of the community, but had more recently settled in this place. They participated, without prejudice, in everyday affairs along with those who had been there since the distant past, and they intermarried as well. But they didn't even think of participating in the search, and as they felt it had absolutely nothing to do with them, they merely gossiped about this preposterous thing that had happened. In one sense, these

*A village
in Gifu Prefecture.
August 1941.*

people were outside of the community mind, and it can be said that in times of emergency, they were of no use to the community.

On this occasion, a young man had gone off in search of the child but after some time had passed, he hadn't returned. Someone said, "Knowing him, he's probably gone off drinking somewhere," and someone else said, "No, I think he's gone to Yamadera." It was finally decided that he'd probably gone as far as Yamadera, and sure enough, that's what had happened. He came back after more than an hour and, chasing the child around, said, "you really fooled me." Then saying, "fool me one more time and you'll be sorry," he went home.

The man was a heavy drinker and always yelling at the children, but he was popular with them. When he heard that the child was missing, he'd gone to Yamadera where the boy's best friend lived. That was deep in the mountains, in the most lonely and out of the way place.

Chapter 13

Tosa Terakawa Night Tale

[Kōchi Prefecture, formerly the Tosa Domain, December 1941]

What is life like for the farmers who live in the mountains of Tosa? Twenty-four miles northeast of Yusuhara, there is a place called Terakawa. I tried writing about that village once, but left those writings in the bottom of a box. That was more than ten years ago. It was December 9 [1941] and the war had just begun. I'd crossed the mountains from Komatsu, in Iyo, to Terakawa, in Tosa. I'd also gone to Terakawa in January of that same year. At that time I was told, "Travelers say they'll be back, but no one's ever come a second time," and I had made the mistake of saying, "I alone will not fail to come again."

So, feeling responsible to go again, I headed off. The road was awful. Barely distinguishable, a narrow path climbed steep precipices, crossed rivers without bridges and took me back farther and farther into deeply wooded valleys.

In the middle of that primeval forest I met an old woman. It was a woman, although at first glance I couldn't be sure. Her face was all lumpy, I couldn't tell if she had hair or not, and there was nothing resembling fingers on her hands. She was wearing a kimono that was literally falling apart and a cloth bundle hung from a sash draped over her shoulder. She had a horrible case of leprosy.

I was utterly taken aback. The path being narrow, there was no way to step aside. So I just stood there. When I did that, she asked how far it might be to Bō, in Iyo. Unfamiliar with those parts, I tried getting out a Land Survey Department map, but not being able to figure it out, I told her I didn't know. Having become a little more composed, I asked, "Grandma, where are you from?" She said she was from Awa [the feudal domain name for Tokushima Prefecture, approximately ninety miles northeast]. When I inquired how it was that she'd come this far, she said she had followed the signs. "Having an affliction like this, I can't walk on the front roads that others take. And because I can't pass through where people live either, I've traveled only on mountain paths like this one." She told me this in a husky voice that was hard to make out. According to the old woman, many in Shikoku were so afflicted, and there were mountain paths that only they traveled.

My heart ached. If what this old woman said was true, she'd come all this way on paths like this one. But that was my only experience of that kind and when I asked others about it later, I wasn't able to make a clear confirmation.

After seeing the old woman off, I took the path she'd come down and came out in Terakawa. In the vicinity of Shirai Pass, the snow rested beautifully, like flowers, on the branches of the trees.

Terakawa was a settlement deep in the mountains, a mere seventeen homes scattered here and there in threes and fours. To hold a simple village meeting, many had to walk half the length of the road. Why would people go to the trouble of living here, deep in the mountains?

We know, from land surveys from the Keichō period [1596–1615], that there was already a village here more than three hundred years ago. Being at the border with Iyo, [the feudal domain north of Tosa] it was apparently an important lookout. A watchman squire lived to the east of Terakawa, in Erimon, and a forest-ranger official came, in turns, to Terakawa from the castle town of Kōchi. The villagers served as rangers as well, and they

House and terraced fields.
Terakawa, Kōchi Prefecture.
January 1941

patrolled the mountains in search of people coming from Iyo to secretly fell trees and steal timber. In exchange for their troubles, I was told, the villagers were not required to pay any tributes or taxes.

Here, in the back end of Tosa, in the area around the upper reaches of the Yoshino River, a splendid virgin forest grows so dense and dark as to make this a lonely place. But across to the north, in the Iyo Domain, there were so many people that they were short of just about everything, so they often crossed the mountains and came to these parts to steal trees. Most came for timber to build houses, and it was difficult for the seventeen families of Terakawa to watch over this much land.

According to an elderly man I met—he was ninety-four at the time—when they found someone stealing trees, they'd fire a shot into the air. The villagers would then come running and chase after the thieves. The old man said the villagers found paths in places they'd never thought of, where they would absolutely not find the poachers' comings and goings. "If there are paths traveled by thieves, there are probably also paths traveled by lepers."

There are also trails traveled by animals. I was told that the boar trails are quite distinct. In Terakawa, they call these trails *uchi*. For a long time there were no paths large enough for a cow in these parts. In fact, many of the villagers died without ever seeing a cow. "I recall that cows came to this place in 1902. They were driven along as far as Erimon with a slap on the butt, but from there, their legs were tied and they were hung from a pole and carried." The old man told me the people risked their lives when they carried the cows on the path above the river.

The story is still told of an old woman from the village who, upon seeing a cow, said, "This horse has horns." When she was told, "This is what's called a cow." She said, "It may be a cow, but it still has horns."

The forest ranger officials had a large influence on the people of the village. Some helped out the villagers in various ways, including teaching them how to read, and enjoyed their lives with these farmers. It was probably one such person who lived here during the Hōreki period [1751–64] and wrote an interesting book titled *An Account of Terakawa Village*.

There were also bad officials who were resented by the villagers. On one occasion, they all chased after a timber thief together but for some reason, the official didn't come back. One of the villagers said they ought to leave him be since he wasn't a good man, while another, fearing a reprisal, thought they should search for him. The man who suggested leaving him won out, and they all returned to the village. But when the official didn't come back that night they decided that meant trouble and everyone went looking for him. They found him at the bottom of a deep gorge. He had died a cruel death. His arms had been tied to a large cedar log, like the horizontal portion of a cross. The horizontal log acted as a hindrance so he couldn't walk among the trees, yet somehow he'd walked through the forest. Coming close to the gorge, and having exhausted his strength, he'd probably fallen from the precipice to his death. Later, in the Meiji period, an official from the forestry office was tied to a tree by a thief and killed. To this day, his gravestone remains standing in the mountains.

Once there was a bad official who really vexed the villagers, so they conspired that someday they would take out their vengeance on him. When it came time for him to be replaced and return to Kōchi, they made a plan to throw him in the river. Ranger officials always rode in a mountain palanquin from Terakawa to Omoiji, so when the villagers came to a precipice above the river they made as if they'd lost their footing and dropped the palanquin in the river. It is said that this samurai warrior, not knowing how to swim, died an untimely death in a deep whirlpool.

There were those who came like the wind and left like it too—merchants from Osaka who came to these mountains to buy honey and beeswax. In the old days, apothecary merchants bought these things, and old bills of sale remain to this day. Bees abound in these parts, and one can find bee boxes all over these mountains. The boxes were of an old design, some making use of the hollows in trees. The merchants came all the way across the ocean [across the Inland Sea] for the honey and wax gathered from those old boxes. And after buying it up, they would return home.

Another thing in these mountains that was profitable was tea. Tea is interesting—it's said that when one cuts down a large tree, without fail tea will grow in and cover the ground. On occasion one will find large tea plants as undergrowth in the woods. Steam the leaves from those plants and after squeezing them in a press, allow them to ferment. This is called *sencha* [a unique variety of green tea, sold in tiny, hard round cakes], which was also sold. Apparently people came from Iyo to buy it.

This is a lonely place, deep in the mountains, but there were a number of paths that, though narrow, led to more open spaces. By way of those paths, the people of the village came to know of the world as well. And where people live, there are tidings of love. It's said that long ago the young men would cross over a large mountain to the south and call on girls in the night, in the vicinity of Mt. Mominoki. That was probably four, even five miles. They would think nothing of going that far at night, walking by

The path to Terakawa, Kōchi Prefecture. January 1944.

the light of a fire torch, for a good woman.

One young man enjoyed a night with a girl and having to work in the morning, left early. But fatigue got the better of him and he took a nap at the base of a tree beside a large rock. A large man with one eye appeared.

"Was last night good?" the man asked.

"Yes, it was."

"What do you think of mine?"

Looking, he saw that the man was sitting on the rock, his kimono open in the front, and that enormous testicles were dangling there.

Saying "They're big," the young man suddenly slashed the balls with the short sword at his waist. When he did this, there was a scream and right there in front of him an old raccoon dog writhed in the agony of death.

There were many stories like this in these mountains. The farmers would fell trees way back in the valleys and farm there. On such occasions, even in the absence of a wind, they would hear what sounded like a terrible gale or the sound of trees falling. The villagers believed this was the work of *tengu*, the long-nosed goblins from nearby Mt. Ishizuchi, or from Mt. Kuromori. Apparently there were a large number of mountains with *tengu* in these parts but when this area started to smell of people, they flew off to a land far across the sea.

There are mountains wherever one looks. In these forests, the farmers practiced slash-and-burn agriculture and lived wherever they pleased. Walking in the mountains, one finds signs of this slash-and-burn agriculture everywhere. As the land was spacious and people were few, in times of famine large numbers of people would come along from Iyo. They'd help cultivate the millet, and were pleased even to have the husks. The husks were indigestible and only served to fill one's stomach, but the people tried eating them anyway. At the time of the Tenpō famine [1833–36], lots of people came from Iyo, built huts in Shirai Valley, and lived there. The valley was full of *shirai* [spider lilies]. Originally the Tosa clan had these bulbs planted on the ridges around the paddies and fields as a hardy food alternative in times of shortage. To this day, if you go to the Shirai Valley in early fall, these flowers bloom in concert, as if on fire. In the midst of the dense green growth that covers these mountains, this red color is quite cheerful, and I was told that it enchanted passersby.

The people of Iyo lived there for nearly a year, digging up spider lily bulbs, boiling them, soaking them in the river, and after extracting the poison, pounded them into cakes called *shirai mochi* [spider lily cakes]. A little of this wasn't bad to eat, but it was not food one would be grateful to eat every day. The people of Iyo ate spider lily, millet, and millet husks.

It was May. They had raised flags and carp streamers beside their shacks, probably merely as a token celebration for their children, but it lent a vital, bright color to those miserable thatched huts. Because they didn't practice such customs here, the people of Terakawa were amazed by this scenery. In *An Account of Terakawa Village*, it was written: "The boys' festival on the fifth of May is even less eventful than the girls' festival on the third of March. There are no decorative banners, and since long ago, this being late in the season, and without seasonal or special clothing to wear, young boys and girls only put irises in their hair or possibly insert them in their sashes. This acts as a charm to ward off illness." These seasonal festivals had been utterly cheerless, but struck by the beauty of the flags and streamers, thereafter the villagers took to buying them in Iyo and displaying them. How that must have brightened life in the mountains.

More than a year passed, and the people of Iyo returned to their villages. They cleared away their huts and the land returned to its original state. It's said there were large mounds of human excrement in the pits they had dug that over the years, washed by the rain and wind, lost their odor and viscosity and became millet husks once again.

The old man from Terakawa said, "That was just something they tried putting in their stomachs. They were contented just to have something in their stomachs." Though the millet husks had only passed through their stomachs, perhaps in so doing the people of Iyo had gained some nourishment, because apparently no one died of starvation.

The old man told me that, at this time, the villagers were so desperate they made spider lily cakes too. One boy who went into the mountains to cut wood packed a lunch with spider lily cakes. They were so bad that he placed the last one on a tree stump when he went home. When he went back after more than a year had passed, the cake, bleached white, was still there on the stump.

Starting around the time of this famine, the people of Terakawa began to get along a little better with the people of Iyo. Some married women from Iyo, after which a clearly defined though narrow path between the two villages came into being. At the same time, little by little, a bright wind began to blow in from Iyo. I was told that most of the unusual customs subsequent to the writing of *An Account of Terakawa Village* came in from Iyo to the north.

The kind of occurrences described in *An Account of Terakawa Village* gradually decreased.

People from the Matsuyama-seijō territory [in Iyo] often sneak into the mountains and steal cypress. The government places mountain guard stations two and a half and five miles from the border. . . . The thieves sneak in during the daytime, select trees, light a fire in the late evening, fell the cypress, and cut them into thick boards. . . . They complete their work during the night, and before dawn they take the boards across the border into their own territory. The watchmen, vigilant, go to their lookouts and discover the light of a fire. So the thieves have come! Each wanting to be the first, the watchmen head in the direction of the fires and there is a cutting and clashing of swords deep in the mountains. In the mountains are the many graves of those who have been cut down. Or, sometimes their ears and queues [long, braided ponytails] are cut and they are chased off. . . . Now there are mounds of ears in three locations.

Only the small birds that come here by way of the sky have not changed. There are a considerable number of robins, wrens, mountain doves, woodpeckers, cuckoos, and kingfishers. All day long, the mountains are filled with their beautiful voices. But a dam has been built in the long valley below Terakawa, the trees in the surrounding mountains have been cut by degrees, and the road widened, so it will probably change a great deal in the future.

Chapter 14

Village Meetings

It's the same everywhere. Farmers feel a strong attachment to their land. At the time of land reform [following World War II], while it was fairly easy to reach an agreement with the larger landowners, many problems arose with those who owned only a small amount of land. In not a few cases the liberation of land was itself unreasonable. When a son was called off to war his father would ask someone else to farm a tiny plot of land, only to have it taken from him. Or a farmer would break his back to own a quarter- or half-acre of land, only to find that he had to give up another piece of land because he was not presently farming it. Farmers suffered, to the point of screaming, the anguish that their long labors were ignored, and this was the cause of countless problems between small landowners and tenant farmers.

Right around that time I heard an interesting story from a friend who was overseeing the redistribution of land in a village near Lake Suwa in Nagano Prefecture. He was experiencing great difficulty in the handling of these matters when an old man who was over sixty told him, "If you look at individual people, no one acts properly all the time, and over the course of three generations in any given family someone will have done something wrong. So people must be ready to compromise with one another."

There was an explanation for the advice this old man had given to my friend. In that village, when a person turned sixty they entered the old people's group. The old people would gather now and then and discuss various problems in the village, problems that were not out in the open. There was nothing to be gained by letting these problems become public knowledge, for they were all matters that would bring shame to one family or another. While the old people talked about these problems amongst themselves, they didn't talk about them with anyone outside their group. In fact, no one even knew that the old people were discussing these things.

My friend didn't know of such conferences among the old people until he was more than forty. He wasn't told anything regarding what the old people had discussed, but when he was at a loss as to how to handle the land emancipation, an old man told him, "Have the courage to do what is right," and this helped him. Then, at a meeting regarding agrarian reforms, when everyone was selfishly asserting their own interests, my friend said: "If there's anyone here who can, alone in the dark, place their hand on their chest and clearly assert 'I haven't done even the slightest thing wrong, and my father and grandfather acted properly as well, and my family's land was acquired without any injustice,' then please speak up." Hearing this, those who had spoken out grew silent. Thereafter, whenever talks reached an impasse, if someone opened with "I place my hand on my chest in the dark of night . . ." an answer was generally found.

I can still remember the time, as a child, when I went to a village meeting. I cannot recall whether I followed my grandfather there, or my father. Many had gathered and were in discussion. One man was asserting himself incessantly in a loud voice. Being a child, I had no idea what he was talking about, but I distinctly recall that he was talking alone. At this point an old man said, "Consider who you are before you speak." At this, the speaker fell silent. I have a truly vivid memory of that moment. Thereafter, when I started to travel, I often had the opportunity to meet old people of this kind. And I came to have a clear understanding of just how important a role they play.

Quite recently, at a party celebrating the publication of Nōda Tayoko's *The Older Sister Whose Arms were Cut Off,* I was interested when Imano Ensuke commended her, saying "Nōda-san, you're a mediating grandmother." Imano-san was a native of Fukushima Prefecture, and his grandmother was a "mediating grandmother" as well. Elderly people with stable lives and a good understanding of things generally take on this role. They are quite familiar with every aspect of the village and are forever reaching out to the unfortunate, which they do in such a way that others know nothing of it. Apparently at one or two in the morning, Imano-san's grandmother visited unhappy women in neighboring villages, delivered food to people who were without something to eat, and counseled the young wives who called in the middle of the night.

It would be easy to divulge people's wrongs, but some problems cannot be solved by contrition alone. Accordingly, the women sought the means to a solution among themselves. The perspective and aid of sensible and wise old women became barometers and supports for the young women. To know everything but appear to know nothing—this was necessary to the resolution of the various strains upon the village.

The tiny villages were so small that communal living was claustrophobic. The happenings in every house naturally became known to all, and knowing too much about one's neighbors made life stifling for everyone. One could not enjoy the ease of living to be found in cities. Nowadays, with a growing number of opportunities for employment other than farming, it is less common for members of the community to be face-to-face all day long, and life has become that much more comfortable. But when everyone was farming, when they were planting, weeding, and harvesting rice in close proximity, one could tell at a glance who was working and how hard, so a person couldn't shirk their work. When individuals tried to match their lives to

Nails embedded in a tree. Saku Island, Aichi Prefecture. October 1956.

the pace and rhythm of the world around them, they overexerted themselves. Often this constricting environment crushed free and easy behavior. Furthermore, daily life was exceedingly simple, as one was compelled to walk down a single, straight path forever.

Some people sought salvation by letting out pent-up energy at festivals and family parties and forgetting themselves in inane play. Others sought the private fulfillment of their wishes, doing their best to take actions out of sight. In addition to acting out against one's mother-in-law or daughter-in-law, a person might steal, or pursue a physical relationship. It seems that the physical relations between young men and women were looser than they are now, and this continued well into married life. When a woman could not handle the situation on her own, she often had to turn to a "mediating grandmother" for help.

On Saku Island in Aichi Prefecture, I was shown a tree into which dozens of six-inch nails had been driven. Hammered in to form the shapes of people, much like driving nails into straw dolls, they were evidence of one person cursing another. The tree into which the nails had been driven was in a forest behind the shrine. When the large broadleaf had withered and died, the shrine had sold the tree and the buyer, intending to use it for firewood, had cut it down. While the buyer was chopping it up, he apparently found nails buried some six inches down beneath the bark. It had probably taken more than a hundred years for a nail to become this deeply embedded. Not knowing what this was, the man who'd been chopping up the tree took it to a mediating grandmother to find out. She immediately recognized that this was a curse but held her tongue.

This elderly woman had counseled a substantial number of women in the community. She told me that women came to her more often regarding relations with men than because of problems with other women. The nails in this tree were most likely related to problems between men and women, but she told me that no particularly grave complications had occurred in her lifetime. Before any problems progressed that far, they were usually resolved.

The wide world beyond the village's borders offered one solution. When a problem could not be solved within the community, a person was asked to leave. In the distant past, forcing people out was not as easily done; whatever happened in the village had to be resolved there. I was told that, of late, when things became tangled people rarely had to be sent away. Instead, they left of their own accord.

Those who became mediators had to hand over their position as the head of the family to their children. Only when they were no longer encumbered by social responsibilities could they take on this role.

It must have been at least twenty-four or twenty-five years ago that I was walking along the west coast of the Tateishi Peninsula, west of Tsuruga in Fukui Prefecture, when I heard voices coming from a small temple above the road. I climbed up and found ten elderly women sitting in a circle inside a tiny hall, eating lunch from a large, tiered picnic box. When I asked what they were doing, they told me they had confined themselves to the temple for a meeting of the Kannon [Goddess of Mercy] Club. When a woman turned sixty, she joined this group. Now and then they spent the night at the temple or gathered at one of their houses for food, drink, and talk.

They encouraged me to join them and I, together with a friend, sat down on the verandah, shared in their feast, and talked with them for a while. Half in jest, and while offering us this and that to eat, they said, "The two of you haven't found wives yet, have you? Marry a good woman. A bad wife means a lean life." Because we were young men and strangers they spoke freely about anything and everything. When I inquired about the Kannon Club in detail, one of them broke in with "the club is for bad-mouthing our daughters-in-law." But this was amended immediately by another who explained, "old people complain a lot and, in spite of ourselves, we are tempted to criticize our daughters-in-law. By talking with one another in a place like this, we can get by without saying things directly to them that would be hurtful."

But if they spread what they had heard throughout the village, would that not be more than the daughters could bear? "We do no such thing," they explained. "We too were daughter-in-laws once, and it never came back to us from someone else that our mother-in-laws had been complaining about us." This was a grievance club exclusively for elderly women. I found the idea quite interesting. Of their own accord, they had created a place that was removed from society.

Such groups were particularly common in Western Japan, where a person moves up through a clearly defined age grade system [becoming a member of various social groups based on age] as they grow older. When they reach a certain age the elderly retire, whereas in the Tōhoku and Hokuriku districts [in northeast Japan] the elderly most often continue to control the household until an old age. In such cases, the daughter-in-law forever occupies the position of daughter-in-law without becoming the mother and similarly, her husband cannot sit at the head of the table. All things considered, where a clearly defined retirement system was in place, the role of the elderly was clearly defined as well.

I have not attended many village meetings. While I have come upon quite a few, I have refrained from joining in for fear that, as a stranger, I will disturb the atmosphere. There were times, though, that for various reasons I had to participate, or I was looking for someone who happened to be attending a meeting, and when I found them there stayed on to participate.

Once, in the mountains of Tosa, when I said that I was from Tokyo, I was pulled inside the local meeting hall while a meeting was taking place. It had been held to make arrangements for cutting the underbrush on a community-owned mountain. The villagers were deciding who would cut where. The headman would say the name of a location on the mountain and ask who would go there, whereupon two or three people who had exchanged looks with one another offered their names. They didn't draw lots and the groups appear to have been decided right then and there, and yet the work of deciding proceeded quite smoothly. It seemed that conditions would be pointedly different depending on where one was on the mountain, yet the people didn't appear to be competing for the better locations. I wondered how this could be but did not have the opportunity to ask because, after the meeting had ended, the villagers asked me to tell them about life in Tokyo.

Most meetings are gatherings of household heads, and only on rare occasions do women attend as their proxies. When they do come, they sit in a corner and speak little. There are meetings that only women attend, though few are village-wide. They are generally voluntary, not related to village government, and most often are social, religious, or work related. Gatherings to drink tea are held frequently in the area around the Inland Sea. The fare is quite plain—usually tea and pickled vegetables—and only a small number of women get together for an hour or two of talk. Often women will gather for events that there is no need for the men to attend: to celebrate the first washing of a baby's hair; the naming of a baby; the first visit to the local shrine; for a service one hundred days after a person's death; and other such occasions. Women also share simple food and drink at the beginning and end of various work duties, or when they gather for a moxa treatment [when mugwort is burned directly on the skin]. Most of the gatherings that are accompanied by food, with the exception of those related to religion or work, end in idle talk, and I have had many opportunities to join them. About half the time is spent in playful conversation with a lot of laughter, but information about the village is also exchanged, and one is given an adequate sense of what each family is like. Such gatherings are called "tea parties."

What began as gatherings to drink tea became meetings for work as well. In places where rice growing or sericulture thrived, decisions regarding the schedule for the collaborative raising of silkworms or the planting of rice were generally made at women's meetings. And there were gatherings for house-building parties, funerals, and other occasions when there was cooperative work performed only by the women.

There are many examples of old documents surviving in the possession of specific old families. Not a few of these are families who, by virtue of heredity, were village headmen for generation after generation. However, there are also numerous examples of villages in which the headman kept old documents in a chest or register box that was used specifically for that purpose. Though there may have been one or two families that did not participate in community groups, most of the families did. When people participated in age-dependent groups [youth groups for the young, old people's groups for the elderly and so on], if a gap

in the power of the individual families existed, the group func-
tioned less effectively. Thus, it came to be an important condition
that, when participating in a group, no distinction be made in
keeping with a family's status.

Based upon my travels to date, my impression is that the age
grade system made a strong appearance in Western Japan, became
diluted in Eastern Japan, and in the vicinity of Iwate Prefecture
[far in the northeast], there were many villages in which youth
groups did not even exist. These days the characteristics of east
and west have melted together, and there are a number of villages
that fall between the type wherein patriarchal family bonds are
strong and the type where non-kinship bonds are strong.

In places where the age grade system is well developed, a retirement system generally has a strong presence as well. Villages
of this type had an exceedingly large number of village-wide community activities and shared labor. In places like Tsushima, where
many old customs remain intact, it would appear that individuals
dedicate more than one hundred days a year to community activities, work details, and public services. Villagers work together
in the mountains and along the shore. They build roads, organize
and attend festivals, memorial services, and public gatherings,
and they do farm work on community land. On the remaining
days they do their own family farm work, but given the limited
time remaining the management of one's own affairs naturally
suffered. And the farther back one goes, the more public service
work there appears to have been.

In order to reduce this community labor and public service
as much as possible, people tried to give up their position as head
of the household quickly, for once a person had retired, they no
longer had to participate in public service and community work.
Thus the practice came into being where people tried to find
wives for their sons as soon as possible, hand over the household to them, and then exert themselves on behalf of the family.
Studying the family history of the Saitōs, a family of hereditary
village heads living in Torikai Village on the west coast of Awaji
Island, I found that—generation after generation—the eldest

son married when he had turned twenty and, at the same time, the father retired and moved into a retirement house that had been built for him on the property. The retiring fathers were in their forties, an age at which they could look forward to working still more. In this manner, early in the modern era, over the course of three generations the Saitōs cleared more than twenty acres for rice paddies.

In Western Japan, where there was still land that had not been cultivated, there are numerous examples of this sort of young retirement. The creation of a branch family at the time of retirement, and inheritance by the youngest male child, went hand in hand with young retirement. In this context, the position occupied by the village elderly was clear: they quickly withdrew from village politics and public service but continued to participate in festivals. In this respect, they continued to be connected to the village's public affairs. And they often attended village meetings in place of the head of the household. Because the father had removed himself from the public affairs of the village, he was seen as a retired person. But, because he was not bound by village affairs, he was immensely free, and his way of thinking was not restricted.

It would seem that the fact that Japanese literature from the Middle Ages was preserved by hermits shares some common ground with the family retirement system—within the village, the retired were responsible for the handing down of culture. As regards transmitters—those who passed down information, stories, culture, and the like—it would appear that there are some differences between the east and the west [in Japan]. Most of the transmitters Mizusawa Kenichi [a folklorist] relied upon when he recently gathered a large number of fine, old tales in Niigata Prefecture were elderly women. Prior to that, when Sasaki Kizen collected many old tales in Iwate Prefecture, most of his sources were old women too. However, in Western Japan, stories are more often handed down by men. Grandpa Sashi on Okinoerabu Island, Grandpa Kuttan on Tsushima Island, and when one looks at other locations, there are more male transmitters as well. I should not make this statement rashly without first mapping out the distribution of transmitters, but I find this matter fascinating. I can infer that stories passed down in Western Japan most often concern the community as a whole, while in Eastern Japan they are passed down within and focus on individual families.

Up until the beginning of the modern era, a rural samurai family lived in my home village. They built temples and shrines and were popular with their fellow villagers, though no one from the family was ever the village headman. They did act as head of the local community, however [the village being made up of a number of distinct communities]. On one occasion the rural samurai was nominated to the position of village head, and several leaders from the village went to call on him. He scattered straw chaff on the floor and said that a village head, like straw, produced a lot of waste and got dirty as well. He then rejected their offer, saying that rather than make a mess, it would be better for him to be of service to everyone.

Generally the person nominated by the villagers to become the village head was then officially appointed by the district governor. The heads of individual communities were also appointed, and a farmer's representative was nominated as well. This person served as the chair at meetings, convening the gatherings and making arrangements for various village events. Usually the farmer's representative was replaced every year. It is not clear when the institution of village meetings came into being, but it would appear that villages shared similar social customs at the beginning of the modern era with the system of self-government found in villages today. The elderly oversaw village matters at a higher level, though they did not have the authority to make final decisions. At the same time, at the discussions themselves, people gave careful consideration to one another, and more than finding solutions, a sort of exchange of knowledge took place. Individual opinions were then consolidated by the farmer's representative and the community head and put in writing.

Chapter 15

The Story of Kawame

[Aomori Prefecture, June and August 1963]

I. HAPPENINGS IN KAWAME'S PAST

Kawame is a community within Sai Village (in the Shimokita District of Aomori Prefecture) that branched off from Hata of the Kawauchi Township, in the same district. Hata is a *matagi* [hunting] village, and when I learned from the people there that the people of Kawame had split off to live separately, I wanted to see what differences there might be between the parent village and its branch village.

Located on the west coast of the Shimokita Peninsula, Sai was once known for being an old port town. There are two reasons for this. First, this was the departure point for a ferry to Hakodate, Hokkaido. Hakodate began to grow around the end of the Tokugawa [Edo] period. Many of those who made the crossing to Hokkaido via the Nanbu Domain traveled along the north coast of the Shimokita Peninsula until they reached Sai and took a boat from here. There was a harbor in Ōma on the north end of Shimokita Peninsula, but Sai was better suited for landing a boat. In those days ports on the Shimokita Peninsula didn't have a breakwater, jetty, or pier, so boats were brought right up onto the beach. A gangplank was then laid down between the boat and the beach, and people stepped up onto the land. In this way beaches where it was easy to land a boat became ports.

The other reason for Sai's renown as a port was that a wonderful natural-growth forest of cypress and cedar was to be found in the mountains around Sai. Boats came from various places along the Japan Sea coast and carried off cypress to be used as building material. They also took cedar, mostly to Hokkaido, for the building of boats. The mountains around Kawame grew thick with such trees, but the people who settled there had no interest in logging work and mostly made a living hunting.

Wanting to learn about hunting, I first visited Grandpa Kamiyama Kanetaka and asked him all sorts of questions about it. I learned, however, that almost no hunting is done here now and that Kawame has become a logging village. And because this was originally a community of hunters, they own almost no land. Yet there are now twenty-eight households. There must be a good reason for a single tiny community to grow in such a remote place in the mountains, and a great personal effort must have been involved. There is a good explanation for this, one that I heard from Grandpa Tsuboya Torazō on my second visit. Hearing his story, I was filled with a youthful enthusiasm as I descended the darkening valley to Sai. I had been touched by the life of this farmer.

In the beginning there were no homes in Kawame, but the *matagi* came from Hata to hunt the deer and serow [a species of goat antelope] that lived in abundance in this valley. They built huts and stayed in them during the hunting season. Then, around the end of the Tokugawa period, two families settled in a place that people refer to as Old Kawame, a short distance behind what is now known as Kawame. These were the ancestors of Tsuboya and Hatanaka. Shortly thereafter, Kawaya and Nitta came as well. While these four families first came here to hunt, they settled here to work as woodsmen. Tsuboya Torazō's grandfather was among the four families who settled in Old Kawame. He worked cutting down cedar in the vicinity of Sai. Large cedar trees grew all the way from Kawame to Sai.

Other *matagi*, who continued to hunt, also came and stayed in the four houses that had been built and went out hunting from there. Two of these hunters decided to settle as well, and they moved to what is now Kawame. In this way there were now six households, the two families that were primarily living as *matagi*—the Kamiyamas and Shimoyamas—having come later. That was late in the 1880s.

Although these mountains had previously been owned by the domain, when state and privately owned land were divided in the first years of the Meiji period, forestland that had been planted by private citizens generally became privately owned forest. But because the people here had secretly planted trees on land that was not their own and feared punishment, no one came forward when the government—knowing this was not a natural growth forest but one that had been planted—asked those who had planted trees to give notice of this. Finally, those who could hide no longer timidly filed notices. Fearing the consequences, they sold their land to Marushō, a merchant in Sai who bought up the land for close to nothing and became the owner of a large forest.

After the division of state and privately owned land, people were given the right to cut down trees on the land for which a notice had not been filed, with the understanding that 20 percent of the profits derived would go to the government and 80 percent to the individual. For forestlands planted in the Meiji period, profits were to be divided 30/70. This is to say that the logging of rented land was allowed. Being in the possession of vast forestlands, Marushō established a lumber mill and continues to manage it to this day.

Walking in the mountains in this area I found a surprising number of mixed-growth forests. I was told that these were places where the cypress trees had burned down in forest fires. Apparently when the cypress burn, a variety of other trees grow in thick in their place. These trees are then cut down, and, after the land is used for slash-and-burn agriculture, cedar are planted on it. Around 1900 the government's forest management office went into the business of logging cypress trees. The people of Kawame did not participate in this work, so laborers came in from elsewhere, many from Tsugaru and Akita.

Then, in the Taishō period [1912–26], a man by the name of Takefuji Hitoshi became the head of the local forest management office. He was a fine and compassionate man, and he avidly promoted the participation of local labor in the logging work. There had to be at least ten people in each work crew, but they weren't able to come up with ten people in Kawame. So they decided to increase the number of families in the community [by setting up branch families]. The number of families grew, and they were able to form a work crew. When these crews were formed, ten people came from Kawame and thirty from elsewhere, and Tsuboya Torazō became the foreman. Until then, the people of Kawame had worked as part-time laborers, planting trees on government-owned land when this work was available. But with government logging, they worked as regular laborers, their wages were good, and they had work all year round so their lives became markedly more stable. They called theirs the Tsuboya Crew. At its largest there were as many as forty members. When there weren't enough people, they brought in fishermen from Sai.

The people of Kawame had close ties to these fishermen, who all had boats they fished with along the shore. The hulls of these boats were made by hollowing out the logs from large trees. Boards were then attached along the sides to make the boats deeper, so they could go out into the waves without taking in water. *Katsura* and beech trees were best for making them.

The people of Hata specialized in making these hulls. No one else could do this work. Those who had left Hata for Kawame also had these skills. Accordingly, they made hulls for the fishing boats in Sai and the villages on either side of it along the west coast of the Shimokita Peninsula. In this way they came to have a deep connection with the fishermen.

The trees used for the making of hulls had to be large. If one wanted the hull of the boat to be three feet wide, the tree had to have a diameter of more than that. These trees were felled with a saw, cut to boat's length, and roughly hewn with a hatchet. They were then refined with a broadaxe. The inside was gouged out with a blade to make it boat shaped. This was difficult work.

In the days when hulls were made from a single piece of wood, they were gouged deeply, and the sides didn't have to be made particularly high. But as the number of large trees decreased, it became more difficult to make a hull with only one tree. So trees were cut in two, and one half was used to make one side of the hull and the other half was joined to it to make the other side. And the hulls became shallower.

When a hull had been completed, it was floated down river to Sai. Because the river was small and shallow, they made dams here and there. When water had accumulated it was released to float the hull downstream. One person would ride in the hull and push off with a pole, while another used a rope to pull the boat along. This was not something an amateur could do. In this way, the people of Kawame made ten or twenty hulls every year.

II. THE LIFE OF THE *MATAGI* [HUNTERS]

Hunting continued to flourish in Kawame up until the Taishō period. People came from Hata to hunt the many serow and deer in this area. In the summer they built lean-tos to sleep in, and in the winter they stayed with the Tsuboyas and Hatanakas. Kamiyama Yauemon was also able to do carpentry work and bought an old house in Sai. After pulling lumber down the river and rebuilding the house, he moved in. About ten years after he had fixed up the house and settled in, the number of deer suddenly dropped off and he was no longer able to make a living as a hunter. Just the same, he continued to hunt a little at a time into the Taishō period.

Some bears also remain, and three were caught three years ago. Around November, before snowfall, the bears look for holes in rocky areas and the hollows of trees to hibernate for the winter. When a tree has fallen and its roots are hollowed out they call this *futade*, and when there is a cavity in a tree it is called *takashi*. The bears are most often found in these places. They are particularly easy to find when they have left claw marks on the trees. The *matagi* take their dogs to hunt the bears when they emerge, around March. The hunters root about in the *futade* with a spear and if they find a bear there, set the dogs on it and shoot the bear. In the old days they also speared them.

When they hunted deer, the *matagi* went out as a group with their dogs. Chased by the dogs, the deer generally came out by the river, so the *matagi* would wait there to shoot them. If the hunt was near the coast, the deer usually headed for the ocean. When that happened, the *matagi* would ask fishermen offshore to catch the deer alive. Deer that went into the ocean were easy to catch.

The *matagi* also used the dogs to chase after serow and usually cornered them in the back ends of valleys. They mostly hunted serow with spears. They had matchlock guns too, but because it took time to load the next shot, spears were most often used. But when they hunted bear, they used both spears and matchlocks. Now, there are good hunting rifles so spears have fallen out of use.

As for the *matagi's* attire, they wore a kerchief headband tied in the back, an undershirt, a shirt, a quilted cloth kimono, a sleeveless top made of dog or serow skin, and a straw raincoat on top of that. They wore close-fitting trousers, but began wearing pantaloons gathered at the ankles around the end of the Meiji period. On their feet they wore straw sandals or sometimes serow skin shoes. At their waist hung a satchel made from the skin of a bear's head. A hatchet and hemp cord also hung there, and they always carried a tinderbag containing a flint stone and steel. Attached to one end of the string used to close the tinderbag was a piece of bamboo that had been cut so its joint remained. A piece of charcoal was kept inside the bamboo with a lid on top. The flint and steel were struck to make a spark that fell onto the charcoal in the bamboo. In this manner, the charcoal was lit. When the end of a rope made of finely shredded and braided cypress bark was inserted into the charcoal fire that smoldered in the bamboo tube, it caught on fire as well. The lit rope was then pulled out of the bamboo tube and used to ignite a matchlock. When a bear is killed, it is skinned on the spot, but its head is left intact. Before the bear is skinned, it is positioned as if walking to the west and then turned over so that its stomach is facing upward. The *matagi* chant an incantation while sharpening the blade. The skin on the bear's "branches" (the four limbs) is stripped off using tree branches, and the meat from the "limbs" is carried back separately. Originally, the *matagi* ate the meat themselves, and anything left over was dried and kept. Now they sell the meat in Sai.

In April, in a spear dedication ceremony, the spears used over the previous year are all offered up, and the year's hunting comes to an end. At this time everyone gathers in the head *matagi's* house for *Niibone*, a memorial service for the bears that were killed. An offering of *sake* is made, and everyone eats and drinks together. The head *matagi* is a person who knows the mountains well.

I should add that when a bear is killed, a celebration is held right then and there. If a bear is killed in the spring, a "bush warbler" banner is placed at the head of the bear. For a fall bear, a "dead tree" banner is prepared. These banners are cut differently for a male or female bear. Kudō Ishimatsu of Hata knew these banners well, so when someone forgot how to make one they went to him to learn.

From the beginning, few *matagi* lived in Kawame, and it was rare for them to hunt together in large numbers. When hunting, nothing resembling a territorial border existed and often, when chasing a bear, the *matagi* would enter mountains that belonged to other villages. But there were no territorial disputes among the *matagi*.

Furthermore, when something was caught, the meat was divided evenly among all who had participated in the hunt. If the meat was sold, the money was divided evenly as well. On occasion the dogs were also given a share, but it was truly a scanty one.

For the most part fishermen bought the bear skins to make arm covers that kept them warm and protected them from getting cut when they fished. Because it wasn't possible for one fisherman to buy a whole bear skin, a group of friends would go in together and divide it among themselves. Serow skins were often used to make sleeveless tops. The *matagi* didn't convert skins into leather. They sent them to tanners in Aomori and Hakodate.

In the days when *matagi* hunted bear, a bear's gall brought a good price. People came from Toyama to buy it, and one *monme* [0.132 oz.] sold for two thousand yen. Because people drank portions that were about the size of two grains of millet, one *monme* was enough for dozens of portions.

Bear bones were also used as medicine. Burned and pounded into a powder, they were quite effective against colds, diarrhea, and the like. The bones from bear, deer, and serow, burned, ground to a powder, and mixed together, were called *sankoyaki*, a highly valued medicine that was effective in treating a lot of illnesses. Accordingly, when these animals were caught, their bones were set aside and charred.

As long as there was a lot of game, hunting paid well, but in the Taishō period there was a sudden drop in the animal population, and the *matagi* had no choice but to focus their efforts on logging and charcoal-making.

III. THE GROWTH OF THE VILLAGE

In 1887, Kamiyama Yauemon and Shimoyama Sannosho came to Kawame from Hata. In the course of three generations the Kamiyamas created four branch families and now have a total of five households. The Tsuboyas, who came to Kawame first, now have three households. Hatanaka Sakichi's family, also among the first to come here, left for Sai. Their house and paddies remain, however, and are being rented to people in Kawame. This is be-

cause only the women in this family remain alive now. The Kawayas continue to live in Kawame. Their branch family has taken the name Minatoya, and there are now three Minatoya households. The Nittas went to Hokkaido so are no longer here.

The Komagines also came from Hata. Husband and wife, they came to Kawame to do logging work and then settled down, but the husband died and the wife, taking her child with her, re-married Suzuki, who had come here from Akita to work. Others have moved here from elsewhere. Takahisa Kaneharu came here as a mineworker and settled down. Manabe Aguri also came as a mineworker and has been here for ten years. Kon is from Miyata, in the Higashi Tsugaru District. He came to make charcoal and stayed on. Katō came from Harada to make charcoal, married a girl from Kawame, built a house, and settled down. Higashide is from Sai, and he came here to do logging work in the government-owned forest. There are also the Miyazawas.

The above twenty families have lived in Kawame since before

the war. Others set up branch families after the war, and there are those who repatriated from Manchuria, making for a total of twenty-eight households now. Two Tsuboyas and two Kudōs went to Manchuria. One Kudō died and the other three returned, built homes, and set up branch families. Add the schoolteacher's family and at present the population is overflowing. Those who established branch families after the war, and those who repatriated, have no land.

Ten people in Kawame are doing government logging at present, though they originally numbered more than twenty. Even then, there weren't enough people, and they hired fishermen from Sai. Logging work has continued to drop off. One reason is that trees are now cut selectively rather than by clear-cutting. The people doing this government logging work are all over forty years old and the heads of their households. The others are mainly off doing logging work in the Kamikawa region of Hokkaido as this pays much better.

As for the women, of those who graduated from junior high school, four are in Hokkaido doing farmwork and three are in Shizuoka working in the *mikan* [mandarin orange] orchards and in a cannery. This is all seasonal labor, so the women return home in the winter when work is slow. It can't be said that traveling for work is all that popular. But as there are only about ten people in the community who are doing government logging work, the others will have to start finding other employment, and the number of people going away for work will probably grow.

The number of households in Kawame reached twenty before the war. The number of households increased at the request of the government forest management office's head, but also because farmland was cleared and people were increasingly able to grow their own food. The families that were added later did not come into existence because they had work but because they were repatriating, or because they were unable to form branch families elsewhere and had to do so while remaining in the community.

IV. THE HISTORY OF RECLAMATION AND THE FOREST

The people who first settled in Kawame, while working in the mountains, also performed slash-and-burn agriculture to grow millet and secure a food supply. The settlers had practiced slash-and-burn agriculture [*yakihata,* literally "burned field"] extensively in their native village of Hata; it was probably for this reason that Hata was so named.

Even before the people of Hata settled in Kawame, slash-and-burn agriculture was practiced in this valley by the people of Isoya. Though now a fishing village, Isoya, across the mountains on the coast, was originally a community of woodsmen who made a living cutting down cypress. In areas where they had cut down the cypress, the people of Isoya burned what remained and grew millet for two or three years, and then planted cedar instead.

When I crossed the mountains from Isoya to Kawame I found places where slash-and-burn fields had become permanent fields; areas where the cedar had just been cut, the undergrowth burned, and a field planted; and sections where large cedar trees remained standing. The stands of cedar were half to three quarters of an acre at the most, suggesting that in the old days this was probably about the area of cypress that was cut down in one year. The larger cedar trees were about fifty or sixty years old, and they would likely be cut down before they grew much older. These stands of cedar were everywhere and were probably planted by individual families. There were also large sections of trees that had been planted recently by the community as a whole.

In this way the people of Isoya had advanced into the Kawame valley and long repeated a cycle of cutting down cypress, practicing slash-and-burn agriculture, and planting cedar. The people of Kawame had followed their example.

In the old days, most slash-and-burn farming was performed in the valleys rather than high in the mountains but when the number of families increased, and slash-and-burn agriculture no longer produced enough food, the people of Kawame asked the government forestry office to select land for them to clear permanent fields.

Millet was planted in the first year, soybeans in the second, and *daikon* radish in the third. Millet was the staple food, the soybeans were used to make *miso*, and *daikon* radish was pickled. Millet was eaten at all times except *Bon* and New Year's, and a lot of it was grown. The millet was cut and tied in bundles. Still in bundle form, the ears were then beaten to remove the seeds. The seeds were then fanned to separate out the shells, cooked in a pot, and spread out to dry. Once dry, the seeds were ground in a mortar until they had been polished. If ground poorly, they were reduced to powder. Millet was ground by two people using a pestle and a large mortar. A board was placed atop the mortar to keep the millet from flying out.

Originally, the people in Kawame didn't grow much *awa* [foxtail millet]. They started growing it in the middle of the Meiji period when the number of permanent fields increased. A sticky variety of foxtail millet was often grown and used in place of rice to make "rice" cakes. Buckwheat was almost never grown until the Taishō period, and when the fields became permanent, a lot of *adzuki* beans were grown.

There was very little variety of foodstuffs in this area. The people of Kawame almost never dug up and ate fernbrake roots and, although there were horse chestnuts, they didn't know they could be eaten.

Since they settled here in Kawame, the villagers have never experienced a crop failure to the point of having nothing to eat. They were poor but somehow found a way to survive. One reason for this may have been an abundance of edible wild plants. At any rate, prior to the turn of the century there were few families and very little interaction with the surrounding communities. The people lived quietly. Surrounded by a vastness of nature and a substantial number of deer and serow as they were, one can imagine that they did not lack for something to eat.

Then, around 1900, the government forest management

office began logging this peaceful place. Loggers came in large numbers from Akita and Tsugaru and began cutting down the cypress trees that grew in the surrounding mountains. Unlike the cutting performed by individuals prior to that time, large areas of land were clear-cut. Where the incline of the exposed slopes was gentle, the land could then be used for growing crops. Until that time, the only people in Kawame with permanent fields were Tsuboya and Hatanaka. I don't know how it came to be that these families had privately owned farmland, but during the feudal era land that was owned by the domain apparently became the possession of whoever cleared it.

Temples owned a lot of land long ago, and lumber merchants had extensive forestland as well. In the Noto Store in Sai, old documents show a record of several hundred acres of privately owned forestland behind Ōhata. At the time of the division of government and privately owned land, in the first years of the Meiji period, the owners didn't have their land surveyed, thinking that an acknowledgment of ownership would lead to an increase in their tax burden. So it all became government land. Much later the people filed a lawsuit in an effort to get their land back from the government, but they lost the case. Now only an oral tradition remains, and there is almost no understanding of who originally owned what. Accordingly, since the time of its inception the community has not jointly owned land, and no individual family has profited from land ownership. It can be said that there is extremely little attachment to the land.

Now people talk of rights and obligations, but until the Meiji period people didn't even have a clear understanding of what rights were or what their own property was. Tsuboya Torazō became the community's representative when he was twenty-five. He was young, but he was selected because he was able to read. But he didn't know anything about the world. In the end of Meiji, around the time Tsuboya-san became representative, the peo-

A log storage area near Kawame, Aomori Prefecture. June 1963.

ple of Kawame cleared forty-five acres of land along the river below Kawame and farmed and planted cedar on it. This was private land, owned by the people of Sai. The story had been passed down among the people of Kawame that Sai had given it to Kawame in the beginning of Meiji. But the people of Sai protested, saying they had no recollection of giving away the land. When the matter was investigated, no written document was found. So after the trees had been cut, the land was returned.

On another occasion when the people of Kawame sold cedar and the land it was on to build a shrine to the community's guardian deity, the people of Sai complained, saying the land was Sai's. But the cedar had been planted by the people of Kawame during the feudal era and therefore should have been in the name of those who had planted it, in keeping with the division of government and private lands in early Meiji. So the people of Kawame went to Sai and had the land returned.

As a result of these experiences, the people of Kawame became cautious with regard to the borrowing of private land. As much as possible, they either borrowed government-owned land or bought it. When they formed a crew for the logging of government-owned forests, they had to have at least ten permanent households in order to have enough people to organize a work party. To increase the number of permanent residents, they promoted the clearing of farmland. The government forest management office approved the use of this land with relative ease. Of those who had bought permanent farmland and cleared it before the war, the following people owned paddy land:

Tsuboya	1.5 acres
Kamiyama	.5 acres
Kon	1.25 acres
Miyazawa	.5 acres
Hatanaka	.5 acres

This paddy land is immediately south of Kawame. Tsuboya Torazō was the first to clear land there and to grow rice on it. Apparently his crop did not yield a single grain in the first year. But he didn't give up, and his harvest grew a little every year.

As stated above, the government forest management office also permitted the use of other gently graded land after the cypress and cedar had been clear-cut. The people then cultivated it and divided it so each family had between 1.25 and 1.5 acres of land. This remains borrowed land, however.

In 1930 a track was laid from Sai to some four miles behind Kawame for the logging of cypress and cedar. From then until just after the war, a truly immense amount of logging took place in these mountains. This was a busy time for Kawame. But the track was removed in 1960, so now trucks carry logs that are not clear-cut but selectively culled, making it difficult to convert land that had been logged to agricultural use. After the war the government forest management office's afforestation activities began to flourish. As a result, there is no longer land that can be used for farming.

In the Shōwa period [beginning in 1926], life in the community has improved markedly thanks to the villagers' participation in the state logging effort. While the people of Kawame used to eat millet and foxtail millet alone, they are now mixing those grains with rice. People used to buy their rice, but an increasing number wanted to have their own paddies and grow their own rice. Then, seven or eight years ago, plastic seedling trays [in which seedlings are raised before they are transferred to the paddy] came along, and a strain of rice that could be grown earlier in the year was developed. When rice cultivation became possible here, the number of people who grew millet dropped, and the people of Kawame turned their energy to the development of paddies. In the tablelands along the coast where there was water, paddy land was cleared. Four people from Kawame participated in the reclamation of these coastal tablelands between Sai and Harada and thereby acquired land there.

Tsuboya-san had noticed this land, overgrown with grasses, and suggested to Takahashi Toshikazu that it be cleared for paddies. Around 1920, hearing that the national government provided subsidies, Takahashi-san asked an official from the prefectural government to look at the land and was told that he would have to pay seventeen hundred yen out of his own pocket. Not having that much money, Takahashi-san cleared four acres of land that was submerged in water.

After the war, when the decision was made to clear this land, because the idea had originally been Tsuboya-san's, people from Kawame were allowed to participate. Kamiyama Yukio, Kawaya Yoshitarō, and Miyazawa Shigezō have half an acre apiece, and Kon's younger brother has .63 acres. Now they borrow a car and all ride in that to farm their land. After the harvest, they have their rice polished in Sai and then take it back home to Kawame. So nine households in Kawame are able to grow their own rice now. But given the present circumstances, this number will probably not grow.

Meanwhile, various expenses are incurred in the administration of the community, making it desirable for the people of Kawame to have shared assets as well. Toward this end, the community borrowed fifty acres of land from the government forest management office in 1928 and planted cedar on it. These trees are now one foot in diameter at eye level. Again, in 1950, they borrowed fifty acres of land and planted it as well. These trees are now about four inches in diameter. Profits from the sale of trees are to be divided 30/70 between the government and the people. The trees planted in 1928 are now ready to be cut, and it is anticipated that this harvest will significantly enrich the community.

As the community-owned forest grows, the matter of how to handle the membership of branch families has become a problem. When a branch family is set up within the community, the main family builds a house for them and gives them a suitable portion of their own land. In the past, a branch family could also pay to join in the ownership of the community forest. Around the end of the war, three hundred yen was enough to join. But now, no matter what one pays, they cannot join. Twenty households are joint owners of the first tree planting and twenty-five households share ownership of the second. At the time of the second planting several households bought two shares apiece. These were families in which a younger brother would be establishing a branch family soon, and they paid two shares in money and in labor so they could hand over one share to the younger brother when he formed a branch family.

Yet this was not enough to solve the ownership problem. Because people who had come later or who had formed branch families later were not included, there are plans for a third community planting on forty acres of land to be borrowed from the government forest management office.

Partners in the community forest must all participate in planting and other related labor, and those who do not participate must pay. In the past, as long as one person participated from each household, all labor was given equal value regardless of gender. Now the people of Kawame conform to the government forest management office's pay scale as follows:

Adult male	700 yen
Male under 18	550 yen
Female	400 yen

When there is community forest work to be done, if an adult male participates on the one hand and a woman on the other, the woman's household must pay the difference of three hundred yen to the partnership or put in that much extra work.

The distinguished service of Takefuji-san, the head of the government forest management office, was influential in making community afforestation more popular than individual planting in this area. Takefuji-san taught the people of Kawame how to plant cedar, and after setting up parcels of land, he had the people plant on them. Kawame's first planting was on just such a parcel. In celebration of the Crown Prince's marriage [in 1924], Takefuji-san lent 7.5 acres of land to the Young Men's Association and had them plant cedar there. Forty years have passed since, and this is now a fine forest.

Around the same time, Takefuji-san set up a charcoal-making association. Saying that the management of this association would run more smoothly if they had their own endowment, he loaned them 4.5 acres of land and had them plant trees on it. He did this not only for Kawame but for Isoya as well. But the people of Isoya had a long tradition of individual families planting cedar, and it was a tradition that was not easy for them to part with. So, while they borrowed a parcel of land as a community, they divided it up into sections that were then planted individually.

Long ago the term for the loaning of forestland was eighty years, but now the trees are cut down after forty years, and it is rare for the loan to be extended. Instead, afforestation by the government forest management office has increased.

V. THE VILLAGE YOUTH AS PERFORMERS

For the people of Kawame to have cohesion, they needed to

have something at their core. They determined that this should be an *ujigami* [a guardian deity]. So they went to the Mito household in Sai and brought back an Inari [fox] shrine and placed it at the southern edge of the community. For a community of only twenty households, the shrine was almost too fine.

That was around the end of the Meiji period. The festival day for the shrine is March 3. To make things lively, people from the community went to Yagoe and hired a *kagura* troupe to come and perform sacred music and dancing in Kawame. Then, in time, when the number of households had grown and there were seven or eight young men, the community hired a teacher from Mena, in Higashioke Village, to teach them *kagura*. Thus it came to pass that they performed their own *kagura*.

There was no school in Kawame until late in the 1890s, and the school in Sai was nothing more than a shack. Not a single child from Kawame attended that school; for this reason no one knew how to read or write. When Tsuboya-san was young, he gathered the other young men into a group. They built a small shed in the village where they met every evening to discuss things, and sometimes spent the night. After talking it over, the men decided that they would study together. They visited the elementary school teacher in Sai, asked him to write a few characters and teach them how to read them, then went back to their shed and practiced writing together. After a week had passed, they took what they'd written to Sai for the teacher to evaluate and asked him to write down new characters. Learning to read and write together, the group of young men became exceptionally close.

In 1912, when the [Meiji] emperor passed away, all musical and other performances were suspended. Around that time, a theatrical troupe led by Nakamura Umejirō had come to these parts but, due to the ban, they were unable to perform. They were utterly distressed, but hearing talk of a group of young men who lived together, studied hard, and ardently performed *kagura*, they came to Kawame. The theatrical troupe was from Akita, and when they came to Kawame they discovered that it was only a small community, not the kind of place to hold a performance. But the people living here were all good people, and the young men were enthusiastic. Drawn to this place, the troupe's leader stayed on. He disbanded the troupe and its members scattered in all directions. Nakamura-san encouraged the people of the village to try their hand at acting. Tsuboya Torazō, twenty-five and the head of the young men's group at the time, readily agreed and formed a troupe with the young men at its core, including other members of the community as well. They were all eager and made quick progress. The principal plays they learned were *Matsumaeya Gorōbē*, *Iwami Shigetarō*, and *Account of the Ichinosedon Army*. Though not much, it was enough for three or four days of performances. Their teacher was so good that they learned quickly and reached a level where they could go out and perform without embarrassing themselves. And having inherited the Nakamura troupe's costumes, they had a complete wardrobe.

What is more, shortly thereafter a Kabuki troupe came to Ōma, but for some reason very few people came to watch them. When they couldn't pay for their lodgings, their costumes were taken from them and they fled. Kawame bought the costumes for three hundred and fifty yen and, together with the other costumes from the Nakamura troupe they had seven wicker trunks of clothing. So, in terms of being equipped, no one in the vicinity held a candle to them. In the Taishō period, when the Abeshiro Mine opened in the Kawauchi Township, the troupe received an invitation and performed for three days to much praise. Though Kawame was but a small community in the mountains, when it came to performing, it had no equal.

Kabuki had long been performed in these parts, in Ushitaki, Fukuura, and Isoya. In Fukuura's case, an actor had fled there in the old days and taught the villagers his trade. Thereafter, the villagers performed every year at festival time, and this continued until recently, but it was rare for them to travel elsewhere to perform.

Kawame, however, had an able-minded teacher who was also popular, so the troupe traveled here and there to perform, and for a time made a living acting and working in the mountains. But when the war grew in intensity, such things were forbidden, and they never performed on the road again.

Nakamura Umejirō married a girl from Kawame, but the couple was unable to have a child, so they took in one of her older brother's children and raised him. The child married the Kawaya's daughter and is now living with them. Nakamura-san was loved by the community, and when he died recently, a splendid tomb was erected.

Others also learned to entertain. They brought the art of dancing in accompaniment to a *samisen* with them from Hata. In Hata, where the entertaining arts flourish, this is called *tsukiage*, and in Kawame as well. In places where *tsukiage* is performed, generally Noh is not, so the people of Kawame have not learned it. *Tsukiage* was passed down by the Kamiyama family, who were talented performers generation after generation. Kinnosuke-san was quite skilled, and when traveling players came along he'd perform with them. Now Kanetaka-san is a fine dancer as well.

In this humble community of people who have convened here, these performing arts have helped everyone get along quite well. In the early days, no family had special rights, and the people lived ordinary lives. Then, around the Taishō period, with the presence of a group of able-minded young men who gave their energies to public projects, this collection of people naturally came to have order and to function as a community. These young men generally led the way, and the other villagers collaborated in preparing a place for a school, building roads, and so on.

At *Bon*, New Year's, and other festivals, the household heads met to discuss work and other matters. The women, mostly housewives, also gathered often. They'd pay group expenses by working on their days off, cutting grass or participating in road construction work, and would pool their earnings. The grand-

Kawame,
Aomori Prefecture
August 1963.

mothers hold gatherings, too, meeting every month at a small temple in the village to chant a million prayers to the Amitabha. Since they don't have any large prayer beads of their own, they borrow them from the temple in Sai.

Such behavior was to be found in the surrounding communities as well, so it could be said that the people of Kawame had learned from others. But they all had to work together to make a living. If anyone was pushed beyond their means, it would have affected everyone. So, since long ago, they have discussed and decided on matters as a community and worked within the limits of everyone's abilities. Whenever a minor decision had to be made, the community head and a five-member council would meet and decide together.

When work was available year-round—government logging work, acting engagements, and charcoal-making work—things were fine. But this balance was easily disrupted. When the number of households grew and some could not be included in the logging work, or when charcoal-making hit hard times, there were those who suddenly found it hard to get by. People had to start traveling elsewhere for work. The first from these parts to cross the water to Hokkaido for work was Nitta-san. That was around 1890, before the government logging had begun and before people had begun to make charcoal. At that time people from the communities of Okotsube and Ikotoma had farmland in Hokkaido, and Nitta-san was hired to work there. Next, Hatanaka-san went away to work canning herring.

When the people started performing plays and doing government logging work, travel for work dropped off for a time, but travel to Hokkaido for work has increased since the war. What is more, among the families who are doing government logging work, women are increasingly taking care of the household and doing most of the farmwork. Accordingly, the level of farm technology is very low.

VI. NEW YEAR'S, FESTIVALS, AND THE MOUNTAIN GOD

Life in the community was uneventful. Everyone took a holiday on the first day of the New Year and spent a quiet day at home. On the second, people visited one another's homes, greeted everyone, thanked them, and wished them a happy New Year. The families all put out *sake* and treated their guests to a drink. The third day, there was *kagura*. The youth took a mythical lion's head kept at the shrine and, while playing a flute and beating on a *taiko* drum, went from house to house, extending wishes for the new year to everyone. On this same day, the grandmothers took a feast to the Goddess Kannon's temple and shut themselves up together there.

On the fifth, the first meeting of the year was held, when the heads of all the households gathered at the home of the community head to decide matters for the following year and elect the next head. Before the war the community head was decided by recommendation. Responsible for all administrative work, the head also had to unify and lead the community. In the old days the community had no expenses, but now expenses are about seventy or eighty thousand yen annually. Originally the money made on acting engagements was used to cover these costs, but now funds are generated by thinning out and selling trees from the community forest.

Because the community doesn't have a long history, there are very few special events. The diversions here are the *Bon* festival in Sai on August 14 and 15 and the festival for the mountain god. At three in the afternoon on August 14 objects of Shinto worship are placed on a palanquin. After being carried around Old Sai, they are taken to the home of a Shinto priest in Ishishimizu. The palanquin is kept there overnight. The next morning it is taken around Big Sai and returned to the shrine at midnight.

On the fifteenth a *tengu* [long-nosed goblin] leads the festival's procession. The more earnest men in the community draw straws to determine who the *tengu* will be. The *tengu* then puts on a mask, an ancient ceremonial court robe, carries a spear, wears one-toothed wooden clogs, and leads the procession. Behind him are the guards and portable shrines. Big Sai and Old Sai each have a portable shrine, and they are followed by four *matsuriyama* [literally "festival mountains"]. The *kagura* troupes follow them, walking around Old Sai on the fourteenth and Big Sai on the fifteenth, making this a truly slow affair. During this time the *kagura* troupes go from house to house, perform *kagura*, and receive monetary gifts. The young people under thirty carry the portable shrines and pull the *matsuriyama*. Those over thirty dress up as samurai and form the guard. The portable shrines are carried along quietly but the *matsuriyama* are made lively by the accompaniment of a flute, *taiko* drums, and dancing.

In the past the people of Sai decided what roles Kawame and the other communities would play; those who were not in the *kagura* troupes participated in keeping with these roles. On the night of the fifteenth the gods were returned. On the sixteenth a stage was built, and people from each community gave a performance. On this occasion Kawame performed a play.

When the *Bon* festival is over, fall comes. People are busy in their paddies and fields, and working in the mountains. Before long, winter arrives.

November 24 is called *Daishikō*. On this day rice porridge is cooked in a large pot and offered to the mountain god using reed chopsticks. Later the rice porridge is eaten by the family. It is said that the mountain god has twelve children, and because she is poor and has difficulty raising them, rice porridge is cooked and offered to her to help with the raising of her children.

In December many gods celebrate their birthdays. Prominent among them is Ebisu [the god of fishing, farming, and commerce], on the fifth. A meal is prepared for Ebisu, offered to him on his birthday, and eaten afterwards by the family as a side dish together with *sake*. The ninth is Daikoku's [the god of wealth's] birthday. Beans are added to rice flour, and these are cooked together and offered to him. There are birthdays for all kinds of other gods as well, such as the God of the Oven and the God of the Well. And last, on New Year's Eve, humans celebrate their own birthdays [as everyone in Japan, regardless of what month they were born, traditionally added a year to their age at the end of each year]. A single pine branch is placed on the household Shinto altar, and a braided straw festoon is hung there. A braided festoon is also hung around a tree in the mountains as an offering to the mountain god.

Last, I will touch upon the festival for the mountain god. Held on December 12, it is also referred to as the mountain god's birthday. When people enter the mountains, before they do any work, they always erect a shrine to the mountain god. A large tree may be the object of worship, or a stone may be carried there. A *torii* gate is then built in front of it. Thereafter, a *torii* is built every year on the occasion of the mountain god festival. So by counting the *torii*, one can determine how many years the woodsmen have been working there. When their work is done, they leave these symbols of the mountain god intact. Accordingly, in the mountains of Sai and Kawame there are an enormous number of these tributes to the mountain gods.

On December 11, rice cakes are made in the home of the

leader of the mountain work crew. Using ten pounds of rice, the women pound two rice cakes and place one on top of the other. *Sake* is also prepared for the god and taken into the mountains. If the men are still working there, the women bring the offering in on their backs. If the men are at home, they carry it, and the women accompany them. A new *torii* is then built in front of the mountain god, the rice cakes and *sake* are placed there in offering, and the people bow in prayer. The work crew then goes down to the mountain shed and spends the twelfth drinking there. The women carry a feast from home, and they spend the entire day in the shed, eating, drinking, and dancing. Officials from the government forest management office also attend the mountain god festival, each bringing a half-gallon bottle of *sake*. People from the mountain work office participate too, so this small mountain shed fills with people, and there is a feeling of intimacy not to be found at festivals off the mountain. In recent years the officials no longer attend.

It is said that the mountain god brings people together and makes them one. Indeed, through this festival people do become truly unified. It used to be that one could not cut down a tree that was a mountain god, but there are times when, owing to the circumstance of clear-cutting, they must be cut down. In this case a priest is summoned and asked to offer a prayer. Recently, as not everyone shares the same feelings about these things, most of the trees that were once worshipped as mountain gods have been cut down. Only the stone gods carried up from the riverbed remain here and there in the mountains. It would seem that the custom of bringing stones is extremely old; one can find stones that are covered with moss.

VII. IN CONCLUSION

The people who came to live in Kawame were not thinking to create a utopia or expecting to secure a special privilege. They just came to live here, and in the course of living, a little at a time, they came to have a community structure and to live as a group that protected its common interests. This village had very little in the way of vested rights. Individuals had little property, and life was extremely unstable, but the ease of living with others of like mind kept people here. These people are quite pure. Nothing about them is mean-spirited. It is a truly wonderful community. They plant trees in the mountains even though the land is not their own. It is forestland that must be returned to the state, but just the same, they plant trees there. There isn't enough work here these days, even in the government-owned forests, forcing people to travel elsewhere for work, which I think will lead to the gradual deterioration of community bonds.

Because Grandpa Tsuboya—a man who understood the world—lived here, a settlement of six shacks grew into a harmonious village of twenty households. Thanks to the people here, the forests in this area have grown to become what they are today. So can we not find a way to more warmly protect the lives of these people? The sale of government-owned forestlands would not seem that difficult, and it would fill this community with hope as it looks to the future. Reaching out and assisting in the growth of a community like this—now that would be true governance.

Chapter 16

———

Totsukawa Landslide

[Nara Prefecture, 1936–39 and April 1965]

The first time I set foot in Totsukawa, Nara Prefecture, was June 7, 1936. I spent the previous night in a place called Jōdo in the back end of Gojō and set out walking from there. Climbing up the valley south of Jōdo one comes out on the top of Amatsuji Pass, the divide between the Kino and Kumano River watersheds. Looking back to the north from the top of the pass, one can see the Yamato plain and to the south, the rugged rise and fall of tall, steep mountains. Cross the pass heading south and the valley suddenly becomes deep.

The Kii Mountains are a rugged range running east and west, but the Totsu and Kitayama rivers have taken a bite out of them and flow from north to south. Accordingly, the valleys they have made are deep and steep. When I spoke with an old man who knew this valley's distant past, he told me that until The Flood of Meiji 22 [1889] the river had flowed more than one hundred feet below where it does now, and from the path above, the river could not be seen. He said that one could take a puff on a pipe in the time it took for a rock thrown from the road to strike the river below. And while this story may have been a slight overstatement, it did convey a sense of what the landscape was like.

Though rugged, the Totsu River valley was an important

*Totsukawa,
Nara Prefecture.
April 1965.* route long ago. Referred to as the Kumano Highway, it came from Gojō, crossed the Amatsuji Pass and, by way of Uenoji and Yamasaki, arrived in Hongū. Many a pilgrim traveled this path on the way to Kumano. In the mountains to the west of the valley, the Kōya Highway—from Mt. Kōya to Hongū via the Nose and Kanno rivers—also played an important role as a direct route through the mountains, joining Kōya and Kumano. And the east-west path that passes through the Nogawa and Tenkawa valleys, on its way from Mt. Kōya to Mt. Ōmine, was an important route for believers in these holy places, making the mountains in between a place of many comings and goings. The believers were not particularly troubled by the rugged and out-of-the-way nature of these mountain slopes. Rather, they saw them as another trial to overcome.

The first time I entered the Totsu River valley I turned east from Amatsuji, descended into the valley, climbed back up along the Ten River, and took a bus out from Kawatani to Shimoichi. I had walked the Ten River valley from the west, and after passing through the communities Sudare, Shiodani, and Shiono, I could see an area of about five to seven acres of gently sloping ground atop a tall cliff, across the river from Shiono. It was rice paddies. Just getting there to tend the rice must have been a terrible struggle, and I was moved by the thought that people would go so far to cultivate land. Later, when I asked, I learned of the flooding and landslides of 1889. Before the landslide, it was as if the valley had been scraped out from the top of the mountain down to the river. I was told that a downpour gouged the soil from the top half of the mountain and dropped it into the river, leaving a flat area of some seven acres that the farmers had turned into rice paddies.

As if by prior agreement, when I talked with old people, they spoke of The Flood of 22. It was that memorable. To learn more about it I went to the Nara library, where I was shown a variety of documents and took notes. I learned that the flood had been an event of unparalleled scale, but for the most part, it had been forgotten by the general public.

Yet flood damage of this magnitude could well occur again, so I think we must forever keep disasters like this in mind. Some had attempted to predict this terrible flood damage; Shimada Komatarō of Kamiichi was one of them. Shimada-san had been the mayor of the Kamiichi Township for a long time, and over the years he had diligently kept a record of water levels on the Yoshino River. He was intent on predicting the weather and had investigated the possibility of a relationship between the number of sunspots and the quantity of rainfall. According to folk wisdom, when bees build their nests up high, there will be a flood and when they build them low, there will be strong winds. Year after year he tested this and found it to be generally true. It was the opinion of this man, based on his experience, that predictions would be of inestimable value even if facilities to prevent disasters could not be created.

People say that "Disasters come along right around the time you forget them." Up until the end of the war [World War II], the people of this valley had certainly not forgotten. They were

House on stilts.
Totsukawa, Nara Prefecture.
April 1965.

even afraid to build a large road because they said that would summon landslides.

Between 1936 and 1939, I entered the Totsu River valley five times. In October 1939 I followed the river south, climbed Mt. Tamaki from Yusenchi, came out in Shingū, and returned to Osaka. When I spent the night in Yusenchi a dreadful tremor continued on and off for nearly thirty minutes and I got under the futon and stayed still. When I woke the following morning, I found that just to the north of the lodging an area two hundred feet high and one hundred feet wide had broken away and fallen into the river. The road there had disappeared entirely. The villagers told me that even without rainfall one or two such landslides occur somewhere in this valley every year and that even now the valley is unstable.

The following day when I woke in a lodging on Mt. Tamaki, a mist was rising up from the valley. I asked an elderly man about this, and he told me this portended an impending downpour. He said I should leave as soon as possible because there was a chance that transportation would be suspended, so I went to Dorohachō along the Kitayama River and took a propeller boat to Shingū. Later I learned that, due to damage caused by heavy rain that fell that night and through the following day, all transportation from the communities along the Totsu River was suspended for more than a week.

* * * * *

There was a long spell of dry weather in the summer of 1889, and the crops were drying out. Although some of the communities along the Totsu River were located in the bottom of the valley beside the river, most were located on somewhat gentle slopes atop the tall precipices that lined the river. This meant that to visit a community just across the river one first had to climb down into the deep valley. There are stories, told in fun, like the one about a person who yelled to a relative living on the other side of the river, saying, "we're pounding rice cakes [a task that takes several hours], so please come over and help." By the time the relative had arrived, the cakes had been pounded.

That summer, the soil had dried out from the drought, so there was no greenery in the communities that had been built on the tops of the steep precipices. Then, on August 17, there were sudden showers in Nutanohara, Asahi, Uguhara, Uenoji, Takōtsu, and Yamate. These were only brief showers and, depending on the location, they came in the morning, afternoon, or evening. Everyone was delighted by the rain, and they all toasted and celebrated what they anticipated would be a good harvest. Then, on the eighteenth, a heavy rain fell, and was accompanied by unusually strong winds. Trees were pulled up and houses were blown over. At night, the winds grew even fiercer.

On the nineteenth the winds weakened but the rain became more violent, bringing thunder and lightning in the night, reaching a dreadful extreme around midnight. Beginning in the evening of this day, landslides occurred that are beyond the power of words to describe. Then, at six o'clock on the morning of the twentieth, the downpour that had continued for two days stopped, and the sky began to clear to the north and by eight o'clock the weather had cleared.

The belt with Ōmine and Odaibara at its center has the largest rainfall in Japan, with 158 inches [13+ ft.] annually in the vicinity of Odaibara. In the Kitayama watershed, although its headwaters are in Odaibara, there is no record of flood damage like that experienced by the Totsu River. These two rivers come together in Miyai, in Wakayama Prefecture, become the Kumano River, and enter the ocean at Shingū. While the Kitayama River is clear and flows through beautiful ravines like Kitasankyō and Dorohachō, most of the Totsu River's canyons are buried in sand and there is a wide, white riverbed.

It is thought that the enormous rainfall is caused when a moist wind blows up into these mountains from the sea to the southeast and collides with a cold northwest wind. The tall peaks of the Ōmine Mountains, stretching north and south and squeezed between valleys cut by the Totsu and Kitayama rivers, are apparently responsible for this phenomenon, and nearly all of the trees near the tops of these mountains are bent eastward, which tells us that while there are strong winds from the east and southeast at the lower elevations, there are strong winds from the west near the mountain peaks. At any rate, the air currents in these mountains are complicated and appear to satisfy the conditions necessary for rainfall.

* * * * *

The following is a look at water levels at important points along the main branch of the Totsu River, showing how they were affected by the flooding brought on by this rainstorm, starting upstream in Dorogawa and moving gradually down from there:

Location	River Height	Location	River Height
Dorogawa	8 ft.	Yamanishi	66 ft.
Tsubonouchi	12 ft.	Hayashi	271 ft.
Kawai	11 ft.	Shiono	89 ft.
Iosumi	15 ft.	Kawatsu	99 ft.

Sakamoto	30 ft.	Nagatono	154 ft.
Kazeya	50 ft.	Hiratani	119 ft.
Tsujidō	53 ft.	Uguhara	210 ft.
Ikeana	60 ft.	Kominoue	119 ft.
Ui	169 ft.	Tanise	219 ft.
Obara	99 ft.	Oritachi	179 ft.
Shimizu	164 ft.	Uenoji	261 ft.
Yunohara	129 ft.	Yamatedani	179 ft.

In particular, the numbers for Uenoji (261 ft.) and Hayashi (271 ft.) tell the frightful story of just how rapidly the torrent rose in this narrow valley. And one must be attentive to the low water levels in nearby Sakamoto and Kazeya. This striking difference was the result of landslides that blocked the river's flow. In time, these were washed away and the water rushed down like a *tsunami*. Where water levels were low, there were relatively few landslides. Here, I have made a record of the major landslides and the lakes they created.

Lake Name	Circum-ference	Water Depth	Height x Width of Landslide That Dammed the River
New Shiono	7.3 miles	298 ft.	2,863 ft. x 2,088 ft.
New Kawarabi	7.3 miles	unk.	5,369 ft. x 1,193 ft.
New Ushinohana	3.7 miles	unk.	formed when New Kawarabi washed out
New Ui	2 miles	unk.	1,074 ft. x 1,193 ft.
New Tsujidō	3.7 miles	unk.	1,790 ft. x 895 ft.
New Hayashi	16 miles	unk.	775 ft. x 2,267 ft.
New Uchino	2.4 miles	unk.	1,193 ft. x 1074 ft.
New Yamate	1.7 miles	unk.	8,948 ft. x 1,193 ft.
New Nobiro	3.4 miles	unk.	5,369 ft. x 2,863 ft.
New Obara	2.4 miles	unk.	1,193 ft. x 1,193 ft.
New Katsuragama	1.4 miles	149 ft.	2,386 ft. x 2,983 ft.
New Kashiwakei	2.4 miles	unk.	1,432 ft. x 1,074 ft.

Each of these lakes was similar in size to the lakes found at modern-day hydroelectric dams and, with the exception of one or two, they were all created before daybreak on August 20. If one adds the smaller lakes, the total number climbs to 53, and if one considers the number of locations with landslides of a height and width greater than 300 feet, this number reaches 247.

These lakes continued to take on water, and in about two hours they began to collapse, though some among them continued to act as reservoirs until September. Many lakes formed in the mountainous area to the north. In the south, in the vicinity of Hiratani, until the morning of the nineteenth, people thought this was a commonplace flood. Some of the villagers pulled out wood that was floating in the river while others went off to fish for *ayu* [sweetfish]. Then the water level suddenly dropped, and they all looked on in wonder. A person who understood such things explained that this was caused by a landslide upstream blocking the river, and that they should flee to higher ground because before long the dam would break The dams upstream collapsed one after another, each time sending a rush of turbid water down the narrow valley, taking everything along the western shore with it.

A similar phenomenon occurred upstream in the vicinity of Sakamoto. Because water that had been rushing along suddenly retreated, travelers on the south side of the river, rolling up the cuffs on their trousers, were able to cross over to Sakamoto on the north side and each of the ten beggars at the shrine downstream in Yamasaki was able to catch dozens of the cherry salmon that were flouncing about in the mud on the river bottom. The villagers said they thought perhaps the water had begun to flow down into the ground, or that the mountains had split and maybe the water's course had changed direction. This impression grew stronger when at eight o'clock on the morning of the twentieth the rain stopped and the sky brightened. But a person from Sudare came along and explained that a large lake had formed in Shiono and encouraged them to take flight because who knew what would happen when the dam broke. Surprised, the villagers began to evacuate. In quick succession more than thirty people came to the rescue from Sudare and were able to help the villagers move their belongings to higher ground. Because Sudare was located up high and there had been few landslides, they had suffered almost no damage and had helped their neighbors in Sakamoto.

Thus the evacuation was complete, and at three o'clock in the afternoon of that same day, New Shiono Lake began to give way. Once an opening had formed, the force of the water washed away sand and earth in an instant. The water reached the eaves of the farmers' homes in Sakamoto, but because this was the only newly formed lake above Sakamoto, there was comparatively little damage. Downstream from Sakamoto, in Tsujidō, sixteen homes were washed away.

The flooding swept away bridges and cut through mountain roads everywhere, making it difficult to even reach the district office in Gojō with information of the disaster. Reports to Gojō were eventually made by the people of Tanise, a community located downstream, beyond Tsujidō. Looking to report on the state of the disaster, the people of Tanise appealed to the community's youth, but the roads were in shreds and they were at a loss for what to do. An old man by the name of Tamada Tadaharu, who had hunted in these mountains when he was young, knew the topography well. "I don't think much rain has fallen to the west, so it's probably best to take the trail west to the Kōya Highway and on to Mt. Kōya. From there you can go down to the Kino River and take a riverboat upstream to Gojō." Making Tamada Tadaharu their guide, a group of five young men carrying sickles, hatchets, and a two-day supply of food, cut their way through what barely passed for a path up to the Kōya Highway. They crossed the Obako Ridge, overnighted once along the way and brought the first report of the disaster to Gojō on the twenty-third. The people in Gojō were dumbfounded by what they heard. Above all, government officials at the district office grew pale when they learned that Tamaoki Takayoshi, who had administered the Uchiyoshino District since 1880 and was the best-qualified person to head up the disaster relief effort, had died a violent death in a landslide in Uguhara, above Tanise.

Tamaoki Takayoshi was from Oritachi, one of the communities that make up Totsukawa Village. Early on he had thrown himself into the imperialist movement and had gone to work for the Nara Prefectural office when the Meiji period began [in 1868]. In 1880 he was appointed head of the Uchiyoshino District and had worked hard for the advancement of this, his birthplace. On August 17, 1889, he had attended a celebration for the completion of the excavation of the Tado Highway in the Yoshino District. On the eighteenth, as the rain and wind showed signs of becoming exceedingly severe, he set out for Gojō early in the morning, heading back up the Totsu River. Due to the violence of the weather, he took refuge in the Deaf Store, in Uguhara. Takayoshi rode in a palanquin and had three porters with him. The Deaf Store was so called because its master was deaf. It was a restaurant, with lodgings as well, run by Kitamura Etsushō and his wife. Their daughter was refined and trim and had become Takayoshi's sweetheart. So when Takayoshi traveled back and forth between Gojō and his home, it was his custom to stay for two or three nights. As the rain was heavy just then, he spent the night of the eighteenth there, and the nineteenth as well. Then, just before dawn on the twentieth, an area directly below the lodging began to give way and Masutani Tomosuke, who had also been staying there, rushed outdoors. He yelled to those inside to evacuate, but Takayoshi and the others stood, lanterns in hand, and made no effort to go out. At this, Tomosuke ran up the slope alone, and the surface of the mountain that until then had slid slowly down, surged toward the valley floor, taking the Deaf Store with it and letting out a thunderous roar. In an instant, the lodge and the people in it had disappeared. To this day, their bodies have not been found.

With this information in hand, Nishimura Kōhei took over the Totsu River relief effort. Kōhei was from Totsukawa and was born in Tenpō 11 [1840]. He had been in Kyoto at the time of the Meiji Restoration, working diligently for the imperial cause, and subsequently became the secretary-general of the Uchiyoshino District. In 1889, in the capacity of chief secretary-general, he administered the district government. He was forty-eight years old and in the prime of life.

Even before the government relief and recovery work began to produce results, the local people pushed forward with their own relief efforts. The damage was indeed great. Like the innumerable landslides and newly formed lakes, the damage to people and livestock defies description. In all of the Totsukawa Village's 334-square-mile area, there were a mere 2,000 homes. While many of these homes were located on slopes atop steep precipices, most of the homes in the communities located along the river and at the base of cliffs were washed away or flattened. Two hundred homes were completely destroyed, 364 homes were washed away, and another 260 were partially destroyed. Twenty-one public offices and fourteen temples and shrines were destroyed as well. Thirty people were wounded, 255 people died, and as many as 2,600 others lost their homes and were rescued by others. As for damage to the cultivated land, it was even more extreme. Seventy to 80 percent was ruined.

The Totsukawa downpour did not greatly effect Shingū, at the mouth of the Kumano River, until around eight o'clock on the morning of the twentieth. The rain had stopped and a blue sky had come into view, when suddenly an unthinkable amount of water came rushing along from upstream. In an instant even Honmachi, the highest ground in Shingū, was submerged and people could be seen getting around town in boats. Damage to homes in the lower areas was tremendous—several hundred homes were washed away, three thousand homes sustained damage, and as many as fifty people drowned. What is more, this happened under a brilliant blue sky. Enormous quantities of lumber, including wood slats used in the making of *sake* barrels, were washed away. It is thought that 70 percent of the property in the Shingū Township was lost.

Is it possible to predict such disasters? If we pay careful attention, a warning sign may be found somewhere. The landslide in Yamate was one example. A full 1,800 by 1,800 feet in size, the first landslide razed two homes and formed the New Yamate lake. Thirteen homes were originally located in a place called Nakamine, but after a long spell of rain in May 1789, a second landslide stamped out the entire community. An old woman was picking lettuce in the field in front of her house at the time, and just as she was about to go in the landslide came. She was buried in her field, but a crack in the earth allowed the air to circulate and she lived there, underground, for seven days, eating her lettuce to stay alive and calling out for help until a fellow villager heard her and dug her out. Then, in Kaei 1 [1848], in Hirayama, an area more than 700 feet high and 900 feet wide slid down into the Yamate River, forming a new lake more than a mile long.

Aside from these large landslides, small landslides occurred repeatedly, and every downpour brought damage. Geologically speaking, this area is susceptible to collapse, and when one location falls, it becomes easier for the same phenomenon to repeat itself in the surrounding area. Although the people of Totsukawa knew this well, they had experienced so many landslides that they were no longer apprehensive of the smaller ones. And this, it may be said, contributed to the size of the catastrophe that did occur.

* * * * *

After reports of the Totsukawa flood disaster reached Gojō, the government authorities took action, private individuals began to make contributions of money and goods, and the locals concentrated their energies on recovery. Their first action was to clear the roads and resume communication with the outside world. Not only did all of the villagers join in this undertaking, but Nara Prefecture also sent a large number of "black-hoe" laborers into these mountains. Black-hoe laborers, used for civil engineering and construction, had experience with this kind of work.

In many of the places where the bridges had collapsed and the villagers were no longer able to communicate with people across the river, arrows were used to send messages. Rope and wire were also stretched across the river and used to cross to the other side.

String was tied to an arrow and shot, and when it reached the other side, a rope was attached to the string and pulled by the people on the other bank. In Kazeya, on August 25, a steel wire was pulled across the river using this method, and a straw basket was tied to it. A person would get in and, using a long rope, they were pulled across the river by people on the other side. Called *yaen* by the locals, this method was used until early in the Shōwa period. The residents of Kuwatani used a *yaen* to cross the river and also built an ark to ferry people to the other side.

Where new lakes had formed, and where it did not appear that the dams were likely to break soon, rafts, called *kamo* [ducks], were built. In locations where the dams were weak they were blown up and the water was drained. The engineering corps of the fourth army division from Osaka was dispatched for this purpose, and the third division from Nagoya collaborated. Maeda Takahiro, a native of Totsukawa, was in Osaka. Takahiro, who was in the third division and would later become a lieutenant general, requested of Kasa Yoshiharu, a second lieutenant in the engineering corps who was also originally from Totsukawa, that the third division be sent to participate in the disaster recovery effort. The Ministry of Agriculture and Commerce and others also collaborated in the destruction of one new lake after another. On September 7, they had begun work on one of the largest of these, the New Kawarabi Lake, but were unable to burst it completely, and for a long time thereafter a lake some four miles in circumference remained. Earth and sand were pushed from the Kawarabi River out into the main branch of the Totsu River, resulting in the forming of the New Ushinohana Lake. Then, with a downpour on September 11, the dam collapsed. This rain led to the lake's destruction but, at the same time, large quantities of soil and sand caused the bottom of the Totsu River to rise markedly. In the vicinity of Uenoji, the bottom rose more than a hundred feet at its highest point.

Making use of these various methods, by the end of September people were able to come and go without hindrance. But how the victims would eat and live their lives in the future remained to be resolved. There was nothing they could do because their farmland had been ruined. With regard to supplying food, members of the Gojō Club took action. They prepared three thousand pounds of white rice, two casks of *umeboshi* [pickled plums], and twelve sacks of salt at eighty-eight pounds apiece, and set out to recruit porters, but, as Totsukawa remained in a state of collapse, the porters did not readily agree. Only when the cost of transporting sixty-four pounds of rice from Gojō to Sakamoto was raised from thirteen *sen* to fifty, were they able to find fifty people. They divided the porters into two groups. One passed through Mt. Kōya and on to southern Totsukawa, and the other distributed foodstuffs in the north, centering on Sakamoto.

Around this time, the donation of money and supplies from around the country had gradually begun to increase, and the newspapers had all collaborated in this effort. The aid of people living in the capital who were originally from Totsukawa was important as well. Not only did they help with the provision of relief supplies, they also gave thought to the future lives of the victims. In early September, thinking that emigration to Hokkaido was the most suitable solution, Maeda Masanori and Nakashima Genjirō began to look into this matter. Then, on September 11, they came to Gojō and met with Nishimura Kōhei and volunteers from Totsukawa Village, and finally decided upon emigration to Hokkaido. In the creation of a new Totsukawa Village, they found the road to relief. They drafted a plan, passed it out in those areas where the damage was most severe, and pressed for this resolution. On September 23 the secretary-general of the district, the village mayor, and the assemblymen gathered to discuss how they should counsel the residents with regard to emigration, and how the new village should be managed.

It so happened that Miyamoto Chimanki, the head of the Kushiro District [in Hokkaido] was visiting the capital, so they invited him to Gojō, and on September 28 he delivered a talk to the people of Totsukawa with regard to conditions in Hokkaido.

This talk gave the villagers resolve, and on the same day six hundred households made the decision to apply. Winter would come soon, and they had to make the crossing to Hokkaido before then. The national government took an active interest in this matter, but it was not until October 16 that Nara Prefecture approved the move. Word of this decision reached Totsukawa on the seventeenth. Two hundred households and 790 people from North Totsukawa and Totsukawa Hanazono, who had been on standby, left Totsukawa the following day, the eighteenth, and headed for Kobe. Most were on foot. They boarded a boat, the *Tōe Maru*, on the twenty-fourth, and arrived in Otaru, Hokkaido on the twenty-eighth.

Then, on October 23 and 24, villagers from West and Central Totsukawa left their communities. There were 204 households and 830 people. They boarded the *Sagami Maru* in Kobe on the twenty-eighth and arrived in Hakodate, Hokkaido on November 3. There they transferred to the *Tōkai Maru*, arriving in Otaru on the fifth.

The third group were 196 households and 860 people from North, Central, and South Totsukawa who left their homes on October 23 and 27 and set sail from Kobe on the *Hyōgo Maru* on the thirty-first. They arrived in Otaru on November 6. In this way, 2,480 people from 600 households, or one third of the population of Totsukawa, left their birthplace in a virtually unplanned frenzy. Moreover, Hokkaido was already cold, and they had to travel winter roads by sleigh to Takigawa and spend the winter in militia barracks there. Then, the following year, they would cross the Ishikari River at Takigawa and set to the clearing of the wilderness on its right bank. In this way, enduring great hardship, the building of the New Totsukawa Village began.

Totsukawa had been located in the mountains, and the people had been woodsmen, wood workers, barrel slat cutters and hunters—trades that made the mountains their object. Cultivation had been limited to farming the fields around their homes and to slash-and-burn agriculture so these people had not experienced full-scale farming. But emigration to Hokkaido meant becoming farmers; it meant they would have to transform their lives. Once they were in Hokkaido, the feeling among the villagers that they had been abandoned deepened. In 1892 the village head, Saratani Kiei, resigned and returned to Totsukawa. Feeling betrayed by their leader, many of the residents of New Totsukawa longed for their homeland, and quarrels broke out. Consequently, Nishimura Kōhei was selected as the new village head and made the crossing to Hokkaido. Resolving to live out his years in Hokkaido, Kōhei poured his energy into the building of New Totsukawa, and, though he left at one point to be district head, he ended his life as a resident of the village. He had given his entire life to Totsukawa.

Up until the war, the people who continued to live in the Totsukawa valley did not want to build a large road because they thought it might bring on another major disaster. For this reason, a motor road did not pass through before the war, and this played a large part in keeping this area behind. When the people of Se, in the northeast corner of Totsukawa, attended a village meeting at the government office in Komori, it took them three days—two days for the round trip and one for the meeting. But people put up with such inconveniences and asked only for peaceful lives. The development of the Totsu River Valley is a large task for the postwar years. It is the quiet hope of the local people not only that a roadway and dams will be built, but that construction will not bring with it a disaster beyond their imagination.

They say that disasters come along around the time they are forgotten, but the people here have not yet forgotten. However, those who are doing the construction work have forgotten, and the people fear what will come.

POSTSCRIPT

After the above was written, dams were built on the Totsu River in Sarutani, Kazeya, and Futatsuno, the road along the river was widened, a bus from Nara now passes through this valley and on to Shingū, and leisure facilities such as the Totsu River Hot Springs have been completed. The valley is utterly changed, but the topography and the geology are the same. The mountains are still rugged, the valleys are deep, and deep in the mountains logging progresses.

Chapter 17

Birth of New Totsukawa Village

[Hokkaido, November 1945, 55 years after resettlement]

I visited the New Totsukawa Village on November 3, 1945 when Hokkaido's fields were covered with snow. Having lost my workplace in Osaka to war damage, I left Osaka on October 16, taking with me a group of people who wanted to become farmers in Hokkaido. I accompanied them as far as Horonobe, near the north end of Hokkaido, and after passing through Kitami and Kushiro, spent the night of November 2 in Takigawa. On the following morning, I took a ferry across the Ishikari River in heavily falling snow. The lodgings in Takigawa were five yen and thirty-five *sen* [approx. 40 cents] and the ferry across the Ishikari River cost ten *sen* [less than 1 cent], an indication that, for the most part, inflation had yet to begin.

I was interested in visiting New Totsukawa Village, because I had been to its parent village, Totsukawa, in Nara Prefecture, and wanted to see what had become of its branch village.

A thirteen-year-old boy by the name of Ushirogi Kisaburō was in the third group of households that left Totsukawa for Hokkaido following the disastrous flooding and landslides. He was born in Chigo, in the South Totsukawa District. Following his parents to a world he'd never seen, he had a vague feeling of anticipation regarding the work ahead. They spent the first night in Shinnogawa and the second in Ōhata. On the third day, they crossed over Mt. Kōya and stayed in Kamiya, and on the fourth day they descended into the Kino River valley, climbed Kimi Pass, and spent the night in Mikkaichi. This daily climbing of mountains was hard on a child of thirteen, and it took its toll. At last, in Mikkaichi, he was no longer able to move, and on the fifth day he was placed on a litter and coming as far as Sakai, spent the night there. The following day he had recovered and walked from Sakai to Hakkenya in Osaka, stopping for the night at a lodging called Kyōya. The following day, the group took a train to Kobe, and there they boarded the *Hyōgo Maru*, arriving in Otaru, Hokkaido on November 6.

In those days, Otaru was still a lonely, one-street town. And it was buried in snow. The train went as far as Ichikochi, so they rode it there and walked on in the snow. The snow was a foot deep. Convicts had come and pressed down the snow [prisons were built in Hokkaido as part of its colonization and prison labor was commonly used]. Unused to these conditions, it was a real struggle for everyone. Finally, they reached the detention camp in Naie and stayed there. To this day when the people of New Totsukawa want to describe utter fatigue, they say, "like when we reached the detention camp in Naie." The following day, under the protection of the convicts, they came as far as the Takigawa barracks with their belongings loaded on horse-pulled sleighs. The ringing of the horses' bells was the sound of hell to them. In Takigawa they would stay in the barracks. Four families lived together in houses about 21 x 24 feet in size, and this life continued until the following June when the snow melted.

Their dwellings and food were provided, but the settlers had to find their own firewood and every day went out into the snow to search for more. Because they had to burn it on the hearth that same day, the room was thick with smoke to the point that their eyes were adversely affected. Unused to life in the snow, they caught colds that worsened and one after another, the children and the elderly died. It was the convicts who came to their aid. Many were accustomed to the snow, and on orders from the authorities, they came to help out with building or any other work that required an extra pair of hands. When the convicts pulled the sleds along by hand, they sang, *"yanse honse, the emigrants from Yamato [Japan] are the compost of Sorachi."* The emigrants knew they were being sung about, but no one complained. They all thought they would die in obscurity in this place and return to the soil.

But when the snow melted and the sun shined brilliantly, their hopes were raised once again. On June 15 they were allocated land, but there were not even roads on which to enter the fields grown thick with Japanese elm trees. Some among the settlers didn't enter their land, while others who had received land that showed some promise began to clear it and on the edge they had cleared, they planted *soba* [buckwheat] and potatoes. They cleared some 540 acres in 1890, nothing more than small plots here and there in the middle of a forest. The conditions there were by no means good, but there was no room for complaints or the expression of one's discontent. Their lives back home had been poor, and to recover from the flood they would have had to work even harder than in Hokkaido for their labors to bear fruit.

One after another, those who had been allotted land in poor condition, those who were caring for someone who was sick, and so on, returned home to Totsukawa, or wandered off to other parts of Hokkaido. But the Ushirogi family was determined to continue farming this land, come what may, and little by little they cleared it. In 1891, in addition to buckwheat and potatoes, they grew foxtail millet and broomcorn millet, and that fall they were able to eat grains that they themselves had grown. But none of the families were used to farming in the north country and many crops failed. If things continued in this way, it appeared that they would, like the lyrics of the convicts' song, become compost in Sorachi. Fortunately, in 1892, an agricultural instructor came and taught them about land reclamation and how to plant new crops. They began to grow rapeseed in 1893, hemp in 1894, and flax in 1896, which would become a source of cash. In 1894 the area of cultivated land had grown to more than 3,700 acres. Around that time the villagers began to prepare the land for rice paddies as well. In no time trees were felled and the paddy lands expanded. The number of settlers from Toyama Prefecture—who were also flood victims—increased, and the village became lively. With their own paddies now, the Ushirogi household finally became stable.

By chance, I had called on the Ushirogis, and they took me in for two days. They told me that about ten of the six hundred families that came from Totsukawa remain on the land they first settled when they arrived. Many of the others have moved to the city.

Chapter 18

The Wanderers' Family Tree

I. IN THE BEGINNING

Because they are numerous and divergent, it is no easy task to consider how it was that those who wandered came to do so. It would appear that in Japan, few wanderers were without roots. Those who had a base and wandered out from it did so because they were not able to make an adequate living at home, or they traveled for religious purposes. And there were a few who had to travel for the government.

It seems the farther back one goes, the more wanderers there were. Those who devoted themselves to hunting or fishing found it difficult to make a living staying in one fixed place. Of those who farmed, whether by slash-and-burn methods or by other means, many lived in a different place in the summer than the winter.

Here I would like to summarize what I have been able to observe with regard to those who were compelled to make wandering a way of life.

II. WANDERERS OF THE SEAS

There is a town called Ama in Wajima, on the Noto Peninsula. When summer came, the people here traveled to Hegura Island, above Hokkaido, where the women dove for abalone and the men for fish. In the fall they returned to Wajima, and the women walked the villages along the Noto Peninsula selling their catch. Most often, rather than sell, they traded for grains because the people of Ama did not cultivate fields or paddies. This practice of living in a different place in the summer and the winter seemed strange to natives of the Noto Peninsula. It all began when people from Kanegasaki, in [what is now] Fukuoka Prefecture, drifted ashore here in the middle of the sixteenth century. In 1649 [a century later] they were given four thousand square yards of land in Wajima, and they settled down.

Kanegasaki was an old fishing village. The people there made a living fishing with nets and diving for seaweed and shellfish. In the beginning of the Kamakura period [around 1200], this area was a possession of the Sō clan. When the Sō clan was appointed to guard Tsushima, fishermen from Kanegasaki traveled from the Kyushu mainland to Tsushima to fish and acted as messengers as well. In the oldest text to be found in Magariura, Tsushima, dating from 1463, it is written, "The use of nets in the Tsutsu District (in Tsushima) is to be permitted. If anyone complains of this, contact us [the Sō clan] immediately." From this we understand that the Kanegasaki fishermen were fishing with nets at that time.

In writings from 1542 I found, "On June 11, 1542, thirty-seven boats made the crossing. They stopped at Iki Island for about twenty days. One boat, with a man named Tōjirō on board crossed over to Tsushima on July 1 or 2. The remaining thirty-six boats also made the crossing in July." This tells us that the fishermen formed fleets of boats when they came. At the end of the seventeenth century fishermen who had been coming every year started to settle in Tsushima. Some also settled in Ozaki, on Iki Island. The fishermen from Kanegasaki who had crossed over to

A houseboat moored in the Inland Sea. Hiroshima Prefecture. August 1968.

Tsushima traveled on to the Korean Peninsula as well and may have developed the fishing grounds there. The Kanegasaki fishermen also settled on Shikano Island, at the entrance to the Hakata Harbor, and in Ōura, in Yamaguchi Prefecture. People from Kanegasaki appear to have settled in many of the other places they traveled to for work as well.

At first they lived on their boats, draping rush mats overhead and sleeping under them at night. Boats of this type were called "houseboats." When I was doing research in Magari, on Tsushima, in 1950, only one houseboat remained. By turning a boat into a house one could easily wander the seas, so houseboats were found not only in Kanegasaki but also in Seto and Kakinoura on the Nishisonogi Peninsula. The people of Seto are thought to be an offshoot from Kanegasaki and a branch group from Kakinoura is in Kashinoura, on Fukue Island, in the Gotō Archipelago. Mainly fishing with nets, they fish in seven-boat fleets.

Fishermen who made houses of their boats were to be found in the Inland Sea as well. One of their centers was in Noji, Mihara City, Hiroshima Prefecture. Using small seine nets that could be pulled by a single boat, at first they threw these nets in and pulled them up, but later they would submerge the net, put up a sail, and pull it along. In Kyushu they did not form fleets, but they did fish in this way. Then, when they found good fishing grounds, they settled, although when someone died, their remains were still taken back to their birthplace. Why did people wander in this way? For one, they may have wanted to live beyond the government's reach, where they didn't have to pay taxes or perform compulsory service. But this also meant that they had no rights. They'd go to an inlet somewhere and make a trifling payment for permission to fish there, catch some small fish and give them to their wife, who would put them in a shallow wooden tub and, resting that on her head, walk from farm village to farm village. These wanderers were looked down upon by the average fisherman, but as long as they didn't take this to heart, they were able to survive. They were poor, and as their numbers steadily grew, they set up as many as one hundred branch villages along the shores of the Inland Sea. This was an unusual phenomenon, given that elsewhere population growth had stagnated in the Edo period.

Few wandering fishermen were to be found in eastern Japan, but in ancient times the movement of fishermen appears to have been extensive. In Oita Prefecture there is a Kaifu [literally "ocean region"] District. In Hiroshima Prefecture one can find towns named Amasato [literally "ocean home"] and Kaisō [literally "seaweed"]. In Tokushima and in Wakayama there are also Kaifu Districts and in Aichi Prefecture there is an Ama District. The fishermen also ranged as far north as the Kasumigaura and Kitaura regions of Ibaraki. On the Japan Sea coast, in Niigata's Iwafune District, and in Sado there are also villages called Kaifu. One can see that fishermen had spread this far, but whether or not they were living on houseboats is unclear.

Fishermen from Sano, in Osaka, traveled as far as the west coast of Kyushu, beginning in the fifteenth century, and to the Kanto Region in the sixteenth. These fishermen did not dive for shellfish, but caught them with nets. When a person has a boat, the area of their activity inevitably grows. Chasing fish, people went everywhere.

III. MOUNTAIN WANDERERS

Like the wanderers of the sea, there were mountain wanderers as well. First there were those who traveled in pursuit of game. In the northeast these hunters are called *matagi*. In Suzuki Bokushi's *Trip to Akiyama* there is a story of *matagi* from Akita who came to the Akiyama Valley, at the north end of Nagano Prefecture. They traveled upstream, catching fish along the way, and selling them to guests at the Kusatsu Hot Springs. The *matagi* tracked bear and wild boar as well. The *matagi* in Matsugiuchi, Akita Prefecture, fished with cormorants and traveled as far as the mountains of Yoshino, in distant Nara Prefecture, to catch bear. It is said that they walked this distance without, for the most part, passing through places where people lived, so it would seem that paths existed for such travel.

I also heard it said that hunters from the mountains of Yoshino in Nara Prefecture, walked as far as Yamaguchi Prefecture [a distance of several hundred miles] to hunt. Exceedingly few villages are made up entirely of hunters. Although such villages were probably abundant at first, they dissolved quickly, and most of the *matagi* settled in twos or threes in farming villages where they hunted the wild boar and other animals that ravaged the crops.

The *sanka* [mountain gypsies] were probably related to the *matagi*. As Misumi Hiroshi stated in his fine research regarding the *sanka*, not only did they make winnowing baskets, but many were freshwater fishermen as well. The *sanka* I met in the mountains of Yoshino all fished the rivers as they went, traveling as far as the Osaka plains at times. I have seen their tents pitched along the Yamato River, near Sakai City. Many of the *sanka* who live in the mountains of Hiroshima Prefecture have settled and formed communities, using them as bases from which they set out to catch freshwater fish. They are especially talented at catching eel.

Sanka are everywhere, and it seems there was originally quite a large number of them, but in no time they settled down and melted into the general population. Many groups of *sanka* were in Kyushu. They moved from place to place and were particularly skilled at making baskets. One of their larger bases was the village of Morotsuka, in Miyazaki Prefecture, but I have heard that they no longer wander. They now live in a valley in the upper reaches of the Gokase River, on the southeast side of Mt. Aso. They first went there to fish for eel. Finding good bamboo, and being skilled at making things from bamboo, they settled. They also farmed and have started to grow tobacco. In fact, now they have given up bamboo work and become farmers completely. It seems there were many other *sanka* bases in Kyushu, but this has not been confirmed.

In Kyushu *sanka* and hunters are seen as two distinct groups, but did not hunters also originally catch freshwater fish? When hunters hunt wild boar or deer, they carry dried stonefish with them and show them to the mountain god so that the god will bestow a successful hunt on them. Most hunters did this, and I believe it is evidence that they caught fish as well.

At any rate, there were many *sanka*, and while some freshwater fished, others did bamboo work. In the mountains of Hiroshima Prefecture, I often heard talk of *sanka* who made and sold bamboo whisks. Bamboo whisks, or *chasen*, are used when mixing *matcha* [powdered green tea]. The bamboo's joint is left intact, and the bamboo is finely split. When a *chasen* strikes a stick or is brushed against it, it makes a unique sound. In the mountains of Western Honshu during rice planting, the bamboo whisk often accompanies a flute and *taiko* drum. As an alternative accompaniment, holes may be drilled in two small pieces of board and a string passed through them. A sound is then made by rubbing the two boards together, an idea that may have come from bamboo whisks. Bamboo whisks are not only used for the making of tea, but were originally used as pot cleaners. Even today one finds them in rural farmhouses.

Unable to make a living on fishing alone, it would seem that the *sanka* made these whisks and sold them as they traveled. Some *sanka* played bamboo whisks and chanted, going door-to-door for money, which was called "whisking." In *An Illustrated Guide to Humanity* there is a drawing of a man walking along and striking a gourd. He is carrying a bamboo pole with a bundle of straw tied to one end into which numerous whisks have been stuck. The drawing's caption explains that a hunter, upon hearing a sermon by the holy priest Kūya, decided to give up hunting and go door-to-door chanting, dancing, and striking a gourd. It would appear that there were many others like him, and when traveling in the Kinki Region and in Western Honshu one comes across numerous villages called Chasen and Sasara [both meaning "bamboo whisk"]. These people have given up their chanting and are now farmers, but originally theirs was a wandering way of life. It seems that they too fished and hunted long ago.

Among those who wandered the mountains, not only were there those who fished and hunted but many who cut down trees and worked the wood, traveling from mountain to mountain in search of good trees. Some carried lathes and made wooden bowls, trays, tables, pots, and the like. They were called *kijiya*. Some among them did not carry lathes but split boards and used them to make things like ladles, while others bent thin boards that were used to make buckets and boxes. Some people made shingles, handles for hoes, and slats used for barrels. Many of these people lived the lives of wanderers. The lathe-carrying *kijiya* in particular, while based in the mountains of the Eigenji Township, in Shiga Prefecture, were active throughout the country. The people commonly found in the northeast these days who make limbless wooden dolls are also from this group, as are those who make the wooden tips for umbrellas and the spindles used in spinning factories. At first they lived and worked in the mountains, but when they started to make umbrellas and spindles they moved into town and blended into the population.

I think it was probably from among these mountain wanderers that wanderers who centered their lives on religious faith were born. Those who cut down trees worshipped the mountain god and acted in compliance with a divine will. This was true of the hunters as well. Hunting festivals, wherein hunters asked for permission to catch prey, were strictly observed. Even now festivals related to hunting are held in Miyazaki and Kagoshima. In these festivals one can observe the practice of old customs such as the killing of game and its placement on an altar in offering, followed by the performance of *kagura*.

I think the *yamabushi* [mountain ascetics] and mountain-dwelling priests also evolved from these mountain wanderers. There is a remarkable semblance between the etiquette of the *yamabushi* and the *matagi* when they enter the mountains, leading one to believe they are from the same world. If not from among those who lived in the mountains and made them the object of their lives, true mountain worshippers would probably not have been born.

With the support of other believers, the *yamabushi* strove for asceticism. They traveled to the mountains they worshipped—Hiko, Ōyama, Ishizuchi, Ōmine, Haku, Ontake, Fuji, Dewa Sanzan—and opened countless training halls nearby.

The *yamabushi* were in a strong position because they had their own beliefs. The villages at the base of Mt. Haku, around Shiramine, were probably *yamabushi* villages as well until the villagers took up Shinshu Buddhism in the beginning of the modern era. When the snow began to pile up, these people would head for the plains to beg for food. They were called "Mt. Haku beggars," and it is said they traveled from the fields of Kaga and Echizen to Ōmi and Kyoto, begging for food along the way. From the area around Hida, east of Mt. Haku, the beggars would also go to the plains of Mino when winter came. I heard similar stories in the mountains of Hiroshima Prefecture and Yamaguchi Prefecture, so it would seem that those who did not have faith had no alternative but to go from door to door, bowing their heads and asking for food. When one had faith, one could offer a prayer and purification, receiving food and lodging in return.

There were also those who lived in the mountains without faith. Without begging for food they, like the *sanka*, made and sold winnowing baskets, bamboo whisks, and bamboo baskets. Such villages abounded. People everywhere made straw raincoats,

Rural Kumamoto Prefecture.
October 1962.

sieves, straw sandals, vine baskets or brooms, and carried them along for sale. I have heard it said that they forced their wares on people, and that if a person said "no" there was a chance their house would be set on fire. But many of these people could not have survived without the compassion of others. That's how hard life in the mountains was.

IV. MOUNTAIN TRAVELERS

Besides the poor who had to rely on the sympathy of others, there were also many who were unexpectedly forced to wander. Famine was one such cause of this. On my travels I often heard stories of people who, having run out of food, had left their homes to wander here and there, finally finding a place where they could settle down again. In the northeast in particular, famine was common. I once visited a farming family living at the foot of Mt. Kurikoma, in Miyagi Prefecture, that long before had lived in the Kitakami River watershed, in Iwate Prefecture. They told me that during the Tenpō famine [1833–36] they had headed farther and farther south and along the way, by chance, they had strayed off the path and into the woods. Finding an abandoned home, they moved in, and have been living there ever since. The former occupants, too, had moved south during a famine.

In this way, whenever there was a famine, people moved from the north to the south and many came to live in homes that others had abandoned. In the villages along Hiroshima Bay too, I was told that a number of families had come down from the mountains during times of famine and settled there.

Such movement was not limited to times of famine. Many were forced to move by the disturbances of war. Villages of fugitives were one such example, though most of these people, after moving, did not wander. Therefore, while it is difficult to include them in the wanderers' family tree, one cannot say that none of them became wanderers.

While it would appear that villages composed entirely of wanderers all set out together at a fixed time, traveling far and wide, wanderers who lived in permanent settlements in the mountains set out individually as they pleased. In the mountains of Gokanoshō, in Kumamoto Prefecture, several villagers told me that their ancestors had traveled a lot, and were constantly down on the plains. Some had been as far as Osaka and Kyoto and back again, and after the Meiji period many had gone to work in a coal mine in Kita Kyushu. In Iyayama, in Tokushima Prefecture, and in Totsukawa, in Nara Prefecture, I heard tell of people who had traveled far and wide from communities that had been virtually forgotten by the outside world.

Those who took up farming generally settled down, but people in other professions had a strong tendency to wander. Even if they were living deep in the mountains, as long as they were not living in a dead-end valley, many traveled far, following common transit and transport routes. Horsemen living in the Ina Valley in Nagano Prefecture tied mountain wares to their horses and traveled as far as the Mikawa District to sell their loads. They then tied salt and other provisions to their horses and returned to Ina.

In the Owari Domain [Aichi Prefecture] cows were more often used than horses, and were referred to as "land boats." Cows in Kiso carried plain wood to Gunma Prefecture. They dropped their load in Kuragano and it was taken by riverboat to Tokyo.

In a village where iron was mined in the Kitakami Mountains, in Iwate Prefecture, cowherds would put the iron on the back of a cow and travel all the way to the central districts. Once there, they would sell the iron and the cow, and walk back north through the mountains. For this reason there were a lot of Nanbu [Iwate] cows in the Kanto and central regions. What is more, if one led their cow in the summer, when the grass was thick, there was no lacking for food.

The cows that had been sold were also useful. I have heard that the salt made along the coast of Niigata Prefecture and carried into the mountains of Nagano Prefecture was carried mostly by Nanbu cows, and it was Nanbu cows that carried hemp grown in Yamagata to Echigo.

The practice of loading cargo on horses and cows, and of using cows in the mountains, was common in eastern Japan and in Western Honshu as well. In the most rugged areas, however, there was no choice but to depend on human shoulders. Crossing over the Hida Mountains people called *pokka* transported goods from Gifu and Nagano, and tiny settlements formed here and there where the *pokka* passed through. Many of the *pokka* lived in villages at the base of Mt. Haku, in Fukui Prefecture. Carrying hoe handles, mushrooms, and paper mulberry bark, they traveled from the mountains down to the plains. For a long time Hidashirakawa was unexplored, but when gunpowder was found there, again it was the *pokka* who carried it to the plains of Etchū. Along these paths were the homes of the *pokka* bosses. One *pokka* would carry as far as the bosses' place, then another would take the load down to a merchant on the plains, and so on, in what appears to have been a division of labor. Wherever in the mountains you were, there were comings and goings. Being in the mountains did not mean seclusion. From the perspective of people in populated areas down below, it appeared to be a

Man carrying wasabi.
Shimane Prefecture.
August 1955.

closed world far away, but those who lived there were connected to a vast world.

Walking in Totsukawa and elsewhere I was overcome by a variety of deep emotions. In Tenkawa, at the northernmost extreme of the Totsukawa valley, curved boards, the slats for making barrels and ladles, were made by the men and carried by the women. Every morning the women woke in the dark, shouldered their loads, and carried them down to the town of Shimoichi. After selling them, they returned home. Women from communities on the west side of Tenkawa carried such wares to a place called Fukibata, east of Mt. Kōya. And from the villages on the western shore of the Totsu River, they carried loads over several passes to Mt. Kōya.

Not only did people live in these mountains and carry loads out to merchants, but religious travelers came and went as well. *Yamabushi* who had worshiped at Mt. Kōya were able to reach the Ōmine Mountains by following the Nose and Amano River valleys. So those who traveled between Kōya and Ōmine passed through these valleys. Until the beginning of Shōwa, many large lodgings remained along the way. The people of Tenkawa worked as guides for religious travelers going to Ōmine. So while they were woodworkers, they themselves were also *yamabushi*.

Heading southeast from Mt. Kōya and crossing over Obako Pass, one descends into the Kanno River valley. Follow that valley down, and you will come out at the Totsu River. Continue down along the Totsu River, and you will arrive in Kumano Hongū. This is the shortest path connecting Kōya and Kumano, and long ago it was well traveled. Around the middle of the Kamakura period [in the 13th century], the holy priest Ippen took this route. And many of the Kōya sages—priests who repeated Buddhist prayers while they walked—took this route from Kōya to worship in Kumano. A truly remarkable number of people walked these mountain paths. And when one studies the towers erected beside the road for the souls of the dead, one will sometimes find the name of someone who has come from quite far away.

Not only did people go from the mountains to the towns, they often went in the other direction. In a remote village in Terakawa, Kōchi Prefecture, among writings from the beginning of the seventeenth century, I found deeds for people who had come from Osaka to purchase beeswax and brick tea. Brick tea involved an old production method whereby tea was fermented and pressed. It was made in these mountains, and people came from far away to buy it.

Walking in the mountains, one is forcefully reminded that in an age when people had to walk everywhere they went, a great number of people could not do business or make a living without walking. In particular, those living in mountain villages could definitely not make a living staying at home.

V. STRAGGLERS

The people described above had a home somewhere that provided a base, and that was probably maintained from generation to generation. But many wanderers did not have a home. Wanderers of this sort most likely died out in one generation but were followed by others who fell into similar circumstances. Lists of the various types of wanderers can be found in *A Record of Modern Manners and Customs* and in *An Illustrated Guide to Humanity*. First I will provide a list of those who traveled, performing door-to-door, begging for food and money, as found in *A Record of Modern Manners and Customs*, published in 1853.

Shinto priests; beggars wearing Sarutahiko masks; con artists pretending to be from the Kashima Shrine; priests who play the flute and wear feminine clothing; Shinto music and dance groups; Shinto street performers; beggar priests who pray on other people's behalf; beggar priests who beat on wood gongs and chant imitation sutras; priests who place papers with characters written on them in people's homes as life lessons; nearly naked beggars with torn umbrellas who pray for better weather on rainy days; beggars who dance and pray for other's recovery from smallpox; beggar priests who pray on other people's behalf during the winter months; dancing priest troupes that dance the Edo Sumiyoshi rice-planting dance; priests who write down the names and ages of individuals and pray on their behalf during special times in the sexagenary cycle; beggars who tell historical and war stories; priests who juggle bamboo and perform other tricks; beggars who perform *kyōgen* Kabuki; pairs of Edo comedians who banter regarding celebratory themes; priests who juggle stones and perform magic tricks; show box carriers; *samisen*-playing storytellers; singers of epic songs; impersonators of humans and animals; impersonators of Noh performers; old battle storytellers who read directly from books; old battle storytellers who add their own interpretations regarding military tactics; roadside beggars; mystical lion dancers played by children accompanied by an adult who beats on a *taiko* drum and sings; puppeteers who perform on top of a box hung from their necks; farmers who chant Buddhist chants and dance to the accompaniment of flutes and *taiko* drums; pilgrims who sing chants while on a pilgrimage to thirty-three Goddess of Mercy statues in the Kansai Region; pilgrims carrying a Buddhist statue in a box while on a nationwide pilgrimage to sixty-six hallowed grounds; pilgrims on a pilgrimage to eighty-eight holy sites in Shikoku; homeless beggars interested in food and money; beggars living in shacks who are only interested in money; finely dressed women who play the *samisen* and sing; dead dog collectors; people with performing monkeys; lepers who ask for rice at New Year's; groups of beggars who play small *taiko* drums and bamboo whisks and sing loudly around New Year's; people who dress up as Daikoku [the god of wealth] and sing in celebration of the New Year; finely dressed women who conceal their faces, play the *samisen,* and sing songs asking for good crops in the year to come; people who paint on the ground using white sand; cleaners carrying bamboo brooms; naked single sumo wrestlers who impersonate two people wrestling; beggar priests who wear grass skirts, shake a rattle made from coins, and sing and dance on particularly cold and windy days; people who line up clay figures in front of the door and tell jokes about them.

One can see that a large number of people solicited door-to-door. While *A Record of Modern Manners and Customs* was published in 1853, *An Illustrated Guide to Humanity* preceded it by 163 years, coming out in 1690. But even in those days an exceedingly large number and variety of people performed and traveled from door to door, as follows:

Priests collecting old nails and coins; priests carrying pincushions full of sewing needles asking women for money to honor the needles they have broken so they won't go to hell; priests who pray on other people's behalf; priests who chant sutras for food; priests and pilgrims who burn incense directly on their arms and pierce them with swords in exchange for rice and money; priests who gather and honor old chopsticks in exchange for money; priests who carry a carving of an old woman beside Sanzu-no-kawa [the Japanese equivalent of the River Styx] who steals dead people's clothes and asks women to pray to her so she will not take their clothes from them when they die; men selling cards and images of gods that protect women from women's illnesses; priests who encourage the daily placement of rice in the garden as an offering to Buddhist saints and then eat the rice themselves; priests who strike tiny bells and sing

Buddhist prayers for money; priests who beg for food but do not eat after midday; smooth-talking men who pretend to be god's messengers and to know the future fortunes and misfortunes of others; male and female pairs with *taiko* drums and bells who pray; young people with multiple bells strung around their necks that they spin around; poor men and women who dress as priests, ring bells, and beg for rice; fishermen who have become priests and make and sell *chasen* whisks; people who beat *taiko* drums crazily and play the flute; people wearing dragon heads and beating on *taiko* drums to drive out evil spirits; nuns dressed in kimonos who sing and use sex appeal; pilgrims who sing pilgrimage songs; people who wear tall *geta*, balance wooden buckets of water on their heads, beat on bells and sing; beggar bosses; beggars who sit along the road and read old military stories; people with performing monkeys; puppeteers who perform Noh plays and dance; bamboo-stick jugglers; people who play *samisen* and washboards and sing sermons; street performers who juggle, spin plates, and perform magic tricks; dancing troupes that dance with fans under large parasols; beggars who perform *kyōgen* Kabuki; beggars who play split pieces of bamboo in the manner of castanets and dance; beggars who perform Noh alone; beggars who wear masks and beat on bells to drive away common colds; beggars dressed as priests who carry long-handled parasols and recite Buddhist teachings; sellers and repairers of clogs to be worn in the snow; haggard beggars who claim to have captained ships that were shipwrecked; young women who ask for food at the end of the year; men with fern leaves on their heads who beat together bamboo sticks and beg for money at the end of the year; beggars who travel in pairs at New Year's, beat on small *taiko* drums, dance and talk about good things in the year to come; beggars who play the *samisen* and sing songs asking for good crops in the year to come; mountain ascetics who shake rattles, play conch shells, and talk about miracles; mountain ascetics with tin canes who drive out evil spirits; people who promise others longer lives in exchange for grilled beans and money on the last day of winter; lepers carrying black boxes on their backs and begging for food.

A comparison of the two texts reveals that several of the types listed in *An Illustrated Guide to Humanity* are not to be found in *A Record of Modern Manners and Customs*. Most likely these people did not disappear, but were left out. The number of people who traveled door to door is thought to have actually increased in the end of the Edo period.

Some of these stragglers did something resembling a performance, but most were beggars. This is to say that they were not in the possession of anything productive to contribute, but lived their lives walking door to door and begging, making use of some slight art they had learned or some dubious recitation. It is said that such door-to-door beggars were seen in even greater numbers in Tokyo and its suburbs up until around the time of the Tokyo earthquake in 1923. Many beggars had dropped out of society, but they were able to survive because the general public gave them enough food to eat. It could be said that the affection of the masses was without limit. The future would show that when people stopped giving, this group gradually disappeared.

VI. THE ENERGY TO TRAVEL

Those who walked along peddling their wares were far greater in number than those who performed and begged from door to door. In *A Record of Modern Manners and Customs*, more than one hundred and sixty types of peddlers are listed. Most were in the city of Edo [Tokyo], and one can see just how many people walked the streets selling something. But now such peddlers have nearly disappeared from Tokyo, and only traces of them remain in the countryside.

While some peddlers sold local products locally, many others traveled quite far to sell their wares. The Ōmi merchants [who were based in Shiga Prefecture and sold mainly textiles] provide a good example, but there were also peddlers of tea, fish hooks, and brushes and ink. The Toyama and Yamato medicine salesmen also walked the entire country. Women in Abu Village, in Tokushima Prefecture, and in Masaki, in Ehime Prefecture, peddled fish locally at first, but from Taishō to early Shōwa they traveled as far as Korea, Manchuria, Mongolia, North China, Canada, and Australia. It was not for a lack of something to eat that they traveled so far. Rather, their history suggests that they were in the possession of an unaccountable energy. If political circumstances had allowed it, they would have gone anywhere. Looking at the gentle expression on the face of an old woman from Ehime Prefecture who told me that, even without understanding the language, she was able to do business, I experienced a feeling of wonder.

Among materials at the government offices of Mikawa, in the mountains of Aichi Prefecture, I found a list of people who had disappeared. These were people who had left the village without notice, in the early years of the Meiji period, and whose whereabouts were unknown. In the Edo period these would have been people who had become homeless wanderers. But were they really missing? When I asked about each of them, I was told that their parents knew where they had gone. When I asked what kind of lives they were leading away from home, I was told that some were stragglers but most were living good and healthy lives.

In the past, people often dropped out of village life. Many did not simply drop out, but were seeking a different world outside the village. The religious travel that was popular in the Edo period—pilgrimages to Dewa Sanzan, Kobugahara, Fuji, Ōyama, the Kikō Temple, Ondake, the Ise Shrine, Ōmine, Honzan, Konpira, Miyajima, Hiko, and Aso—was possible with the support of numerous others. Not only was this an opportunity to see another world, but to come into contact with it as well. Thus, even in villages that did not associate closely with their immediate neighbors, one can find surprising connections to distant places, connections that suggest they were by no means isolated.

Looking at things in this way, one finds strong contradictions with the views of scholars who suggest that travel was strictly limited, that it was inconvenient, and that villages were closed off. In Hinokinai, in the mountains of Akita Prefecture [far north on the island of Honshu], I asked the individual travel histories of all the old people. The women had not traveled all that much, but I was able to confirm that most of the men had been on pilgrimages to the Ise Shrine and to Kumano. As *matagi* hunters they had gone to the mountains in Echigo every year. Such travel was not limited to the mountains of Akita. I heard similar stories everywhere. The world of the common people was surprisingly expansive.

Nagano Prefecture. July 1965.
Photograph by Ōmi Shigeo.

Glossary

awa: Foxtail millet. Dating back to the Jōmon period, the production and consumption of *awa* in Japan predates rice; until recently, *awa* was an important staple in the Japanese diet. Once cooked and eaten alone, after World War II it was displaced by rice and is now eaten rarely and in small portions mixed with rice and sometimes used in sweets.

banzai: Literally "ten thousand years." Originally a cheer for the emperor's longevity and national prosperity, after the Meiji Restoration *banzai* became a cheer of celebration and exhortation.

beriberi: A condition resulting from a vitamin B1 (thiamine) deficiency. *Beriberi* may occur when a person eats only white rice, which is low in thiamine because the thiamine-bearing husk has been removed in the polishing process.

big rice planting: The occasion when a large number of people—often women—worked together to plant a rice paddy. Planters were accompanied by *taiko* drummers, a flute, and one or more singers who gave rhythm to the work. Cows would often first trample and turn the soil, lessening the chance that the paddy leaked water through mole and other rodent holes. These plantings were often to celebrate someone's recovery from a long illness, the building of a house, or some other auspicious occasion and were often sponsored by a person of means.

black-hoe laborers: Laborers from farming communities who worked on construction projects. In the Edo period (1603–1868), farmers living in the Owari Domain (now Aichi Prefecture) who were in need of cash revenues were given permission by the domain to leave their homes and work on road, river embankment, and other construction crews. Initially they hired themselves out as laborers only at times of the year when there was no farming work to be done, but as their skills improved the demand for their work grew and some crews worked year-round without returning home. This practice continued until the middle of the Meiji period, around 1900.

Bon: The Buddhist Festival of the Dead, honoring one's ancestors and held in the middle of July on the old lunar calendar and in August now. On this occasion, families gather and visit the graves of their ancestors, and communities celebrate with several days of music and dancing. Often a welcoming fire is burned at the beginning of *Bon,* and the ancestors come down the smoke to return to the world of the living. A send-off fire is then burned at the end of *Bon,* and the smoke serves as a path back in the other direction.

branch families (*bunke*): Households that broke off from and served as extensions to the main, ancestral home. In Japan, where landholdings were generally small, the head of a household and his successor lived in the ancestral home (*honke*), and the other sons and their wives built separate homes and established branch families (*bunke*), thereby keeping the family property intact. Generally, the son who remained at home farmed, while those who moved away—having no land to speak of—often took up a trade or traveled to where they were needed as manual laborers. In the past (as described in "Nagura Talks") a poor migrant would sometimes settle and set up a branch family in affiliation with a home in the community that had greater financial means. In rural Japan, this *honke-bunke* dynamic can still be found today, although it applies only to kinfolk. The practice of taking in strangers has disappeared.

Chōshū: Modern-day Yamaguchi Prefecture. The Chōshū Domain vied with the Satsuma Domain (now Kagoshima Prefecture) for influence in the imperial court in Kyoto in the early 1860s. For a time Chōshū gained control of the imperial court, only to be driven out by Satsuma. When Chōshū tried to regain control they were labeled "enemies of the court." The shogunate sent two punitive expeditions to Chōshū. The first, in 1864, ended without conflict. However, the second, in 1866, concluded with a withdrawal of the shogunate's troops, severely damaging the shogunate's prestige and contributing to its eventual downfall.

Chūshingura: Famous Kabuki play depicting the 47 Rōnin Incident when a *daimyō* was forced to commit ritual suicide for drawing his sword and attempting to kill a protocol official in the shogunal palace. The *daimyō's* domain was also confiscated and the samurai who served him were dismissed. Two years later, forty-six loyal retainers avenged their lord's death by killing the protocol official, after which they committed ritual suicide.

Daikoku: The God of Wealth. One of the Seven Deities of Good Fortune, Daikoku is often depicted carrying a large mallet for the granting of wishes, with a bag slung over his shoulder, and standing on bales of rice. Daikoku is sometimes worshipped as a tutelary god of the kitchen, and sometimes honored during harvest time as a god of the fields.

domains: Historical divisions of territory in Japan. Domains (*han*) existed during the Edo period and the early years of the Meiji period until they were abolished and replaced by prefectures. The size of individual domains varied widely and was defined by the production of rice and other grains. There were approximately 260 domains in the 18th century. Their lords were obliged to live in the capital every other year and to provide military support to the shogunate. Generally the greater a domain's distance from Edo, the more autonomous it was.

Ebisu: The god of one's occupation and often of fishing, farming, and commerce. One of the Seven Deities of Good Fortune, Ebisu is depicted carrying a fishing rod and a sea bream, a symbol of good luck. Because Ebisu is thought to be hard of hearing, devotees bang on his shrine before reciting their prayers.

Edo: Old name for Tokyo. Located along the Pacific coast on central Honshu and literally meaning "River Gate," Edo was the largest city in the world in 1695 when its population reached one million. It was renamed Tokyo, literally "Eastern Capital," when the imperial court moved from Kyoto to Tokyo after the Meiji Restoration of 1868.

ema: Pictorial votive offerings generally painted on flat wooden surfaces. Seen as the messengers of human wishes to the world of the gods, horses were once given to Shinto shrines. They were eventually replaced by *ema* (literally "picture horses"). For many years *ema* were presented as offerings to heal physical disorders or illness, and they were painted with related symbols: eyes for eye problems, a catfish for skin problems, an octopus for warts, and so on. They were also offered when making a wish for success in battle or as thanks for a wish that had been granted. In recent years their use has come to include wishes for success on tests, in marriage, in childbirth, and so on.

Federation of Nine Academic Societies: A federation of scholars in the fields of ethnology, folklore, anthropology, sociology, linguistics, geography, religious studies, archaeology, and psychology. The federation focused on a new location each year, beginning in 1950, and studied it from all nine academic angles. Their first field of study was the island of Tsushima, located between Japan and Korea.

fox fire: A long line of flickering red or orange lanternlike lights sometimes appearing at night, traditionally thought to be the glowing breath of foxes, a light caused by the beating of their tails or the light from balls of fire that they carry. Fox fire sometimes led people astray and sometimes helped them find what they were looking for, and in one region in the north of Japan it was said to be the light from torches carried on the occasion of a fox wedding. Fox fire may come from the decomposition of animal corpses that give off phosphorus compounds.

foxes and fox spirits: Creatures thought to be capable of bewitching people. Foxes often appear in folktales taking the form of women and marrying men. Fried bean curd is said to be their favorite food.

Genkainada: A stretch of ocean between Tsushima and the Kyushu mainland. Genkainada is rich in fish and has long been an important route for travel to the Asian continent.

geta: Wooden clogs. They generally have two crosswise supports that add height and help to keep the wearer's feet and clothing up out of the mud.

Grand Shrine of Izumo: One of the most important Shinto shrines in Japan, located in Shimane, along the Sea of Japan. According to the old lunar calendar, for one week in October all of the gods in Japan gathered in Izumo. For this reason, October used to be called the "month without the gods" in the rest of Japan.

head of the household: The eldest male, or a proxy thereto, required by the community to participate in public service and community work and to attend village meetings. Miyamoto points out that in eastern Japan (north and east of Tokyo) the eldest male often remained head of the household until an advanced age, while in western Japan this role was often passed on quickly to one of the sons, enabling the young and still-able father to work on behalf of the family without the distraction of any commitment to the community.

hie: Millet. Once an important staple in the Japanese diet, *hie* was eaten before rice was grown and later when rice crops failed. As it was cumbersome to mill and did not taste good, millet came to be eaten only in times of extreme hardship and poverty.

Hokkaido: The second largest and northernmost island in Japan. Hokkaido is thought to have been settled by the Ainu, Gilyak, and Oroke some 20,000 years ago. The Matsumae Domain was established at the southern end of the island during the Edo period. After the Meiji Restoration, the Japanese government began a colonization effort, hoping to make use of the island's potential farmland and other resources, and as a defense against a Russian invasion. First peasants and former samurai were recruited to settle here and later—between 1881 and 1894—five prisons were built on the island. Prison labor was used in an effort to speed up colonization and, in the early years, the prisons were fairly porous as the prisoners cleared land and built furniture outside the prison walls. Meanwhile, members of nearby communities relied on the services of the prison doctors and sent their children to schools located within the prison facilities. The victims of disasters were also sent to Hokkaido as part of this colonization effort.

Ikegami Hiromasa (1909–65): Private ethnographer who researched and wrote about mountain worship and religious beliefs and practices.

Ishiguro Tadaatsu (1884–1960): Agricultural administrator, twice the Minister of Agriculture and Forestry before World War II, who largely influenced government policy in the 1920s and 1930s with his belief in agrarian nationalism.

Jizō: A divine Japanese Buddhist being with limitless compassion. Often depicted as a monk with a jewel in one hand and a staff in the other, Jizō helps all who suffer, and while he is seen, in particular, as a protector of children, he also watches over travelers, women, and firefighters.

kagura: Sacred Shinto music and dancing performed to invoke the gods and to pray for a prolonged and vital life. *Kagura* continues to be performed by musicians in the imperial household and by villagers in rural Japan. In the latter case, the performers often wear masks and perform at a festival for a local Shinto shrine, the longer performances lasting through the night.

Kannon: The Goddess of Mercy. Kannon is infinitely compassionate and very popular in Japan. Kannon is thought to protect those in need, especially women wanting to have children or women in the throes of childbirth.

kijiya: Woodworkers who generally used lathes to produce bowls, trays, and dolls. *Kijiya* built huts in the mountains and collected wood for their work, moving on when the trees they needed had become scarce. When forest ownership rights were more clearly defined in the years after the Meiji Restoration, it became more difficult for them to move freely in the mountains, and they turned to agriculture or moved into Japan's cities, where they often continued to make and sell wood products.

kotatsu: A brazier placed beneath a table. *Kotatsu* first made use of charcoal and later electricity to warm one's feet and legs.

land reforms (of 1946): Policy implemented after World War II to limit individual landholdings and thereby to reduce tenant farming and the number of absentee landlords. The government bought land from absentee landlords and land that could potentially be cultivated but was not. This land was then sold to the theretofore tenant farmers. This led to increased harmony in most villages and motivated the new owner-cultivators to pursue new farming technologies. In instances where tenant farming continued, the tenants were granted more rights, and restrictions were made on the level of their payments.

leprosy: A chronic bacterial disease that often produces skin lesions. The Japanese Ministry of Interior Issues conducted a national survey in 1900 and found a population of more than 30,000 individuals with leprosy in Japan. To contain the disease, the decision was made to isolate these individuals, and some eighteen leprosaria were built. Individuals with leprosy were isolated, sterilized, forced to perform labor, and arbitrarily punished. Many of these practices continued even after World War II.

matagi: Hunters who generally lived in the mountains of northern Honshu and, for much of their history, subsisted on collective hunting in the winter months and farming in the summer. Their way of life was greatly altered when extensive logging began and the Japanese serow population dropped. Their language and customs are thought to share common roots with those of the Ainu living on the island of Hokkaido.

Meiji Restoration (1868): The end to 265 years under the Tokugawa shogunate, eventually replacing domains, lords, and feudalism with prefectures and more democratic government, while also attempting to restore the status of the imperial court and opening the country to the West.

miso: A salty paste made by fermenting rice, barley and/or soybeans. *Miso* is used to preserve vegetables and meats and in the making of *miso* soup.

Mizusawa Kenichi (1910–94): A collector of legends and folklore who sought out and interviewed oral transmitters in rural Japan.

Moneychanger Gohei (1774–1852): An Edo-period trader. The title "moneychanger" is misleading given the depth and breadth of this particular merchant's trade network, which included direct and indirect trade with Korea, Russia, the United States, Australia, Tasmania, the Ainu (in Hokkaido), and Hong Kong. His life story supports Miyamoto's depiction of a dynamic society at this time in Japan's history, for it is a prime example of creative individual action and adaptation at a time that is often depicted as static and when the country is said to have been completely closed to the outside world.

Mt. Kōya: The name used for a collection of mountains located south of Osaka on the Kii Peninsula. This area was first settled in the 9th century by Kūkai, founder of the Shingon sect of Japanese Buddhism. Like the Ōmine Mountains to the east, Mt. Kōya has long been a popular destination for pilgrims. With a university that offers studies in both Buddhism and Shinto and some 120 temples, Mt. Kōya continues to be an important religious center.

Nakayama Tarō (1876–1947): An ethnologist and a contemporary of Yanagita Kunio and Orikuchi Shinobu.

Nevsky, Nikolai Aleksandrovich (1892–1937/1945?): Russian philologist who studied the Japanese, Ainu, and Ryukyuan languages and conducted extensive ethnographic surveys under the tutelage of Yanagita Kunio and other Japanese folklorists. Accused of being a spy, he was arrested in Russia in 1937 and, according to some sources, executed later that year. Other sources suggest that he may have died in a camp in 1945.

Ono Takeo (1883–1949): A scholar in the field of agrarian economic history.

Priest Tendō: Legendary priest born in the village of Naiin on the island of Tsushima in 673. A child prodigy, he began his Buddhist studies in

Kyoto at the age of nine before returning home. Tendō had supernatural powers, and when Emperor Munmu became sick he flew from Tsushima to the imperial court and healed the emperor. The locals continue to fear the places associated with Priest Tendō, and on the rare occasion that they go near, they back away rather than show their backs.

raccoon dog: An animal related to dogs and wolves but more closely resembling the raccoon in appearance and temperament.

rural samurai: Called *gōshi* in Japanese, rural samurai who lived and supported themselves on land that they directly managed or farmed. During the Edo period, they were generally ranked below the samurai who resided in castle towns. Among the rural samurai were those who had made the choice to move from the city to the countryside and some who were once non-samurai village heads who had been given permission to use surnames and to carry swords. After the Meiji Restoration, most were classified as former samurai, helping them to retain a certain status as country gentlemen.

Russo-Japanese War (1904–5): Conflict in which Russia and Japan battled for control over Korea and Manchuria. In the Treaty of Portsmouth, in September 1905, Japan was granted exclusive rights in Korea and half of the island of Sakhalin.

samisen: Three-stringed musical instrument, also spelled *shamisen* and literally meaning "three flavor strings." The body of this narrow-necked, fretless instrument was traditionally made using the skin of a cat.

sanka: Mountain gypsies. The *sanka* (literally, "mountain cave") traveled in family units and often pitched tents beside mountain streams; they sold the fish they caught and the baskets, brooms, and other bamboo wares they made. In the years after World War II, they took up a more sedentary life and blended into the general population.

Sasaki Kizen (1886–1933): A collector and researcher of Japanese folktales, folkways, and traditions.

sekihan: Rice boiled with *adzuki* beans on special occasions, giving it an auspicious red color.

sen: One hundredth of a yen. Yen and *sen* were both introduced in 1872; the yen is used to this day, but the *sen* went out of circulation in 1953.

sericulture: The raising of silkworms and the production of silk.

Sericulture came to Japan from China sometime around the third century. Silk exports were an important part of the economy beginning in the Meiji period, with exports going to the United States and Europe for silk stockings in the 1920s and 1930s. Rural families grew mulberry trees and raised silkworms in their own homes—the sound of thousands of silkworms eating mulberry leaves resembled falling rain—and young women left home to work in silk factories. Working in dusty and cramped conditions, many contracted tuberculosis and died. During World War II, silk was used for Japanese parachutes.

Shibusawa Keizō (1896–1963): Grandson of the pioneer industrialist Shibusawa Eiichi. Keizō was a banker and avid ethnologist devoted to the study of the common people and their contributions to Japanese culture. He established the "Attic Museum" (now the Japan Folk Culture Institute) in a building on his own private property in Tokyo, which became a gathering place for Japanese tools and folk crafts and for the young ethnologists who Shibusawa engaged—and generously sponsored—in a wide variety of research.

Shikoku: Literally "Four Domains," one of Japan's main islands, lying to the east across the Inland Sea, and a popular destination for pilgrimages. Particularly popular is a 750-mile circuit of eighty-eight temples that are thought to have been visited by Kūkai, who was born on Shikoku in 774 and was the founder of the Shingon sect of Japanese Buddhism.

Sino-Japanese War (1894–95): The First Sino-Japanese War, fought against China for control of Korea. This was Japan's first step down the road to imperialism. The Japanese won decisive victories on land and at sea. The Treaty of Shimonoseki was signed on April 17, 1895, ceding Taiwan and a part of Manchuria to Japan.

sweet potatoes: An important food crop in Japan. Sweet potatoes came to southern Japan from China via the Ryūkyū Kingdom (present-day Okinawa) early in the 17th century. By the end of the 19th century they were grown in large quantities throughout Japan, often saving the citizenry from starvation in years when other crops failed. In the years immediately following World War II, many Japanese survived by eating sweet potatoes.

taiko **paddy**: See "big rice planting."

tatami: Straw mats. Used only by the wealthy for the first thousand years of Japanese history, *tatami* began to be used by the general public in modern times, replacing or being used in conjunction with wood floors. In the 20th century, a *tatami*-mat maker could be found in most medium-sized communities.

Tenpō famine (1833–36): A particularly harsh famine resulting from poor crop yields beginning in 1833. Cold weather, flooding, and high winds destroyed crops for three continuous years, prices became inflated, and peasants migrated to the cities. In the northeast, many died of starvation and disease.

tengu: A long-nosed goblin and mountain guardian—with an affinity for large trees and special powers—who was thought to kidnap Buddhist priests and children.

Thanksgiving Celebrations: Dancing in the streets in wild attire and other celebrations over the course of a year from June 1867 to May 1868. Celebrations began in the Kansai area and spread eastward to Edo when amulets from the Ise Shrine were rumored to have fallen from the sky. This general hysteria is thought to have been born out of both elation and unrest on the part of the common people in this time of political and social transition.

tobacco: Important cash crop for Japanese farmers for much of the 20th century. In 1904, in an effort to fund the Russo-Japanese War, the government made the sale of tobacco a government monopoly, and it remained so until 1985.

Tokyo Earthquake (1923): Also known as the Kantō Earthquake, a quake measuring 7.8. The ensuing fires resulted in some 100,000 deaths and the loss of homes by 71 percent of the population of metropolitan Tokyo and 85 percent of the population of Yokohama. Most of this loss was due to the spread of household fires that had been lit in preparation for the midday meal.

torii: A gate to and symbol of a Shinto shrine comprising two columns and two horizontal beams, one placed atop the columns and another just below and between them. *Torii* are most often made of wood and sometimes of stone.

Tosa Genji: An allusion to Genji of *The Tale of Genji*, one of the most famous seducers of women in Japanese literature.

Toyama medicine salesmen: Itinerant medicine vendors based in Toyama Prefecture, on the island of Honshu. These salesmen walked throughout Japan carrying tiered wicker boxes on their backs. They made use of a credit system, providing their customers with a basic supply of medicines and collecting money only for the medicines that had been consumed in the time since their last visit. This was popular among a rural population that had limited monetary resources.

transmitters: Those who passed down information, stories, and culture, conveying knowledge to future generations and thereby shaping the future of their own families and communities and of the country as a whole. Miyamoto was particularly interested in the role of these individuals and the mechanisms and means by which they passed on what they knew through the spoken and later the written word.

Tsushima: In Nagasaki Prefecture, two islands that lie in the Korea Strait only 31 miles from Korea. Tsushima was an important stepping-stone between Japan and the Asian continent.

ujigami: Originally tutelary or guardian deities, each for an individual clan (*uji*). For the past several hundred years *ujigami* have become local deities protecting small communities that often share a common family name and a common ancestor. When housed in a portable shrine, the *ujigami* is moved from household to household every year.

umeboshi: Salt-cured, sun-dried plums thought to prevent colds, offset fatigue, and stimulate the appetite. Like soy sauce and *miso*, *umeboshi* were, until recently, made by most rural households for consumption by the family throughout the year.

yamabushi: Mountain ascetics, usually male, who practiced austerities and worshipped at holy mountains. They were often called upon to heal the sick or to exorcise fox and other spirits.

Yanagita Kunio (1875–1962): Often described as the founder of Japanese folklore studies. Yanagita worked for the Ministry of Agriculture and Commerce and for the Legislative Bureau of the Imperial Household Ministry from 1900 to 1919 and for *Asahi Shinbun* from 1919 to 1930. Focusing on the country as a whole, Yanagita looked for and wrote prolifically about unifying features, customs, and habits unique to Japan. With its emphasis on regional distinctions, Miyamoto's work can be seen as a response to Yanagita's view of Japan as a single homogeneous unit.

Other Titles of Interest
from Stone Bridge Press

A Different Kind of Luxury: Japanese Lessons in Simple Living and Inner Abundance
By Andy Couturier. 316 pp, 9 x 6, paper, ISBN 978-1-933330-83-9.

Tenryuji: Life and Spirit of a Kyoto Garden
By Norris Brock Johnson. 320 pp, 6 x 9, casebound, ISBN 978-1-933330-81-5.

The Japanese Tea Garden
By Marc Peter Keane. 296 pp, 8 x 10, casebound, ISBN 978-1-933330-67-9.

The Inland Sea
By Donald Richie. 256 pp, 5.25 x 7.25, paper, ISBN 978-1-880656-69-3.

Native American in the Land of the Shogun: Ranald MacDonald and the Opening of Japan
By Frederik L. Schodt. 432 pp, 6 x 9, paper, ISBN 978-1-880656-77-8.

Unbeaten Tracks in Japan: An Account of Travels in the Interior
By Isabella L. Bird. 354 pp, 5.25 x 7.5, paper, ISBN 978-1-933330-19-8.

Milky Way Railroad
By Kenji Miyazawa; translated by Joseph Sigrist and D. M. Stroud. 144 pp, 5.25 x 7.5, paper, ISBN 978-1-933330-40-2.

Basho's Narrow Road: Spring and Autumn Passages
By Matsuo Basho; translated by Hiroaki Sato. 192 pp, 5.5 x 9, paper, ISBN 978-1-880656-20-4.